COLLECTED WORKS OF

BERNARD LONERGAN

VOLUME 15

MACROECONOMIC DYNAMICS:

AN ESSAY IN

CIRCULATION ANALYSIS

COLLECTED WORKS
OF BERNARD

LONERGAN

*MACROECONOMIC
DYNAMICS: AN ESSAY IN
CIRCULATION ANALYSIS*

edited by
Frederick G. Lawrence, Patrick H. Byrne,
and Charles C. Hefling, Jr.

Published for Lonergan Research Institute
of Regis College, Toronto
by University of Toronto Press
Toronto Buffalo London

ISBN 0-8020-4384-4 (cloth)
ISBN 0-8020-8195-9 (paper)

Printed on acid-free paper

Canadian Cataloguing in Publication Data

Lonergan, Bernard J.F. (Bernard Joseph Francis), 1904–1984
    Collected works of Bernard Lonergan

    Partial contents: v. 15. Macroeconomic dynamics: an essay in circulation
    analysis / edited by Frederick G. Lawrence, Patrick H. Byrne, and Charles C.
    Hefling, Jr.
    Includes bibliographical references and index.
    ISBN 0-8020-4384-4 (v. 15 : bound)   ISBN 0-8020-8195-9 (v. 15 : pbk.)

    1. Theology – 20th century.   2. Catholic Church.   I. Crowe, Frederick E.,
    1915–   II. Doran, Robert M., 1939–   III. Lonergan Research Institute.
    IV. Title.

BX891.L595 1988   230   c88-093328-3

The Lonergan Research Institute gratefully acknowledges the financial
assistance of THE LONERGAN INSTITUTE AT BOSTON COLLEGE toward
the publication of this volume of the Collected Works.

University of Toronto Press acknowledges the financial support for its publishing activities of the Government of Canada through the Book Publishing
Industry Development Program (BPIDP).

Canadä

Contents

PART TWO:
HEALING AND CREATING IN HISTORY / 97

PART THREE / 107

General Editors' Preface

As general editors of the Collected Works of Bernard Lonergan we wish to extend our deepest thanks to Fred Lawrence, Patrick Byrne, and Charles Hefling for the enormous work they have done in bringing to publication this edition of Lonergan's essay on macroeconomics.

As their Editors' Preface indicates, this edition takes as its basis Lonergan's last and still incomplete version of the essay, that of 1983, and adds material from earlier versions mainly for the light it throws on the last version, which, we may presume, is the closest of all the versions to what Lonergan himself eventually would have published had he been able to complete his work.

Companion to this volume 15 is a volume of archival material that records Lonergan's 'work in progress' in the 1940s. For the latter volume we have assigned the number 21 in our CWL series (though in our original plan volume 21 would have covered a wider selection of archival materials), and are publishing it simultaneously with this volume 15 under the title *For a New Political Economy*.

In this way the reader will have ready access both, through the present volume, to Lonergan's last version of the essay and, through volume 21, to what seems to be his earliest work on the subject.

Lonergan was regularly concerned with what we are doing when we do theology, or when we do economics, or 'do' any other subject. And that immediately raises the question of what we are doing when we work on his thought on economics; in particular, which of his famous eight functional specialties are we engaged in? It is clear that the three editors have done a laborious, meticulous, and extremely thorough work of research. It is clear too that their Editors' Introduction and Appendix (the latter with its history of the diagram) have made important contributions to the history of Lonergan's thinking. But, of course, it is not possible to separate research and history neatly from interpretation. The general editors are pleased, therefore, to have as editors for this volume researchers of Lonergan's macroeconomics whose interpretation too is especially worthy of our attention. We are convinced that their research will provide data for endless interpretation that will owe much to their own implicit exercise of that specialty.

Turning to matters of lesser importance the general editors assume responsibility for the minutiae of style; here, as in all the volumes of the Collected Works, the *Oxford American Dictionary* and the *Chicago Manual of Style* are taken as guides; there is no attempt to make Lonergan's language inclusive; typos, punctuation, minor faults of grammar, and the like are corrected without notice.

While our debt to the editors can never be sufficiently acknowledged, we must not forget the others who contributed to the volume. The editors' Acknowledgments mention the debt owed to Nicholas Graham, Philip McShane, Eileen deNeeve, William Mathews, Peter Burley, Francis McLaughlin, Harold Peterson, and Joseph Flanagan. We gladly associate ourselves with Professor Lawrence's word of thanks, and would add a special word for Charles Hefling, who represented the Boston College team in the very considerable correspondence we had with them. Our thanks go also to Kerry Cronin, who did much to keep the Toronto-Boston teams in communication; to graphics artist Alexander (Sasha) Kalenick; and to Robert Croken and Deborah Agnew, who assisted in many ways with the production of the manuscript.

FREDERICK E. CROWE
ROBERT M. DORAN

Editors' Preface

This volume of Lonergan's Collected Works has as its basis and core the essay on macroeconomics that Lonergan was working on when failing health brought his scholarly work to an end. It would be a much slimmer volume if its editors had been content simply to publish the contents of Lonergan's typescript, the 'black marks on paper,' as he might have put it. But while everything contained in those eighty-nine pages does appear in this volume, a lot that they do not contain has also been included. We have augmented as well as edited the typescript as Lonergan left it, and having done so we owe the reader an account of what we have done, and why.

This preface aims at fulfilling the obligation. Because our task as editors was complicated, explaining it will be a somewhat lengthy business. The text of the essay we have edited has an interesting and unusual history, of which a sketch, at least, needs to be provided as the background of our editorial decisions. Readers who wish to bypass some rather specialized information and return to it later may go directly to the last part of the preface, which summarizes the work we have done and the conventions by which we have distinguished our contribution to this volume from Lonergan's own.

The typewritten pages in the Lonergan Archives at Toronto that bear the title *An Essay in Circulation Analysis* are Lonergan's reworking of a much older typescript. As the Editors' Introduction will tell at greater length, Lonergan began his work on economics in the 1930s and brought it to a culmination in a long essay that can be dated to 1944. This, the 'original' *Essay in Circulation Analysis*, was not published. Lonergan put it aside and left it unchanged for more than thirty years. In 1977 or thereabouts, he began to revise it, and went on revising until some time in 1983. The result was the existing typescript. The text is complete, in the sense that it is continuous from beginning to end; it may be called 'final,' as we shall call it here, inasmuch as it includes the last changes that Lonergan made; but in certain respects it remains unfinished.

How this interrupted work-in-progress could best be published was the problem we faced as its editors. It is a problem that admits of different solutions, none of them, perhaps, altogether satisfactory. Our decision, to borrow a term from the theater, was to offer a 'performing edition' – a text that gives readers what they need in order to understand Lonergan's argument. The present volume is not, then, an archival record of what Lonergan wrote. It is Lonergan's analysis of macroeconomic dynamics, put into a form that can be studied, used, criticized, and applied. Part 1 of this edition presents that analysis, amplified in ways that will be discussed below. Part 2 continues the analysis, drawing out some of its further implications. Part 3 elaborates one phase of the analysis in a more detailed and technical form. But the amplification, the continuation, and the elaboration are Lonergan's, as well as the analysis itself. We have added much to the contents of his typescript, but what we have added is material which, although it does not belong to the *Essay* in its 'final' form, either did belong to it at an earlier time, or was written by Lonergan and used by him to clarify his argument.

To expand on this last statement: Much of the text that we have included in the present volume comes from the 'original' *Essay* of 1944, of which a photocopy was made before Lonergan began to alter it. But other data were available to us as well, and we have made extensive use of them in the present edition. All these data are connected, one way or another, with the seminar on 'Macroeconomics and the Dialectic of History' that Lonergan taught at Boston College each year from 1978 to 1982. For members of the seminar (which included one or more of the present editors every time he taught it), Lonergan prepared ad hoc handouts that will be discussed below, and he assigned an essay of his own on 'Healing and Creating in History.' More important in the present context are the copies of his *Essay* itself that were made for use as the seminar's principal reading. There are five of these 'textbook' versions, each different from the others. The first of them reproduces Lonergan's typescript as it stood in 1978, and thus includes all the changes he had made in his 'original' text up to that time. The next year's 'textbook' includes subsequent changes, and so forth.

The existence of the 'textbook' versions as well as the "original' and 'final' ones makes it possible to follow in some detail the revisions Lonergan made in his *Essay*, in the order in which he made them. Each of the five provides, as it were, a cross-section of an ongoing process that had its starting point in the *Essay* of 1944 and its term in the existing typescript. What kind of process it was – 'what was going forward,' to use another Lonergan phrase, from 1978 to 1983 – is a question that has to be touched on here, inasmuch as our answer to it has shaped the present edition. It has two aspects. On the more formal side, it asks, What was Lonergan doing? In this regard it is a question about the text as such; about which parts were revised, to what extent, and when. On the more substantive side, to ask what was going forward is to ask, What did Lonergan accomplish by doing what he did? In this regard it is a question about the purposes that reworking the text served, and about how they should be assessed.

To begin with the text itself: As a first approximation, what Lonergan did in changing his *Essay* can be pictured as what the owner of a house does to renovate it without moving out. The order of topics – the *Essay*'s floor plan, as it were – never changed. But instead of tearing down everything and rebuilding from the ground up, Lonergan replaced rooms or walls or windows one at a time, so that the building as a whole was always habitable. When he stopped working, he no longer had the same house he had built in 1944, although some parts of it remained unaltered from the 'original.' Yet it was probably not yet the house he envisioned, either, for there is no reason to think he had finished renovating, and certain reasons to think he had not.

Lonergan's way of working with words on paper makes tracing his 'renovations' a fairly straightforward, if tedious, project. Thinking, as he was wont to put it, was for him a matter of writing and rewriting. But more exactly, in his later years, thinking was a matter of typing and retyping. In rethinking his *Essay*, it is clear that his regular practice was to take whole pages out of the typescript as it stood and insert newly typed pages in their place. Somewhat fewer than half the pages of the 'final' version are identical with those of the 'original'; the rest were presumably added as replacements beginning around 1977. Each page in the existing typescript can, in fact, be dated by reference to photocopies of the earlier versions. But as a page-by-page comparison, taking all these versions into account, showed us at the beginning of our editorial work, Lonergan's revising was more complicated, and more drastic, than the house-renovation metaphor might suggest.

Something of the complexity can be gathered from the chart that accompanies this preface. It is an attempt to summarize in graphic form how the content of each of the versions compares with the others, and also with the present edition. Sequence in time is charted from left to right. Each of the first six columns corresponds to one of the versions of Lonergan's *Essay* for which photocopied evidence survives – the 'original' and the five 'textbooks.' The seventh column represents the now-existing typescript; the eighth, this volume of the Collected Works. Charted from top to bottom in each column is the sequence, only, of pages within that version – 'only,' because no attempt has been made to give equal vertical space to each single page. By reading from left to right the reader can see when a given page or series of pages was first included in the *Essay*, whether it was dropped and if so when, and where its contents can be found in the present edition.

To start, for example, at the upper left-hand corner, in 1944 the *Essay* opened with a one-page 'Outline of the Argument.' Lonergan kept this page at the beginning of the first two 'textbook' versions, those of 1978 and 1979, but after it he inserted a pair of sections entitled 'Circulation Analysis' and 'Method.' By the time the *Essay* was photocopied again, for the 1980 seminar, he had replaced all three of these opening sections with a shorter 'Introduction.' This 'Introduction' remained in the two subsequent versions, those of 1981 and 1982, but was itself dropped from the version of 1983, which begins with a new section on 'Analysis.' Finally, as the right-hand column of the chart indicates, 'Analysis' continues to be the first numbered section of the present edition, but the 'Introduction' from 1980 and the 'Outline of the Argument' from 1944 are included here as well, combined in a preliminary section that we have named 'Preface.'

The chart has its limitations. While the relative dating it sets out seems fairly certain, its absolute dates are less so, since the inclusion of a 'new' page in any given year's version of the *Essay* is no more than presumptive evidence for when Lonergan wrote it. There is reason to think, for instance, that the section entitled 'Method,' although it first appears in what we are calling the 'textbook' for 1978, was composed somewhat earlier. Again, to repeat what was said above, the chart represents only formal changes in the *Essay*'s text. It may be regarded as an overview of 'what was going forward' in Lonergan's thinking to the extent that it shows which sections he worked on, in what chronological order. But only to that extent. It is one thing to say Lonergan changed a page, another thing to say he changed his mind. No doubt the changing pages show he was thinking by rewriting, as was his habit. What he was thinking, however, the chart does not tell. It takes note of newly included pages, not how new their contents are or in what their newness consists. In this regard the 'new' pages vary greatly. Comparing them with the pages they replace shows that sometimes Lonergan seems to have changed only his wording, and not very drastically at that, while sometimes he has thoroughly reconceived a line of argument, in effect writing an entirely new section. Nearly always the revised text is shorter. The chart does not aspire to sort these changes or assess their significance; it only registers the physical indications of Lonergan's having made them.

These limitations notwithstanding, the chart does display one important fact that might otherwise go unnoticed. Lonergan wrote a considerable number of pages for his *Essay* that appear neither in its 'original' version of 1944 nor in the 'final' one of 1983. Some pages were included temporarily, so to say. They served in one or more of the intermediate 'textbook' versions as replacements for earlier material, only to be themselves replaced or set aside before 1983. The sections on 'Circulation Analysis' and 'Method' mentioned above are two cases in point; another is a section on 'Deficit Spending and Taxes.' It is chiefly because of these pages that the versions of 1978 through 1982 claim our interest, because they establish that Lonergan's 'final' typescript is not, accurately speaking, a revision of the *Essay* he finished in 1944. It is a revision of previous revisions.

That fact is a significant one inasmuch as it weighs against one possible interpretation of Lonergan's purpose in revising, namely, that his main concern was to simplify the 'original' *Essay*, which is considerably longer and more technical than the 'final' version, for non-specialist readers. To be sure, he did simplify it, especially in regard to mathematics. Nor have we any doubt that making the *Essay* accessible was one of his aims in revising it. In our judgment, however, he was at the same time taking his analysis beyond the point he had reached in 1944 – developing his ideas even as he pared down his expression of them. The process that can be followed through the 'textbook' versions is an instance of *die Wendung zur Idee*, the 'shift towards theory' that Lonergan often spoke of. We recognize that the shift is partial and incomplete. We are convinced it is real.

The most suggestive of the clues that suggest such a development is one that would most likely have been lost had no 'textbook' versions of the *Essay* been photocopied. It concerns §14 of the present edition, which is not a section in the usual sense but a diagram – 'my baseball diamond,' as Lonergan called it. This 'Diagram of Rates of Flow' is the hinge on which

1944	1978	1979	1980	1981	1982	1983	The Present Edition
page numbers as of 1944	(page numbers for intermediate versions (1978–1982) are added, always in parentheses; because of revisions and replacements, the same number has at times appeared on more than one page)					final page numbers preceded by "EMA" in the 1983 version	
1 Outline of the Argument						} Preface, with Summary of Argument	} Preface, with Summary of Argument
	§2 Circulation Analysis (2)		Introduction (1-2)				
	§3 Method (3-5)					§1 Analysis 1-5	1 Analysis
						§2 Economic Process 6-8	2 Economic Process
						The Idea of History of Economic Analysis 9	
			§2 Circulation Analysis (3)			§3 Significant Basic Variables 10-13	3 Significant Basic Variables
			§3 Procedure (4-5)			14	4 Circulation Analysis
						15-16	5 Procedure
2-4 §4 The Productive Process (6-8)						17-19	6 The Productive Process
					(summary table from Lowe)	20	Additional Note to Section 6
5-11 §5 Division of the Productive Process (9-15)						21-27	7 Division of the Productive Process
12-18 §6 The Basic and Surplus Stages of the Productive Process (16-22)						{ §6 The Basic Stage of the Productive Process 28-31	8 The Basic Stage of the Productive Process
						§7 The Surplus Stage 31-34	9 The Surplus Stage
19-20 §7 Cycles of the Productive Process (23-24)						= §8 35-36	10 Cycles of the Productive Process
21-23 §7bis Cycles of the Productive Process (25-27)						= §9 A Technical Restatement 37-39	11 A Technical Restatement
24-33 §7ter Classes of Payments (28-37)						= §10 40-49	12 Classes of Payment
34-41 §8 Rates of Payment and Transfer (diagram, 40 verso)	§8 Rates of Payment and Transfer {(38-39) (40-42)} {diagram, 42} Revised diagram (42a) (42b)			Diagram: Another Revision (42c)		= §11 50-51	13 Rates of Payment and Transfer
							(Includes material from the 1944 and 1978 versions omitted in the 1983 version)
42 §9 Circuit Acceleration (43)					(§11 continued; 40-41)	52-53	
					§12 Diagram of Rates of Flow (42)	54	14 Diagram of Rates of Flow

the *Essay in Circulation Analysis* turns. In the initial phase of his argument, Lonergan works towards a formulation of terms and relations that are adequate to the task of analyzing macroeconomic dynamics. Beginning in §15, a second phase of the argument moves inversely, bringing those basic terms and relations to bear on successively more concrete, and more complex, problems. Between the two movements is §14, the diagram, which provides an image, a 'phantasm,' in which readers are invited to grasp how the foundational terms and relations define each other.

Parallels could be drawn between the twofold, forth-and-back movement of the *Essay* and the structure of a number of Lonergan's other writings. But for present purposes the point to note is a simple one: If Lonergan was rethinking his basic conceptions, the most likely place to find evidence of his having done so is the diagram. And in fact the diagram did change. Not only does the one in the 'final' version differ in more than detail from the one in the 'original,' but there are three intermediate forms of the diagram as well, preserved in 'textbook' versions. Each of the five 'baseball diamonds' is a modification of the previous one;[1] and to those modifications correspond changes in the text. All this is discussed at some length in an appendix to the present edition. Here it need only be mentioned that, whether Lonergan altered the diagram first and the text afterwards or vice versa, we are convinced that something substantive was at stake.

It is because we find in 'what was going forward' from 1978 onwards a development in Lonergan's thinking that we have used his 'original' text (and its revisions) to explicate the position he takes in the 'final' version, instead of presenting that version (and its predecessors) as *parerga* to what he wrote in 1944. This is not to say that we regard the version of 1983 as definitive. There is no definitive version of the *Essay*, and since Lonergan's death there cannot be one, the present edition not excepted. We do think that in the 1983 typescript Lonergan came as close as he ever did to the position he was reaching for. But we are also aware that, as it stands, it is neither finished nor internally consistent nor easy to understand.

For one thing, it contains not only some of Lonergan's earliest writing,

---

1 This is true even in the case of the 'diagramme,' as it is labeled in the 1944 version. About two years before the 'original' *Essay* Lonergan had written *For a New Political Economy*, which anticipates several features of his macroeconomics, including a 'baseball diamond.' The text is published in Collected Works of Bernard Lonergan, vol. 21, edited by Philip J. McShane (Toronto: University of Toronto Press, 1998); for the diagram, see part 1, chapter 5, §34.

unchanged since 1944, but also some of the last words he wrote. None of Lonergan's prose makes for easy reading, but in his earlier works he does write more expansively, drawing out his argument at length and establishing his points in detail. By contrast, towards the end of his life he wrote in a spare and lapidary style that makes every word count. Readers of his later works commonly find that different discussions of the same topic illuminate each other, and certainly our experience in studying the various versions of the *Essay* was that Lonergan's earlier and ampler way of making some particular point shed valuable light on a more telegraphic formulation written later.

Besides resolving inconsistencies that remain in the 'final' version, we have therefore provided a kind of commentary, by adding to the text, as Lonergan left it, words, sentences, pages, and whole sections of the *Essay* that appear in its earlier versions. The 'original' version is the source of most of these additions, but for reasons just outlined we have also drawn on the 'textbooks' that embody developments leading from the 'original' to the 'final' text. The result is not a variorum edition, but it is, in some sense, a composite edition. We have in effect put back into Lonergan's *Essay* most of what he cut out of it, in that nearly everything which appears in any of the six earlier versions also appears here in one form or another. Also included in our edition are the contents of the ad hoc pages which, as mentioned above, Lonergan wrote for distribution in his seminar. As a rule these 'supplements,' as they will be called here, are directly connected with the text of the *Essay* in the 'textbook' version for the current year. Each is thus associated with one of those versions, and has been assigned a corresponding date, although no attempt has been made to incorporate them into the chart. Their contents are various. Some are in effect replacement pages. Some are detached footnotes, as it were, elaborating on particular passages. Some give instructions for altering the text; in certain cases the alteration Lonergan prescribes corresponds to a change that he went on to make himself, so that it shows up again, on a retyped page of the next year's 'textbook.'

Such was the material available to us as editors. Our edition makes available to readers, in a form that we think they will find usable and useful, all of that material which in our judgment bears on Lonergan's latest understanding of the dynamics of economic process. In so doing, our aim has been to enlist Lonergan himself as commentator on his own position. We have tried, however, to make our editing transparent, so that the reader can distinguish without much difficulty between what we have added and what we have added to. Different ways of marking our interpolations as such correspond to the three ways we have adopted for handling different sorts of material.

(1) Some passages appear in footnotes. This category includes, in addition to passages that Lonergan later omitted from the *Essay* itself, transcriptions from the supplementary pages he handed out in his seminar. It was pointed out just now that some of these supplements also list modifications that he apparently intended to make in the text as it stood at the time. For the most part we have only recorded his instructions; where we have followed them by altering the text, a footnote calls attention to the fact.

(2) Other passages, ranging in length from a few words to several paragraphs, have been included within the body of the text. These interpolations are marked as such either by being enclosed in square brackets or, when they are lengthy, by a vertical line in the right-hand margin. This second method has been used in cases where we considered that inserting older material would not interrupt, but might serve to augment, the later wording. At times, for example in §15, there are interpolations within interpolations, owing to Lonergan's having revised his own revisions.

(3) As the chart suggests, several whole sections of varying length have been added. The 'Outline of the Argument' and the 'Introduction,' mentioned already, are two of these; another is an appendix to §15. Two more, which come from the version of 1980, are drafts of concluding sections, nearly finished to all appearances but dropped after the next year's version. We have edited these sections and returned them to their concluding function at the end of part 1. The eleven further sections we have reinstated constitute much the greater part of our editorial interpolations and call for some further explanation.

As will be clear from the chart, the second half of Lonergan's *Essay*, beginning with the section on measuring change in the productive process, went through two major revisions. Of the last nine sections in the 1944 version, three were rewritten, wholly or in part, before the earliest of the 'textbook' versions was photocopied for the first of Lonergan's seminars in 1978. Later, in time for the version of 1980, Lonergan replaced all nine of these sections with four new ones, which together are less than a third as long as what they replace. These four more recent sections remain in the 'final' version and are included as §§17 through 20 in part 1 of the present edition. All the material they replaced – the nine 'original' sections of 1944, together with the revisions of 1978 – is included here as §§23 through 31 and the 'Additional Notes' to §§24, 25, and 31. It forms, in other words, part 3 of the present edition.

All of this can be summarized as follows.

Part 1 of our edition is Lonergan's typescript of 1983, augmented, in the text or in footnotes, with material he wrote for earlier versions or for supplemental pages given out in his seminar. These interpolations can be distinguished from the contents of the 'final' typescript without much difficulty. Except in certain equations, Lonergan never used square brackets in his *Essay*, which also has no footnotes. Everything that is bracketed in the present edition, and every footnote, has been added by the editors. It follows that anyone who wishes to read the 1983 version 'neat' can do so by ignoring all the footnotes and the bracketed passages, together with the longer passages that are marked with a marginal line.

Part 3, roughly speaking, is the second half of the *Essay* as found in the 1944 version. As with part 1, we have augmented it with later material, mainly from the version of 1978, but also from Lonergan's supplemental pages. The notation has been brought into conformity with part 1, as discussed below, and it can be regarded as an alternative ending to that part – something like the 'Great Fugue' that Beethoven originally wrote as the last movement of one of his string quartets, the final version of which has a briefer and more accessible finale. At the end of §16, that is to say, the reader may go directly to part 3, which deals with the same topics as §§17 and 18 in part 1, but in much greater mathematical detail.

It remains to take note of some related typographical matters. Some of the information set out in the chart is also given in the text. Throughout the present edition we have indicated by year the version in which any passage longer than a few words first appeared. As explained above, the contents of the 'final' typescript were written at different times, and each of its components is preceded by its date, enclosed by upright lines thus: |1980|. The remaining passages in part 1, which are the passages we have reinserted, have their dates enclosed instead in square brackets. In part 3 the components are likewise dated. Although we have not thought it necessary to add a marginal line calling attention to the fact, everything in this part comes from versions of the *Essay* other than the 'final' one. Accordingly, all the dates are in square brackets.

As in other volumes of Collected Works of Bernard Lonergan, editorial changes that affect only spelling, obvious typing errors, and punctuation have been made silently. A small number of editorial clarifications appear within square brackets. It has been necessary to renumber all the sections; Lonergan's numbers (which changed) are indicated in the chart. More serious are the changes we have made in some of Lonergan's mathematical expressions. Altering these has been necessary for one or both of two reasons.

In the first place, Lonergan himself modified the symbolic notation, sometimes more than once, in the course of revising the *Essay*. As a result, there are inconsistencies not only between different versions but also within some of them. The 'final' version is one of these; its notation, as it stands in Lonergan's typescript, is not uniform. An explanation of many of these notational shifts lies in the somewhat complicated history of the 'Diagram of Rates of Flow,' to which an appendix in the present edition is devoted. We have endeavored to make the symbolic notation consistent throughout the present edition, especially, though not only, in restoring earlier material. The conventions we adopted are listed at the point in Lonergan's argument where they first become relevant, and will be found in a footnote near the beginning of §8. Insofar as our changes involve only the substitution of one symbol for another, we have made them silently.

More problematic, in the second place, are certain formulations in the version of 1944 that are not, as they stand there, mathematically correct. Lonergan appears to have become aware of at least some of these mistakes, and this may explain why none of the questionable expressions survives in his 'final' typescript. The sections of the 'original' version in which these expressions appear do, however, have a place in the present edition, for reasons already given. When we have found it necessary, for the sake of incorporating this older material, to correct what Lonergan originally wrote, attention is called to the fact in footnotes, and his own formulation is recorded.

In conclusion, something should be said about part 2 and about the title.

The second part of the present edition, 'Healing and Creating in History,' never belonged to the text of the *Essay* as such. It is a lecture, given and first published in 1975, that Lonergan assigned as reading for his macroeconomics seminar. It has since been reprinted in *A Third Collection* and in *The Lonergan Reader*, and is to be included in another volume of Lonergan's Collected Works.[2] Despite this wide availability, we have given it a place here because, as the title of his seminar, 'Macroeconomics and the Dialectic of History,' suggests and as the Editors' Introduction spells out, Lonergan always regarded his work in economic theory as relevant to

---

2 *Bernard Lonergan: 3 Lectures*, ed. R. Eric O'Connor (Montreal: The Thomas More Institute, 1975) 55–68; *A Third Collection: Papers by Bernard J.F. Lonergan*, ed. Frederick E. Crowe (London: Geoffrey Chapman; New York and Mahwah, NJ: Paulist Press, 1985) 100–109; *The Lonergan Reader*, ed. Mark D. Morelli and Elizabeth A. Morelli (Toronto: University of Toronto Press, 1997) 566–76.

larger questions that are both real, concrete, and practical, and at the same time ethical, philosophical, and ultimately religious. The beginning of such a trajectory can be discerned in the section on 'The Position of This Essay' which in the present edition is the final section of part 1. 'Healing and Creating in History' continues the trajectory, indicating more fully the direction in which Lonergan was heading. Hence its inclusion as part 2.

Finally, the title. Although *An Essay in Circulation Analysis* is the name that appears at the beginning of each of the seven versions discussed above, we have reason to think it likely that Lonergan would have changed it. One alternative for which there is documentary evidence is *A Primer in Macroeconomic Dynamics*;[3] another is *An Essay in Macroeconomic Analysis*.[4] A case could be made for adopting either of these. Calling his work a primer was surely a bit of irony on Lonergan's part, but certainly his concern is with macroeconomic analysis, not with an analysis of circulation in any more restricted sense. Again, what he analyzes is not static but dynamic; that is a fundamental emphasis from the outset. Absent any unequivocal evidence that he had made up his mind, the title that Lonergan was content to keep while he worked on his revisions has been kept here also, as a subtitle to the more properly descriptive *Macroeconomic Dynamics*.

CHARLES C. HEFLING, JR.

3 Letter to Jane Collier, Cambridge University, 12 June 1982 (Archives, Lonergan Research Institute, Toronto).
4 The thirteen pages that are 'new' in the version of 1983 are numbered with the prefix 'EMA,' which Lonergan explained as stated.

Editors' Introduction

Economist Peter Burley has written, 'I know of no work quite like this Essay. Its detailed interest in technical details of macroeconomic dynamics is not the sort of thing one normally finds in social ethical treatises. At the same time its Christian reformist orientation puts it outside the socialist or liberal positivist literatures. It certainly owes many of its technical insights to Schumpeter, but seems to me to have a more systematic core than that many-sided, but unmathematical genius, ever specified.'[1]

This introduction is an attempt to come to terms with the unique character of Bernard Lonergan's *Essay in Circulation Analysis*.[2] To accomplish this task several bases need to be touched. First, because Lonergan's work is otherwise concerned almost totally with issues in philosophy, theology, and generalized empirical method, the story needs to be told of how his writing on economics arose, and of his two periods, separated by about forty years,

---

1 Peter Burley, 'A Summary of Lonergan's Economics,' in *Lonergan and You: Riverview Reflections 1985* (Katoomba, Australia: Bennett & Son, 1987) 1–10, at 1–2. This article was republished, with a slightly different title ('A Summary of Lonergan's Economic Diagram') and other changes, in *Australian Lonergan Workshop*, ed. William J. Danaher (Lanham, MD: University Press of America, 1993) 3–11.

2 As the Editors' Preface indicates, this was the title that Lonergan consistently gave to various versions of the present work. We will use this title (and the abbreviations *Essay* and *ECA*) in this introduction, unless we are referring specifically to the present edition, in which case our abbreviation will be *MD:ECA*.

of concentrated work in economics. Second, at least a tentative and preliminary account of the significance (for his life's work and for the Collected Works) of Lonergan's labors in the field of economics is needed. Third, the *Essay* has to be tentatively situated in relation to the vast and diversified field of conventional economics. And fourth, some brief overview of the content and possible relevance of the work itself has to be given.

Outline of Contents
1 Lonergan's Entry into Economics, 1930–1944
2 Democratic Economics: An Alternative to Liberalism and Socialism
3 Lonergan's Reentry into Economics, 1978–1983
4 Lonergan's Interlocutors in Economics
5 Macroeconomic Dynamic Analysis as a New Paradigm of Economic Theory
6 The Systematic Significance of the Fundamental Distinction between Basic and Surplus Production and Exchange
7 Lonergan's Critique of Secularist Ideologies: The Need for a Theological Viewpoint

1   Lonergan's Entry into Economics, 1930–1944

Lonergan's work in economic theory originally was done between 1930 and 1944. His preoccupations during the 1930s were far-reaching. In his first Roman period Lonergan wrote in a letter to Henry Keane, his Provincial Superior in the Society of Jesus, about the possibility of working out a metaphysics of history that would provide a truly Christian response to the issues raised by Hegel and Marx. And he produced substantial texts on the theory and philosophy of history.[3] In one of these texts, Lonergan provided a statement of what was on his mind at this time:

> ... any reflection on modern history and its consequent 'Crisis in the West' reveals unmistakably the necessity of a *Summa Sociologica*. A metaphysic of history is not only imperative for the church to meet

3 At least some of these texts are extant in the archives of the Lonergan Research Institute in Toronto (henceforth Lonergan Archives, Toronto). On this see Frederick E. Crowe and Robert M. Doran, 'Editors' Preface' (to 'Lonergan's *Pantôn Anakephalaiôsis* [Restoration of All Things],' *METHOD: Journal of Lonergan Studies* 9:2 (October 1991) 134–38.

the attack of the Marxian materialist conception of history and its realization in apostolic Bolshevism: it is imperative if man is to solve the modern politico-economic entanglement, if political and economic forces are to be subjected to the rule of reason ...[4]

Lonergan felt challenged by what he then called 'the heritage of intellectual vacuity and social chaos given by the nineteenth century to the twentieth.'[5] He cast an especially critical eye on the nineteenth century's 'asinine confidence in political economists' that 'has landed the twentieth century in an earthly hell.'[6]

The present economics *Essay* together with those sociological and historical papers make clear that the scope of Lonergan's intent during those years embraced a range of issues that since the eighteenth century have been categorized as 'political economy': (a) a philosophy of history oriented toward the transformation of social practice; and (b) an empirical analysis of the processes and structures in the production of the material substratum of human societies and cultures. One earlier draft of what eventually became our *Essay* bore the typewritten title *For a New Political Economy*.[7] Another draft bears the handwritten superscript *Essay towards a Pure Theory of Social Economics*.[8]

Lonergan's express interest in the economic side of political economy began when he was doing his philosophical studies at Heythrop College, Oxfordshire, while taking an external degree in languages and mathematics at London University. At Heythrop he was taught ethics by Lewis Watt, s.j., the author of *Capitalism and Morality* (1929)[9] and of *Catholic Social Prin-*

4 Lonergan, '*Pantôn Anakephalaiôsis* [Restoration of All Things],' *METHOD: Journal of Lonergan Studies* 9:2 (1991) 139–69, at 156.

5 Lonergan, 'Philosophy of History,' an unpublished typescript in the Lonergan Archives, Toronto, to be dated in the mid or late 1930s, with pagination 95–130; our quotation is from p. 98.

6 Ibid. 99.

7 'For a New Political Economy,' Lonergan Archives, Toronto. Now published as part 1 in *For a New Political Economy*, ed. Philip McShane, vol. 21 of Collected Works of Bernard Lonergan (Toronto: University of Toronto Press, 1998).

8 'Essay towards a Pure Theory of Social Economics,' Lonergan Archives, Toronto. Now published in part 2 of the same volume 21 of the Collected Works.

9 Lewis Watt, s.j. *Capitalism and Morality* (London, Toronto, Melbourne, and Sydney: Cassell & Co., 1929).

ciples (1929),[10] a commentary applying the teachings of the papal encyclical *Rerum novarum* to the English scene.[11] According to Lonergan, Watt related moral principles to what he considered the necessary and ironclad laws of economics. Lonergan was outraged by the way these 'necessary and ironclad laws' led British policy-makers to believe that it would have been morally wrong for England to violate the market's laws of supply and demand in order to relieve the Irish famine.[12] He deeply appreciated Watt's concessions to facts: anyone could see that businesses trying to pay what church teaching speaks of as a 'family wage' were less successful than their competitors who did not attempt to do so. As Lonergan recalls Watt's blunt posing of the problem: 'you starve the workers to keep capitalism going, or you feed the workers and ruin capitalism.'[13]

Through Watt's course on Catholic social ethics Lonergan clarified an all-important insight. As a general command, the moral precept of a 'just' or 'family' wage so stressed by the social encyclicals – in traditional Catholic teaching, more a precept of charity than of justice – was extrinsic to the economic reality of the concrete situation of businessmen and wage earners. This gap between well-intentioned moral demands and economic exigencies prompted Lonergan to inquire how economic moral precepts could be based on or grounded in the economy itself.[14]

When Lonergan returned to Canada from England in 1930 the Great Depression, in which 'the rich were poor and the poor were out of work,'[15] was in full swing. What were the economic forces underlying the Depres-

10 Lewis Watt, s.j. *Catholic Social Principles: A Commentary on the Papal Encyclical RERUM NOVARUM* (London: Burns, Oates & Washbourne, 1929).

11 Watt also wrote over forty articles on social and economic questions, and over thirty pamphlets (mostly the result of lectures he gave), including one entitled *Communism and Religion* (London: Catholic Truth Society, 1934) and another called *Usury in Catholic Theology* (Oxford: Catholic Social Guild, 1945).

12 See Lonergan's remarks in *Caring about Meaning: Patterns in the Life of Bernard Lonergan*, ed. Pierrot Lambert, Charlotte Tansey, and Cathleen Going (Montreal: Thomas More Institute Papers/82, 1982) 30–31.

13 See Philip McShane, 'Features of Generalized Empirical Method and the Actual Context of Economics,' in *Creativity and Method: Essays in Honor of Bernard Lonergan S.J.*, ed. Matthew L. Lamb (Milwaukee: Marquette University Press, 1981) 543–71, at 562.

14 *Caring about Meaning* 31.

15 Ibid.

sion? Even as the dominant neoclassical paradigm in economics was being discredited by the economic events of the Depression, the need to pay special attention to the concrete intelligibility of specifically *economic* events was brought home vividly to Lonergan by propaganda for Clifford H. Douglas's famous Social Credit movement. Lonergan was impressed by Major Douglas's focus upon the permanent gap between the earnings of (fully employed) workers and the cost of a minimally adequate standard of living, since wage rates were low and prices high. He was not satisfied with Douglas's $A + B$ formula and the deceptive simplicity of his inflationary policy implications, which Lonergan thought lacked a foundation in an accurate analysis of actual economic occurrences.[16] Why Douglas's solution was inflationary in character posed a unique challenge for Lonergan. It helped him to formulate the question that inspired his analysis.

Lonergan was concerned about how laborers were to afford to cover capitalists' profits (*MD:ECA* 33, note 34). Several of his book reviews written during this period show that he had a vital interest in such things as cooperatives and Catholic social action generally. In a short review written in 1942, Lonergan spoke of a 'materialistic, anti-traditional tendency' in modern culture:

> Its obvious representative is in the field of economics: eighteenth century capitalism, nineteenth century communism and twentieth century nazism. Such is the great materialist trinity: communism is a collectivist reaction against capitalist individualism; nazism is a nationalist reaction against the international character of finance and world revolution. Despite their differences and oppositions, all three agree in their dedication of man, soul and body, to the goods of this world. None of them acknowledges and submits to a higher end or a higher law for man. Their consequences are not a matter of abstract deduc-

---

16 See Clifford H. Douglas, *Credit-Power and Democracy: With a Draft Scheme for the Mining Industry* (London: Palmer, 1921). See also by the same author *Social Credit*, revised ed. (New York: Norton, 1933). On the 'A + B formula' Philip McShane (note 13 above, at 563) has this to say: 'according to Douglas, there is a permanent discrepancy between A (the purchasing power of consumers) and A + B (the total cost of production [of the goods workers need for a minimal standard of living]). The view leads to a requirement of consumer credit ...'

tion. The experiment has been performed and still is being performed on the quivering body of humanity. The results are not pleasant.[17]

Lonergan grasped how the great orientations of twentieth-century politics – liberal capitalism, communist socialism, and all nationalisms – are all integrally related to concrete economic issues. None of these political orientations actually based its policies on a correct understanding of the dynamic schemes that require human cooperation, that call forth 'some procedure that sets the balance between the production of consumer goods and new capital formation, some method that settles what quantities of what goods and services are to be supplied, some device for assigning tasks to individuals and for distributing among them the common product,'[18] namely, the exchange processes of the market. He realized that failure to understand correctly what is needed if the economic process is to perform well is gravely threatening to democratic liberty. This is why he undertook his serious study of economics.

Schumpeter's statement that scientific analysis is a matter not of 'logically consistent process' but of 'an incessant struggle with creations of our own and our predecessors' minds'[19] is certainly true of Lonergan's path to his own analysis. Archival evidence – we do not know how complete it is – of Lonergan's pursuit of economic understanding exists in the form of handwritten notes, digests of books read, excerpts, and comments.[20]

17 Lonergan, review of Andrew J. Krzersinski, *Is Modern Culture Doomed?* in *The Canadian Register* (Quebec edition), 19 September 1942, p. 8.

18 Lonergan, *Insight: A Study of Human Understanding* (first published in 1957; 2nd rev. ed., London: Longmans, Green and Co., and New York: Philosophical Library, 1958; Collected Works edition, Toronto: University of Toronto Press, 1992). References to *Insight* will give first the 1958 and then the 1992 page numbers (e.g., 626/649); in the present instance the relevant pages are 208/234.

19 Joseph A. Schumpeter, *History of Economic Analysis,* ed. from manuscript by Elizabeth Boody Schumpeter (New York: Oxford University Press, 1954) 4.

20 Much of the extant evidence can be found in *For a New Political Economy* (see above, note 7). Further, the Lonergan Archives show that during his fourteen-year stint with economics Lonergan studied carefully Lionel C. Robbins's *An Essay on the Nature and Significance of Economic Science* (1932); Frank H. Knight's *Risk, Uncertainty and Profit* (1921); C.F. Roos's *Dynamic Economics* (1934); Friedrich A. Hayek's *Monetary Theory and the Trade Cycle* (1933) and *Profits, Interest, and Investment* (1939); and Erik A. Lindahl's *Studies in the Theory of Money and Capital* (1939).

One of the most substantial batches of archival material is made up of Lonergan's notes on the rather forbidding *Lehrbuch der Nationalökonomie* by the German Jesuit Heinrich Pesch, whose views formed the theoretical core of Pope Pius XI's encyclical *Quadragesimo anno*.[21] Besides dealing with the interrelated issues of production, exchange, and finance, Pesch insisted that economics is a matter of natural ethics – a position that recalls Lonergan's own deep appreciation of Thomas Aquinas's way of generalizing and consistently applying the 'distinction between a natural order and a supervening gratuitous order.'[22] Although he agreed with the consensus among secular economists on the intellectual autonomy of economics, Pesch nevertheless disagreed with its denial of any specifically economic end or aim or finality. For both Lonergan and Pesch the properly economic goal is the appropriate standard of living, the betterment of the material conditions of human existence. For both, economic activity provides the material substratum for the cultural creations of human ingenuity and aspiration.

Lonergan probably also found Pesch's insights into subsidiarity congenial. And Pesch may even have helped Lonergan to understand the relationship between economics and the properly political order. For the Lonergan of *Insight* (first published 1957), economic ends fit concretely into an ordered hierarchy: technology, which is the society's concrete possibility for transforming the potentialities of nature into the standard of living, is subordinate to economy, which is the process for producing and distributing the best possible standard of living; and economy is subordinated to a political order embodying a democratic, free-enterprise economy. If the concretely functioning economy disposes of material and technological resources to mediate the material conditions of human living, the task of politics is to constitute an ethos for disposing of the economy, 'an ethos that at once subtly and flexibly provides concrete premises

21 On Heinrich Pesch, see John C. Cort, *Christian Socialism: An Informal History* (Maryknoll, NY: Orbis Books, 1988) 288–94.
22 Lonergan, *Insight* 527/550. And see his *Grace and Freedom: Operative Grace in the Thought of St. Thomas Aquinas*, ed. J. Patout Burns (London: Darton, Longman & Todd, and New York: Herder and Herder, 1971) 1–19; the book is a republication of a series of articles reworking Lonergan's doctoral dissertation and first published in *Theological Studies* 2 (1941) 289–324; 3 (1942) 69–88, 375–402, 533–78.

and norms for practical decisions.'[23] At the core of any ethos, according to Lonergan writing in *Method in Theology* (1972), is a normative scale of values: *vital* values condition and are subordinate to *social* values such as a properous economy; social values condition and are subordinate to *cultural* values that give meaning and value to a society's way of life; these cultural values condition and serve *personal* values – the freedom and dignity of each human being; and all these values condition and are oriented and fulfilled by *religious* values relating us directly to divine transcendence.[24]

Hence, a key to grasping the intent of this *Essay* is Lonergan's recognition that political and economic goods of order are distinct yet not separate. If the distinction is not maintained both in theory and in practical policy-making, catastrophic confusion results: 'the materialist trinity' of liberal capitalism, communist socialism, and nationalism or fascism, each of which illustrates what happens when the proper limits of politics and economics are not respected. Politics then becomes less a mediator of practical intelligence than an arbiter of sheer power; at the same time, economics becomes politicized, not in the sense of a practically intelligent subordination to higher political ends, but in the sense of unintelligent, unreasonable, and irresponsible manipulations of the economic good of order that run counter to the intelligibility proper to economic processes.

Lonergan focused upon the challenge presented by the contemporary crisis of freedom and democracy by grasping the central structures constituting the concrete intelligibility of the economic good of order in modern capitalist exchange economies. This had to be done in order to let economics be economics and politics be politics as people cooperate freely and morally to achieve the common good in the modern world. Lonergan's end was ultimately political; but for the sake of the political goods of freedom and democracy, he dedicated himself to understanding the limits of the economic sphere in its proper autonomy.

2   Democratic Economics: An Alternative to Liberalism and Socialism

Lonergan always liked to insist that the old-time political economists were champions of democracy. Whatever may be true of those older political

---

23 Lonergan, *Insight* 222/248.
24 Lonergan, *Method in Theology* (London: Darton, Longman & Todd, and New York: Herder and Herder, 1972; reprinted Toronto: University of Toronto Press, 1990, 1994, 1996) 31–32, 39.

economists, he himself was certainly a champion of democracy in the sense that the raison d'être of his work in economics was to make it possible for citizens to overcome serious economic problems democratically. He did not develop a full-blown political theory, but he was opposed to relegating the course of the economy to any bureaucracy, whether it be capitalist or socialist in name.

In a 1941 book review Lonergan expressed his worry that in view of the threat of Nazism and Communism democracy might seem to be 'a noble experiment that failed,' an experiment 'doomed to the quiet death of uninspired regimentation under an intellectually insignificant bureaucracy.'[25] Lonergan's conception of human freedom and his correlative idea of democracy led him to take seriously what James Madison in *The Federalist* (no. 39) speaks of as 'that honourable determination, which animates every votary of freedom, to rest all our political experiments on the capacity of mankind for self-government.' For Lonergan the possibility of human self-government is identical with the potentiality for being attentive, intelligent, reasonable, and responsible. Thus, human freedom is concretely realized by attentive, intelligent, reasonable, and responsible conduct in fields of action where no coercion is involved and alternative courses of action are objectively open. It follows that, read in this context, the statement of *The Federalist* (no. 1) about 'government from reflection and choice' instead of by 'accident and force' is a clear rendering of what Lonergan means by democracy.

It is plain then that Lonergan's idea of democracy and of democratic economics is integrally bound up with his notion of human freedom grounded in knowledge. He dramatically contrasts bureaucratic economics and free-enterprise economics: 'The bureaucrat ... gives [people] what he thinks good for them and he gives it in the measure he finds possible or convenient; nor can he do otherwise, for the brains of a bureaucracy are not equal to the task of thinking of everything; only the brains of all men together can even approximate to that.'[26]

Free enterprise for Lonergan is right, and bureaucratically managed economy is wrong, not because of some doctrinaire libertarianism on his part, but because free enterprise is the method of the self-correcting proc-

25 Lonergan, review of M.M. Coady, *Masters of Their Own Destiny*, in *The Montreal Beacon*, 2 May 1941, p. 3.
26 Lonergan, *For a New Political Economy* (see note 7 above) 34.

ess that concrete economies require, whereas bureaucracies exclude the kind of widespread and ongoing learning that progress demands at every level of the exchange process. Lonergan asked in that 1941 review:

> Why does the proletariat today include almost everyone? Why is the control of industry in the hands of fewer and fewer? Radically it is our own fault. We leave our affairs to others, because we are too indolent and too stupid to get to work and run them ourselves. The results are palpably ruinous; our system of free enterprise cannot survive if only a few practise free enterprise.[27]

What Lonergan means by a free-enterprise system comes out in a question-and-answer session in June 1977 when he said:

> Very definitely I should say that the issue of free enterprise is proximately scientific but ultimately existential. It is proximately scientific inasmuch as one has to refuse to mean by free enterprise what has been going on in the West for the past two hundred years. One has to mean what is revealed as possible by a functional analysis in macroeconomics. But the issue is ultimately existential, for one has to choose between praxis and technique.
>
> Planning is a technique by which a few people take upon themselves the office of deciding what vast numbers of other people are to do, whether they are to do it, and what will happen to them if they don't. That is what planning means. And it is not particularly intelligent because it uses old ideas that everybody understands and knows are good; it is not a source of initiative.
>
> Free enterprise is a setup in which individuals are free to figure out what can be done, whether they will do it; and if they so decide they take upon themselves the risk of doing it ...
>
> The issue between planning and free enterprise is existential in two manners. It arises inasmuch as it is doubtful whether or not the people are totally corrupt. If people are totally corrupt then planning is inevitable. They can't help themselves. In the manner that they are not, you have some hope. But it is also existential inasmuch as

---

27 Lonergan, review of M.M. Coady, 3.

one's decision on the issue tells something about the kind of person one is. Our age is an age of technique; our behaviorists, positivists, newsmen, politicians know and think a great deal of technique and very little of praxis, and one can catch the virus. But deciding one way or the other is existential.[28]

2.1 Liberalism and Socialism as Economistic Ideologies

Lonergan was aware that since the nineteenth century most official Catholic social teaching about political and economic matters, while favoring democracy, has tended toward the general advice to steer between the extremes of liberalism and socialism. Although he agreed with aspects of both, Lonergan considered liberalism and socialism to be manifestations of the major 'surrender [of intelligence] on the speculative level.'[29] The relationship between the economic order and the political order in modernity is one fraught with difficulties, and from Lonergan's perspective, the difficulties are exacerbated by what, in the foundations for social theory elaborated in *Insight*, is called the longer cycle of decline.[30]

Adam Smith's *Wealth of Nations* sets forth a theory of the 'natural system of liberty' that lays the basis for a disagreement with John Locke's way of relating economics to politics in *The Second Treatise of Civil Government*. There it is argued that capitalist economy as natural needs political control by the social contract, which establishes a civil government to make laws. Smith's 'natural system of liberty' implies the primacy of the economic order (though this did not mean that he was doctrinaire about rejecting certain government interventions into economic affairs). Today, liberalism has hardened into a position that endorses the primacy of economic forces in the public sphere, while socialism favors the politicization of economics. For Lonergan, these two positions are involved in general bias[31] and so promote the longer cycle of decline. Briefly, then, the bearing of this classification is as follows.

With liberalism Lonergan upholds the strengths of the free-enterprise system when it comes to economic innovation and growth and improvement in the standard of living. Equality of opportunity is praiseworthy. But

28 Lonergan, response to questions at the Lonergan Workshop, Boston College, June 1977, pp. 7–8 in the transcript made by Nicholas Graham of the question session of 24 June (pp. 87–88 in the cumulative transcript for the week).

29 Lonergan, *Insight* 230/255.

30 Ibid. 226–42/251–67.

31 On general bias see Lonergan, *Insight* xiv–xv/8–9, 225–42/250–67.

he does not agree with the liberal tendency to dismiss as ideological any argument not based on market cost-effectiveness, since there are goods people need and attain that cannot be judged in terms of exchange value. Hence he regarded as ideological the liberal assumption that arguments in the political sphere can only be adequately adjudicated in sheerly economic terms.

Lonergan was utterly sympathetic with aspects of the socialist critique of the defects of capitalism: the flagrant and gross inequalities in the distribution of the social product manifest in the proletariat or what today we call the 'permanent underclass'; the callousness and crassness of commercialism that puts money before human beings; the harshness of the consequences for people who cannot compete as producers and consumers: the sick, the handicapped or 'challenged,' the injured, the young, especially infants, and the very old. Yet he profoundly disagreed with the socialist propensity to interpret the primacy of the political sphere over the economic sphere in terms of a bureaucratic control of free enterprise for the sake of general welfare.

Lonergan abandoned the classicist notion of culture and of society and reconceived the modern, empirical idea of culture in terms of a notion of the human good that transposes the classic distinction between the *bonum utile* (good because useful) and the *bonum honestum* (true good based on virtue) into a transculturally valid heuristic structure. Hence, Lonergan's social theory is completely compatible with, and in fact supports, the differentiation of government rule from religious authority. On his analysis of the longer cycle of decline, however, conscience and objective morality would have to be kept in the public sphere so that the ends of society as defined religiously or morally well beyond mere safety and comfort could in some way authorize a public use of power; otherwise, unrestrained self-interest will be both socially and culturally dominant. This situation constitutes the major pitfall for the bias of common sense classically formulated in Machiavelli's teaching that in order for society to function smoothly force or fraud has to substitute for morality. This 'commonsensical' trimming-down of theory to meet the requirements of bad practice was further elaborated by the 'new science of politics' when Locke, Smith, Montesquieu, and Madison explicitly sought to substitute acquisitiveness for morality by establishing 'institutions with teeth in them,' institutions that would liberate greed by protecting commerce and economic rights.

Liberal democracy's original theorists, such as Thomas Hobbes, Baruch Spinoza, and John Locke, inferred from the factually controversial nature of the good, especially the highest good, that conscience and convictions about objective morality can all too easily turn into the chief causes of civil war. Peaceful human cooperation would consequently demand authorization by a democratic consent based on a lowest-common-denominator consensus that tends to overlook or neglect religious, personal, and cultural values. For Lonergan the corresponding normative overemphasis upon the subpolitical laws of the market is destructive in the long run of the social and vital values at the heart of both free enterprise and liberal democracy.

Until the upheavals of 1989 to 1991, there was tremendous pressure for liberal regimes to incorporate socialism as the best remedy for the economically disenfranchised. Lonergan contended that socialism corrects the relentless liberal pursuit of self-interest by means of a bureaucracy, thus eliminating capitalism's problems by abolishing people's freedom.[32] According to Lonergan, if the pursuit of socialist goals lacks true understanding of economic processes, it cannot help but waste capital unproductively.

2.2 Free Enterprise as an Educational Project

In his concern for liberty as the potentiality for the human good, Lonergan was critical of the liberal meaning of freedom as just doing as one pleases, because it assumed that human reason is a calculating faculty in the service of the passions. Accordingly, the liberal conception of the free-enterprise economy embodies the classic economic assumption that the human being is a maximizer of satisfaction or utility in a market. In spite of their scepticism that monopolists and monopsonists would eventually balance each other, Montesquieu and Madison grounded democracy on the strategy expressed in Madison's classic formulation of the foundations of the large commercial republic in *The Federalist* (nos. 10 and 51): a political framework in which countervailing business powers would each cancel out the

---

32 For Lonergan, prediction and control are not legitimate ends of science because they are not the same as verified understanding, which is the true aim of science. Moreover, prediction and control in the area of the so-called applied human sciences conflict with the very nature of the subject matter of human science: on the one hand, prediction and control depend upon and imply the policy of the elimination of human freedom; on the other, human freedom is something that may just spring up even in situations in which people have managed practically to eliminate it.

worst depredations of the other. This is a subordination of the political order to the economic order. In what Lonergan called an amoral devotion to automatism, the new political science thought it could use group bias to defeat group bias.

Similarly, Lonergan was no less critical of the socialist view of freedom, which (according to J.L. Talmon) derives from the social totalitarianism inherent in Rousseau's idea that, if necessary, 'people have ... to be forced to be free.'[33] The socialist appeal to universalism is procedural. In their way of exploiting group bias socialists give universalist rationalizations in order to 'set up a bureaucracy and regiment a people,' in Lonergan's phrase,[34] thus giving up democracy in all but name. Lonergan always insisted that the problems of the economy cannot be solved by suppressing either freedom or free exchange. Why?

According to Lonergan, liberty is an originating value, the principle of the human good. This liberty is actualized whenever people intelligently conceive concrete courses of action in response to the question, What should we do? and reasonably judge that these courses of action are the right thing to do in response to the question, Should we do it? and then responsibly decide and act in the light of their understandings and judgments. Such questions for deliberation intend values conditioned by the technological, economic, and political orders that make them concretely possible. To the extent that people become reasonably sure that their choices of conditioned goods are also, at least implicitly, choices regarding the fulfilment of the prior or concomitant conditions that enable those goods to be achieved, they are humanly operating as fully free. This is the context in which we ought to read the following passage from a fragment of an earlier version of our *Essay*:

> ... the liberal dream of an automatic economy has, like all dreams, at long last broken. The necessity of rational control has ceased to be a question, and the one issue is the locus of that control. Is it to be absolutist from above downwards? Is it to be democratic from below upwards? Plainly it can be democratic only in the measure in which economic science succeeds in uttering not counsel to rulers but precepts to mankind, not specific remedies and plans to increase the

33 See J.L. Talmon, *The Origins of Totalitarian Democracy* (New York: Praeger, 1960; first published in 1952) 42.

34 Lonergan, *For a New Political Economy* 4.

power of bureaucracies, but universal laws which men themselves administrate in the personal conduct of their lives ... [T]o deny the possibility of a new science and new precepts is, I am convinced, to deny the possibility of the survival of democracy.[35]

Lonergan thought of his work in economics as a contribution to a vast educational program 'to train and equip the masses for economic independence';[36] 'to release the spontaneity and the creativeness that reside not in red tape but in human beings, not in ideologies nor in parties nor in the advice of experts nor in five-year plans but in free men.'[37] The ultimate aim of his *Essay* was 'a democratic economics that can issue practical imperatives to plain men.'[38] He considered valid macroeconomic dynamic analysis 'an instrument that democracy must have, for it is the broad generalization, the significant correlation, that effectively organizes free men without breaking down their freedom.'[39] Thus, Lonergan called for an understanding of economics in which the economy is properly subordinated in a properly organized polity.

3   Lonergan's Reentry into Economics, 1978–1983

Lonergan's serious reengagement with economic issues from 1978 to 1983 was a 'second spring,' for those studies constituted a revival of work done in the 1930s and early 1940s. In the 1960s and early 1970s, when Lonergan was pushing to finish *Method in Theology*, political theology was arising in Europe and liberation theology was erupting in Latin America. In those days he frequently mentioned to friends that he had done some work on economics that he had let drop in 1944, after fourteen years of laboring on it whenever other duties were not pressing upon him. That earlier intensive work in economics had culminated in the novel and foundational analysis of productive processes and monetary exchange set forth in roughly 130 pages of typed text entitled *An Essay in Circulation Analysis* and dated

35 Lonergan, 'An Outline of Circulation Analysis' (Lonergan Archives, Toronto, Batch ɪɪ, Folder 58), p. 3 of unnumbered pages; now published in *For a New Political Economy* 110–11.
36 Lonergan, review of M.M. Coady, 3.
37 Lonergan, *For a New Political Economy* 4.
38 Ibid. 5.
39 Ibid. 7–8.

1944. He also spoke of passing the fruits of his labors on to experts in the field and getting little, if any, reaction or encouragement.[40]

Lonergan's way of summarizing what his economic theory was about was typically gnomic. With a twinkle in his eye he would allude to applying some fundamental theorems of calculus in order to grasp economic dynamisms so that one could draw such practical precepts about the proper functioning of any concrete economy as, 'Don't put on the brakes and the accelerator at the same time!' Few listeners in those days had any clue to the meaning of these seemingly cryptic sayings. Although he wondered aloud about returning to his work in economics, he remained characteristically reluctant to publish anything with which he did not feel finished or satisfied. At the same time he was typically willing to hand over his text to any brave soul who, tantalized by his enigmatic summaries, asked for something to study.

Already in the late 1960s he had sent a couple of postcards to Philip McShane in Ireland, stating that the political theology of Johann Baptist Metz lacked anything on economics.[41] Lonergan's talk about the economics work increased exponentially as he approached the closing phases of getting *Method* published. Later on he often told an anecdote about attending a *Concilium* conference held in 1977 at the University of Notre Dame shortly after he became Distinguished Visiting Professor of Theology at Boston College. At Notre Dame he took part in a round-table discussion group at which Gustavo Gutierrez stated that the real problem with liberation theology was that none of the liberation theologians of the day had a serious knowledge of economics. And so from 1978 until illness caused him to withdraw from active teaching in 1983, Lonergan taught the course 'Macroeconomics and the Dialectic of History' for one semester each academic year. The text of *ECA* formed the main reading for the course.

Lonergan was always keenly aware of current developments in secular

---

40 See *The Question as Commitment: A Symposium*, ed. Elaine Cahn and Cathleen Going (Montreal: Thomas More Institute Papers / 77, 1977) 32, 110.

41 As McShane recalls it now (personal communication), this was probably in the summer of 1968, when he received a postcard from Lonergan asking whether he could find an economist to read a work of his (Lonergan's) on economic theory. The following day another postcard arrived giving the reason for the first: Lonergan had been reading Metz on economic justice and considered it was time such reflections were taken out of the context of the family wage and put into that of an adequate economic theory.

economics. In the early 1970s the United States economy was in a recession. Besides declaring a wage freeze, the President caused a minor sensation by stating publicly the truism of u.s. domestic policy: 'We're all Keynesians now.' Even as the liberation theologians abroad were advocating democratic-socialist control of markets, the u.s. economy was experiencing the phenomenon of 'stagflation' – a clearly discernible overturning of the conventional economic wisdom about the tradeoff between inflation and unemployment so neatly expressed in the Phillips curve.[42] So-called 'Keynesian fine-tuning onto the neoclassical track' was not working; and forms of socialist planning only promised to deepen rather than resolve the anomalies of welfare economics.

As he returned to work on economics in the 1970s Lonergan thought that Western economic policies were often based on 'mistaken expectations' (*MD:ECA* 80–86), fostering a lack of adaptation to the demands of what he called 'the social dividend of pure surplus (producer-goods) income' in relation to 'basic (consumer-goods) markets' (*MD:ECA* §27: 144–56). He believed he had an explanation for what, in a statement from the *Essay* we are editing, he described as a 'situation – sometimes thought mysterious – in which consumer prices continuously inflate, new enterprise is evaded, unemployment becomes chronic, and despite the inflation the value of stocks declines' (*MD:ECA* 175).

Meanwhile he had been reading Jane Jacobs, whom he greatly admired, and Adolph Lowe, whose *On Economic Knowledge*[43] had impressed him favorably. But what stirred in Lonergan the hope that he might indeed be able to connect his own ideas with those of current academic economics was his 1976 discovery of Michal Kalecki's *Selected Essays on the Dynamics of the Capitalist Economy* (1971).[44] 'With the discovery of Kalecki,' he said, 'I knew that there was a bridge-head.'[45] And so in 1976 he asked his old friend Eric Kierans (a former student of his who had taught economics at McGill University, and had been for a time a member of the Trudeau cabinet in Ottawa) how he could most efficiently catch up on developments in

---

42 See Mark Blaug, *Economic Theory in Retrospect*, 4th ed. (Cambridge: Cambridge University Press, 1985) 678–86, 690.

43 Adolph Lowe, *On Economic Knowledge: Toward a Science of Political Economics* (New York and Evanston: Harper Torchbooks, 1965).

44 Michal Kalecki, *Selected Essays on the Dynamics of the Capitalist Economy: 1933–1970* (Cambridge: At the University Press, 1971).

45 See *Caring about Meaning* 165.

economic theory since he had stopped studying it seriously on his own in 1944. On Kierans's advice Lonergan began a systematic study of back issues from the 1960s and 1970s of *The Economic Journal,* making his typical outlines, summaries, and excerpts of key articles.[46] He also began studying a broad spectrum of works on economics of which the following list is exemplary: W.W. Rostow's *The Stages of Economic Growth*[47] and his *Politics and the Stages of Growth;*[48] Adolph Lowe's *The Path of Economic Growth;*[49] John Eatwell's and Joan Robinson's *Introduction to Modern Economics;*[50] Joan Robinson's *Economic Heresies*[51] as well as other of her writings; William Breit's and Roger L. Ransom's *The Academic Scribblers;*[52] Robert J. Gordon's *Macroeconomics;*[53] such collections of essays as Alfred Eichner's *A Guide to Post-Keynesian Economics;*[54] and Daniel Bell's and Irving Kristol's *The Crisis in Economic Theory.*[55] He also made use of books going beyond economics proper such as Richard Barnet's and Ronald Müller's *Global Reach;*[56] and

46 *The Economic Journal* (The Quarterly Journal of the Royal Economic Society) was published through volume 84 (1974) in London by Macmillan Journals Ltd. Volumes 85 (1975) through 96 (1986) were published by Cambridge University Press. More recent volumes have been published by Basil Blackwell, Ltd., Oxford.

47 W.W. Rostow, *The Stages of Economic Growth: A Non-Communist Manifesto* (Cambridge: At the University Press, 1960; 3rd ed., 1990).

48 W.W. Rostow, *Politics and the Stages of Growth* (Cambridge: At the University Press, 1971).

49 Adolph Lowe, assisted by Stanford Pulrang, with an appendix by Edward J. Nell, *The Path of Economic Growth* (Cambridge: At the University Press, 1976).

50 Joan Robinson and John Eatwell, *An Introduction to Modern Economics* (Maidenhead, Berkshire: McGraw-Hill Book Co. [UK], 1973).

51 Joan Robinson, *Economic Heresies: Some Old-Fashioned Questions in Economic Theory* (New York: Basic Books, 1971, 1973).

52 William Breit and Roger L. Ransom, *The Academic Scribblers,* revised ed. (Hinsdale, IL: Dryden Press, 1982 [first edition, 1970]).

53 Robert J. Gordon, *Macroeconomics* (Boston and Toronto: Little, Brown & Co., 1978; 2nd ed., 1981).

54 Alfred S. Eichner, ed., *A Guide to Post-Keynesian Economics.* Foreword by Joan Robinson (White Plains, NY: M.E. Sharpe, 1978; 2nd printing, 1979).

55 Daniel Bell and Irving Kristol, ed., *The Crisis in Economic Theory* (New York: Basic Books, 1981).

56 Richard J. Barnet and Ronald E. Müller, *Global Reach: The Power of the Multinational Corporations* (New York: Simon & Schuster, 1974).

Joseph Collins's and Frances Moore Lappé's *Food First*,[57] and Colin Tudge's *The Famine Business*.[58] Finally, Joseph Alois Schumpeter's *History of Economic Analysis*[59] became a *vade mecum*. Lonergan seemed never to cease studying it during these years, and he referred to it often in his lectures, writings, and conversations.

Out of his profound concern for that decade's sufferings and struggles for economic and social justice, Lonergan, in his middle and late seventies, put in long hours of work at his desk. In this edition we have tried to make available all the modifications and expansions and improvements Lonergan made upon his 1944 text.[60]

4   Lonergan's Interlocutors in Economics

Lonergan himself thought his analysis of production and monetary circulation in an advanced exchange economy differed appreciably from classical, neoclassical, Keynesian, post-Keynesian, or Marxian accounts of capitalist economy.

The question motivating his economic analysis was, 'Why are there economic forces, making it impossible for industrialists to pay workmen a wage and for workmen to raise a family?'[61] Such a formulation might cause mainline neoclassical economists to suspect that his answer might lead to government intervention, which they oppose. But Lonergan's concern about inequities in the distribution of the social product did not entail the belief that the unfairness of the free market can be rightly handled through the intervention by state power into blind market forces, thus endangering the free expression of interests that occurs in market exchanges alone.

Lonergan is different from many concerned about social justice and sympathetic with his question about the workers. Since he did not rely on

---

57 Frances Moore Lappé and Joseph Collins with Cary Fowler, *Food First: Beyond the Myth of Scarcity* (Boston: Houghton Mifflin Co., 1977).
58 Colin Tudge, *The Famine Business* (London: Faber and Faber, 1977).
59 Joseph A. Schumpeter, *History of Economic Analysis*, ed. from manuscript by Elizabeth Boody Schumpeter (New York: Oxford University Press, 1954; 8th printing, 1974).
60 On the complicated evolution of Lonergan's text, and the means adopted for presenting it in the present edition, see Editors' Preface.
61 Lonergan, '*Pantôn Anakephalaiôsis*' 150 (see note 3 above).

modified Marxist or socialist diagnoses of capitalist political economy, he did not simply condemn the central capitalist mechanism whereby businesses use money to hire labor and buy materials, to organize production of commodities to sell for more money, and then to employ this additional money they make to hire more labor, buy more materials, and organize more production.

Lonergan was inspired by the events of the Depression, from the stock-market crash in 1929 to the moratorium on the banks in 1933, to discover how to ground objectively correct moral courses of action in an adequate economic analysis of the relationships between capital formation and the production and distribution of consumer goods. In his determination to understand those relationships in specifically economic terms, Lonergan expanded in detail the ethicists' key question regarding a just or family wage for workers. His more comprehensive approach includes (1) the capitalist process of what Marxists call 'realizing surplus' (or earning profit) by the occurrence of significant innovations with prospects of high profits motivating new higher rates of investment, and bringing about a build-up of a layered hierarchy of increasing rates of capital stock production; (2) the eventual overtaking, by the expansion of capital stock, of the growth in the rate of output, which causes a surplus capacity; (3) downturns in prospective profits along with the continued accumulation of debt on the part of entrepreneurs, eliminating motives for further investment; and (4) the unfolding possibilities of recession, depression, or (in Marxist terms) crisis, with greater or lesser convulsions, revulsions, and even the devastation of the organs of finance.

Like Lonergan, such architects of the mainstream approaches in contemporary economics as Alfred Marshall and John Maynard Keynes shared Karl Marx's urgent concern to relieve the specifically modern forms of poverty – the 'paradox of poverty in the midst of plenty.'[62] In a very early fragment of a pre-1944 version of his *Essay in Circulation Analysis*, Lonergan summarized in this way the situation of the then dominant economic paradigms for guiding and criticizing a society's economic performance:

> [Economic criticism and guidance] does not proceed systematically
> from solid premises. It is the intuition of socialists who find a radical

62 John Maynard Keynes, *The General Theory of Employment, Interest and Money* (New York: Harcourt, Brace & World, 1964; first published, London: Macmillan, 1936) 30.

incoherence in individual choices and decisions and leap with a gay
profusion of rhetoric to the *simpliste* solution of subordinating preferences and expectations to the benevolence of a tyranny. In contrast
the criticism of traditional economists is the soul of sobriety. It is
acute, informed, exact, subtle. But perhaps one may doubt that it is
inspired, that it suffers from the imperious pressure of really significant ideas. Too often does one learn that problems are very complex
indeed, that this or that element in the complexity may be singled
out as especially troublesome, that such and such a makeshift perhaps meets the issue more satisfactorily than others which have been
advocated. For as makeshift follows makeshift, it becomes increasingly difficult to distinguish between a democratic and a totalitarian
economy.[63]

Lonergan's intention was 'to formulate the laws of an economic mechanism more remote and, in a sense, more fundamental than the pricing system ... laws which men themselves administrate in the personal conduct of
their lives.'[64] In 1978, he began to refer to Nicholas Kaldor in support of
his judgment that the significance traditionally accorded to price theory by
conventional economics since Adam Smith's *Wealth of Nations* (1776)
amounted to a virtual derailment of economic theory. One of Kaldor's
statements to which he often referred states:

> The difficulty with a new start is to pinpoint the critical area where
> economic theory went astray. In my own view, it happened when the
> theory of value took over the centre of the stage – which meant focus-
> ing attention on the *allocative* functions of markets to the exclusion of
> their *creative* functions – as an instrument for transmitting impulses to
> economic change.
>
> To locate the source of error with more precision, I would put it in
> the middle of the fourth chapter of Vol. I of the *Wealth of Nations* ...
> [A]fter discussing the need for money in a social economy, Smith
> suddenly gets fascinated by the distinction between money price, real
> price, and exchange value, and from then on, hey presto, his interest
> gets bogged down in the question of how values and prices for prod-
> ucts and factors are determined. One can trace a more or less contin-

63 Lonergan, 'An Outline of Circulation Analysis' 109–10 (see note 35 above).
64 Ibid. 110.

uous development of price theory from the subsequent chapters of Smith through Ricardo, Walras, Marshall, right up to Debreu and the most sophisticated of present-day Americans.[65]

Even if economic theory may not have been turned into 'the study of the efficient allocation of a fixed volume of resources' in a market system until Jevons and Walras, Lonergan's interest in Kaldor's sweeping statement was to emphasize that prices and their changes are not explanatory but accountants' entities. For a first approximation of what Lonergan means here, let us draw an analogy to empirical scientific inquiry. The physicist's antecedent job of measuring and plotting measurements on graphs in physical science might be compared to tracing the movements of prices as the exchange economy ebbs and flows. What Lonergan has called 'grasping in the scattered points the possibility of a smooth curve,' or determining an indeterminate function in physics, would then be comparable to working out an economic theory that specifies the channels through which money circulates. Lonergan insists that the mechanism of the pricing system does not furnish economists with distinctions among the significant variables of aggregate surplus (or producer-goods) and basic (or consumer-goods) supply and demand with their determinate yet flexible velocities and accelerations, any more than Galileo Galilei's discrete measurements of distances and times at the Tower of Pisa of themselves provided the law of the acceleration of falling bodies. For Lonergan these distinctions in economics are only brought to light by a dynamic analysis of a concrete evolutionary process (MD:ECA 133–44, 144–56, 156–62). In short, the lack of ultimacy that Lonergan ascribes to prices and price theory can scarcely be overemphasized.

4.1 Lonergan and Marx

Although he sympathized with Marx's critique of classical political economy, Lonergan did not think Marx achieved an explanatory grasp of the intelligibility of the economic sphere as such. Marx's labor theory of value invoked an admixture of political, sociological, and especially proprietarial dimensions. Moreover, Lonergan had no respect for the way an illegitimate importation of sociological categories into the properly economic

---

65 Nicholas Kaldor, 'The Irrelevance of Equilibrium Economics,' *The Economic Journal* 82 (1972) 1237–55, at 1241.

sphere lends support to the simpliste Marxist-socialist penchant for setting entrepreneurs and workers against each other. Marxist advocacy of group bias and the use of propaganda and violence short-circuit democratic solidarity. To Lonergan's way of thinking, a moral vision that substitutes propaganda and force for its lack of intellectual acuity is a self-contradiction much more radical than the 'contradictions' that supposedly drive dialectical materialism.

4.2 Lonergan and Marshall

Lonergan shared Alfred Marshall's willingness in his *Principles of Economics* to make economics utterly independent of ethics and politics, insofar as this meant establishing the intellectual autonomy of economic science.[66] His notes on Schumpeter's treatments of Marshall in the *History of Economic Analysis* and his own comments on Marshall stress the latter's contributions in the development of equilibrium theory within the trajectory leading from Walras to the several editions of the *Principles.* He does not go into the aspect so beautifully articulated in Keynes's memoir of Alfred Marshall regarding the pains Marshall took in his lectures and his footnotes for *Principles* to adjust equilibrium theory to real complications of concrete economic dynamics such as motivated Lonergan to criticize and abandon equilibrium theory.

Lonergan found seriously wanting, as universally valid advice, the policy of laissez-faire for government (conventionally linked with the names of Marshall and Walras, even though this may never have been the explicit intention of either) and thrift and enterprise for individuals. For Lonergan this policy was based on assumptions of equilibrium theory that did not integrate a grasp of diverse and highly contingent equilibria appropriate to different phases of an expanding economy. Thus, the presupposition of the automatic movement of the market toward equilibrium tended concretely

66 Alfred Marshall, book I, especially chapter 2, 'The substance of economics,' and chapter 4, 'The order and aims of economic studies,' *Principles of Economics: An Introductory Volume* (First published 1890; 8th ed., London and New York: Macmillan, 1940, with frequent reprintings) 12–23 and 32–40. On Marshall, see John Maynard Keynes, 'Alfred Marshall, 1842–1924,' *Essays and Sketches in Biography* (New York: Meridian Books, 1956) 39–98; published earlier in *Memorials of Alfred Marshall,* ed. A.C. Pigou (London: Macmillan, 1925) 1–65.

to result in liberal capitalism's exploitation and oppression of the workers that Marshall, too, wanted to resolve through economic intelligence. As Lonergan stressed repeatedly, thrift and enterprise are the correct behavior when an economy is undergoing the vast widening and deepening of capital formation. As soon as capital formation levels off, and a new phase of widening and deepening the standard of living ought to begin, raising workers' wages and extension of their credit balances, for instance, might be more responsible courses of action than thrift and enterprise.

Lonergan thought the adoption of a so-called Marshallian way of thinking about the plight of the worker in the early 1930s led to the general conclusion that unemployment was to be handled not by increasing the quantity of money but by cutting wage rates. This was supposed to restore profitability to enterprise by lowering costs relatively to prices because, with the quantity of money remaining constant, prices would come down more or less proportionately to decreased costs.

4.3 Lonergan and Keynes

Despite his sharp disagreements with Keynes, Lonergan credited him with making macroeconomic analysis possible by showing up the fallacy of the neoclassical argument about full employment being automatically governed by a regime of flexible wages and prices.[67] Keynes realized that if reduced wages and costs usually go hand in hand with reduced prices, there would be no real reason why employment rates should go up. Nor would the burdens of past debts be lessened. The 'Keynesian revolution' called for a new theory that would regard employment as an aggregate concept. The three independent variables of Keynes's general theory – the propensity to consume, the rate of interest, and the schedule of the marginal efficiency of capital – were used to answer the question, What determines the level of employment and national income at any given time? Joan Robinson claims Keynes's breakthrough is 'the highly significant conception that an increase of investment without ... a corresponding increase in the propensity to save raises profits, while an increase in propensity to save without a corresponding increase in investment reduces them.'[68] With

---

67 See *Caring about Meaning* 84.
68 Joan Robinson, 'Kalecki and Keynes,' in *Problems of Economic Dynamics and Planning: Essays in Honour of Michal Kalecki* (Warszawa: PWN-Polish Scientific Publishers, and Oxford: Pergamon Press, 1966) 335–41, at 336.

Richard F. Kahn, Keynes came up with the concept of 'the multiplier – the relation of an increase ... in investment to the total increase in employment that it generates.'[69] With the help of the idea of the multiplier, Keynes thought he had arrived in *The General Theory* (1936) at an analysis of employment that turns on the distinction between the rate of interest and the rate of return on investment. In terms of his three variables, Keynes studied effective demand for consumer goods, and the correlation between the amount that consumers decide to save and the amount that businessmen decide to invest, especially when a discrepancy between planned savings and planned investment causes further contractions in incomes, investments, and so involuntary unemployment.

The marginal efficiency of capital refers to what Keynes calls 'the psychological expectation of future yield from capital-assets.'[70] This idea of the marginal efficiency of capital postulates the existence at any given moment of a schedule of possible investment projects, listed in order of their prospective profitability, with a cutoff at the point where the prospective rate of net profit is equal to the rate of interest to be paid for finance.[71] The propensity to consume refers to the 'fundamental psychological law ... that men are disposed, as a rule and on the average, to increase their consumption as their income increases, but not by as much as the increase in their income.'[72] By way of oversimplification, this psychological factor is to be taken in tandem with the attitude to liquidity and the expectation of return on capital, and combined with wage units and the quantity of money to determine national income and quantity of employment.[73] Hence, book III of *The General Theory* deals with the objective (chapter 8) and subjective (chapter 9) factors affecting the marginal propensity to consume, and then relates the propensity to consume to the multiplier (chapter 10). As Alvin Hansen put it, in Keynes's system, '[d]emand determines employment, and employment determines the marginal product (*i.e.*, the real wage), not the other way round.'[74]

69 Ibid. 335–36.
70 Keynes, *General Theory* 247.
71 Ibid. 135–93, 245–54.
72 Ibid. 96.
73 Ibid. 247.
74 Alvin H. Hansen, *A Guide to Keynes* (New York: McGraw-Hill, 1953) 21–22. According to Hansen, Keynes used the concept of the multiplier to work out the implications of government investment to increase the volume of

Although Lonergan shared Keynes's scepticism about classical solutions to the problems of unemployment, and however much he agreed with him about the need for a macroanalysis, he considered the 'Keynesian revolution' a misnomer, because Keynes was still operating in terms of the equilibrium economics of David Ricardo's 1810 theories. At best those theories would be relevant only to stationary economies, not to dynamic, growing, changing ones in which, as Clement Juglar put it, capitalist prosperity is the cause of depressions. From Lonergan's perspective, this failure truly to work out a new paradigm for economic science had an adverse effect upon Keynesian interpretations of the relationships between monetary events (such as government deficit spending, interest rates, credit volume, and the volume of the supply of money) and the determination of demand, not to mention other economic conditions.

His allusions to Keynes throughout the *Essay* provide evidence that Lonergan thought of himself as joining Keynes's concern to resolve the anomalies resulting from the trade or business cycle (which Keynes, unlike Michal Kalecki and Joseph Schumpeter, did not try to analyze). This is why *The General Theory*'s formulation of the modern problematic figures so prominently in the summary of the puzzles that Lonergan claims to have solved adequately in the light of his own circulation analysis.[75] Unlike Keynes, however, Lonergan examined why business cycles tend towards exaggerating their phase of major surplus expansion and 'systematic profits' into a boom and towards reducing what should become a basic expansion (with a higher standard of living for workers without either unemployment or inflation) into a crash that relegates a 'notable proportion of the population' to 'the reserve army of the unemployed' (*MD:ECA* 115, note 148).

---

employment by bolstering effective demand for consumer goods, and to show that deficit financing could provide an increase in income as a multiple of the insertion of government spending. By discovering the marginal propensity to consume, the multiplier could be derived; and with the multiplier known, the change in income that would result from any change in expenditure from sources such as government taxes, newly issued money, or funds borrowed from the public could be estimated, since total income resulting from the amount spent would be some multiple of the amount spent.

75 See below, Summary of the Argument, *MD:ECA* 5–6.

4.4 Lonergan, Kalecki, and Others

Lonergan felt a greater affinity for the Polish Marxist who also worked in England for a time, Michal Kalecki. According to Joan Robinson, Kalecki explained that 'if monopolistic influences prevent prices from falling when wage costs are lowered ... reduced purchasing power causes a fall off in sales of consumption goods, so that higher profit margins do not result in higher profits.'[76]

Kalecki's ideas about correlating increases in investment, income, and savings, on the one hand, with increases in the medium of exchange, on the other, though not precisely correct in Lonergan's eyes, had the merit of appealing to his deep conviction about the relation between quantities of money circulating in aggregate accelerations and decelerations in the economy (*MD:ECA* 60–65; 137, note 193; 142–44; 169–70). Even more significantly for Lonergan, instead of depending on the theory of the multiplier, Kalecki 'went straight to a theory of the trade cycle, on which Keynes was very weak.'[77] So in his lectures Lonergan often invoked Kalecki's notions about the dynamisms operative in trade cycles; and he was fond of quoting his aphorism about the workers spending what they get and the capitalists getting what they spend (*MD:ECA* 70), since it suggests in a global and compact way distinctions so central to his own analysis.

Both Keynes and Kalecki found the moral ugliness of capitalism repellent. Yet Keynes believed that the policy of greatly expanding the role of government in directing the economy – what he called 'the battle of Socialism against unlimited private profit' – would eventually result in a moral management of the levers of economic control (government spending, interest rates, volume of credit, and volume of money).[78] But Lonergan was sure that the regime of an economic brain trust issuing bureaucratic directives from above downwards would serve neither morality nor democratic freedom.

Lonergan delighted in the attacks upon neoclassical economics by members of the Cambridge school of economists (especially Joan Robinson and her sometime colleague Kalecki). He used Robinson's and John Eatwell's

---

76 Robinson, 'Kalecki and Keynes' 337.
77 Ibid.
78 Roberta Schaefer and David Schaefer, 'The Political Philosophy of J.M. Keynes,' *The Public Interest* 71 (Spring 1983) 45–61 (quoted phrase, 49).

Introduction to Modern Economics (1973)[79] for his graduate course one year, although he found their criticisms more helpful than the positive remedies they proposed for the neoclassical defects. In fact he changed over to assigning the early chapters of Robert J. Gordon's *Macroeconomics*,[80] because he thought the book was pushing towards the kind of theory needed. He admired the clarity of its exposition, diagrams, appendices, and glossaries as most helpful to an audience of whom many were unfamiliar with the dominant paradigm in academic macroeconomics. Aside from Kalecki and a quite significant diagram in Adolph Lowe's *The Path of Economic Growth* (1976), Lonergan was for a time intrigued by the way issues in dynamic macroeconomics were raised by the eleven authors represented in Alfred Eichner's *A Guide to Post-Keynesian Economics*,[81] though they, like the other authors mentioned, mainly aided him in articulating his own state of the question.

4.5 Lonergan and Schumpeter

Ultimately, none of the authors mentioned so far was more important for Lonergan than Joseph A. Schumpeter. He is the only contemporary economist mentioned more often by name in the *Essay* than Keynes. As a young man, Lonergan took copious notes on Schumpeter's work of 1934, *The Theory of Economic Development*[82] (see *MD:ECA* 75). He also worked through the two volumes of the famous *Business Cycles* (1939).[83] In the 1970s he studied (almost surely for the second time) *Capitalism, Socialism and Democracy* (1942),[84] and his esteem at this time for the *History of Eco-*

---

79 See note 50 above.
80 See note 53 above.
81 See note 54 above.
82 Joseph A. Schumpeter, *The Theory of Economic Development: An Inquiry into Profits, Capital, Credit, Interest, and the Business Cycle,* trans. Redvers Opie (Cambridge, MA: Harvard University Press, 1962; 8th printing, 1968; original copyright, 1934).
83 Schumpeter, *Business Cycles: A Theoretical, Historical and Statistical Analysis of the Capitalist Process* (New York: McGraw-Hill, 1939; paperback ed., 1964; original German, 2 vols, 1939).
84 Schumpeter, *Capitalism, Socialism and Democracy,* with a new introduction by Tom Bottomore (New York: Harper Colophon Books, 1975; original publication, Harper & Row, 1942; 2nd ed., 1947; 3rd ed., 1950).

nomic Analysis (1954)[85] was boundless. This book was assigned reading in his course, and by using Schumpeter to state his own problematic in the *Essay* (*MD:ECA* 7–12, 14, 86–91) Lonergan gave expression to the overall affinity he felt for Schumpeter's appreciation of dynamic macroeconomic analysis.[86]

Lonergan agreed with Schumpeter on the importance of a systematic or analytic framework in order to explain, rather than merely to record or describe, the aggregate phenomena of macroeconomics; he agreed with Schumpeter that to be able to explain the booms, slumps, and crashes of the trade or business cycles the economist's analysis had to be as dynamic as the subject matter under investigation; and he agreed that the economist had to know what are the significant variables in the light of which price changes are to be interpreted. According to Lonergan, standard economic theory had successfully achieved none of these desiderata. He credits Schumpeter with 'acknowledg[ing] that dynamic analysis called for new light on equilibrium' (*MD:ECA* 92).

Yet however much, in their different ways, authors like Schumpeter or Kalecki or Keynes pointed toward the need for this 'new light on equilibrium,' Lonergan did not think any of them had actually succeeded in supplying it. 'Such new light arises,' he wrote,

> when, over and above the equilibria of supply and demand with respect to goods and services, there are recognized *further equilibria*

---

85 Schumpeter, *History of Economic Analysis* (see note 59 above).
86 Lonergan was grateful for the way Schumpeter had shown that slumps and crises were related to contractions of plant and equipment, and that there were 'a hundred theories' on why – so that in Schumpeter's estimation there really existed no solid explanation. Lonergan claimed: 'I have an explanation on that.' In addition, he said he was grateful to Schumpeter for elucidating the virtualities of François Quesnay's (1694–1774) *tableau économique* (*MD:ECA* 53). Lonergan appreciated the way the *tableau* (1) allowed the theorist (a) to correlate many things all at once, and not just one at a time, piecemeal; (b) to assign numbers arithmetically to the variables involved; (2) permitted insight into phantasm instead of mere speculation detached from facts. See Joseph A. Schumpeter, *History of Economic Analysis* 222–23, 241–43. Lonergan's own use of his five-point diagram indicates just how seriously he took the need for adequate diagrams. See 'Appendix: History of the Diagram, 1944–1998' below, pp. 177–202.

that have to be maintained if an economy chooses to remain in a stationary state, to embark on a long-term expansion, to distribute its benefits to the vast majority of its members, and so to return to a more affluent stationary state until such time as further expansion beckons. (*MD:ECA* 92; emphasis added)

Only a dynamic analysis of these macroequilibria would make it possible to be specific about 'the conditions of a properly functioning economy.' Only the correct dynamic analysis would make it possible to articulate the conditions that, in the measure that they are met, result in 'aggregates acceptable to the economic society in its entirety' (*MD:ECA* 92).

For both economists and economic agents at large to understand the 'further equilibria that have to be maintained,' a theoretical grasp of monetary circulation is needed. More fundamental than the money supply by itself – or than any of the Keynesian levers of control – is the need to balance two distinct circuits of supply and demand revealed by an adequate macroeconomic dynamic analysis. None of the chief economic currents of thought with which Lonergan was familiar was very helpful to him when it came to answering how economic moral precepts can be based on the dynamisms of the economy itself, because none of them had achieved an adequate macroeconomic dynamic analysis.

5   Macroeconomic Dynamic Analysis as a New Paradigm of Economic Theory

Lonergan's doctoral work on Thomas Aquinas's theology of divine grace and human freedom was a large-scale demonstration of the effects of moving from commonsense descriptions of reality to theoretical or explanatory accounts of it. That work also taught Lonergan firsthand the pitfalls of failing to achieve satisfactory theoretical answers to questions calling for explanatory answers. In the absence of adequate theory, there results just a redescription of the quandaries to be explained. In terms of his exigent sense of theory, Lonergan realized that the familiar phenomena of booms and slumps that can be experienced and empirically verified by anyone – Kitchin or Juglar or Kondratieff cycles (*MD:ECA* 161–62) – can be satisfactorily analyzed only by means of a system of basic terms in which the terms are defined by their relations to each other, and the relations fixed by the terms. The definitions must in other words be implicit, as are the definitions of basic terms like 'point' and 'line' in David Hilbert's rigorous restatement of classical geometry.[87]

A systematic explanation, then, requires a normative (in the sense of what classically was called 'the nature of ...' and today would be called the unspecified correlation to be determined, the undetermined function to be determined) theoretical framework. The basic terms and relations of such a framework would specify the distinctions and correlations that artic- ulate the causes, which are not necessarily visible, of events that are appar- ent to all. The framework would thus stand to the ordinary apprehension of the booms and slumps of the trade cycle in much the same way that the explanatory grasp of acceleration as 'the second derivative of a continuous function of distance and time' stands to the ordinary, commonsense grasp of what it is to be going faster. As Lonergan put it:

> Both *going faster* and *acceleration* apprehend the same fact, but the former merely apprehends, while the latter adds to apprehension acts of analysis and generalization, of deduction and systematic corre- lation. For *acceleration* is *going faster*, but analyzed as d^2s/dt^2, general- ized to include *going slower*, enriched with all the implications of the second derivative of a function, and given a significant place in sys- tematic thought on quantitative motion.[88]

The kind of explanatory framework of which this is an example is 'norma- tive.' In common parlance, anything 'normative' is usually thought of as involving value judgments as opposed to 'descriptive,' factual judgments. For Lonergan, the meaning of 'normative' entails no such opposition. To 'descriptive,' however, he does assign a particular meaning that needs to be noted. A descriptive account, in his usage, is one that treats things in relation to ourselves and our senses. Hence most of what we know – our 'common sense' as Lonergan uses the term – we know in a descriptive rather than an explanatory way. The everyday apprehension of 'going faster' in the example above is an instance of descriptive, commonsense understanding. By way of contrast, an 'explanatory' understanding grasps

---

87 On implicit definition see Lonergan, *Insight* 12–13/37, 392/417, 435/460–61, 437/462, 492/516.

88 Lonergan, *Grace and Freedom* 13.

things-in-relation-to-one-another.[89] In these relations lies the basic meaning both of theory, in Lonergan's sense, and of a systematic as opposed to a commonsense account. Explanatory understanding, as exemplified by the technical sense of acceleration in the example, grasps an immanent lawfulness or intelligibility or regularity in data as empirically apprehensible.

It is this lawfulness or regularity, as defining the intelligible relationships in phenomena perceived, that is referred to by the word 'normative.' Thus, we can speak meaningfully and correctly of the law of falling bodies, '32 feet per second per second,' as being normative, even if no body ever actually falls at that rate. Clearly, 'normative' in this sense does carry implications for arriving at value judgments, in the specific sense that it is a good thing to respect the normative natures of processes and things when it comes to conceiving and judging and deciding upon courses of action.

Lonergan contended that the set of terms and relations capable of explaining the phenomena of the business or trade cycle would not be the same as any given pricing system that automatically coordinates a vast coincidental manifold of decisions of demand and decisions of supply (*MD:ECA* 13, 17). Such a system comes to sight as bookkeeper's entities that form the basis of the preliminary descriptive classifications that need to be explained: they are similarities that are 'first-for-us.' The relevant set of explanatory terms and relations would have to expose similarities that reside in the relations of things to one another or what is 'first-in-itself': namely, both the dynamic elements and the differentials of the economic mechanism which reveal the significance of aggregate changes in prices that by themselves are in need of interpretation. To repeat, then, Lonergan holds that prices as a concern of bookkeepers or accountants are known-first-to-us by description and commonsense classification; and that his own functional analysis of production and circulation reveals an explanatory system known-first-in-itself.[90] Only such an explanatory framework will enable the all-important discrimination either of the causes and the variations in prices (*MD:ECA* 75–80, 113–20) or of 'a relative and an

89 Lonergan, *Insight* 37–38/61–62, 41/65, 77–78/101, 80–81/104, 177–78/201, 181/204, 291–92/316–17, 513–14/537–38.

90 Aristotle distinguishes 'what is first by nature' (*proteron pros physei*) and 'what is first for us' (*proteron pros hymas*) in *Posterior Analytics*, I, 2, 71b 33 – 72a 5; compare *Physics*, I, 1, 184a 17–18.

absolute rise or fall of monetary prices,'[91] and only such an explanatory framework will make possible a correct interpretation of their significance.

Thus, prices provide the contents for something like meter readings in science, data that have to be interpreted in order for their significance for the economy to be understood. For Lonergan the interpretation requires something like the scientific theory in light of which meter readings or other measured data make sense. In economics, Lonergan believes the needed theory is a superstructure of terms and relations that specify classes and rates of payments. In his analysis such classes and rates of payments are determined by both (a) the mutual internal conditioning of surplus *and* basic circuits of circulation considered in themselves; and (b) the mutual external conditioning *between* the two circuits, so that the operations of each are modified according to whether the overall state of the economy is stationary, or is undergoing minor basic or surplus expansion, or is undergoing a major surplus expansion that naturally leads to a major basic expansion.

This rather complex superstructure is needed in order to avoid the static approaches that, according to Schumpeter, have virtually obliterated the dynamic and the differential dimensions of the significant variables in the economic processes since the nineteenth century. As Lonergan writes in the *Essay*:

> While we agree with Schumpeter that Walras's system implicitly includes the aggregates commonly considered in macroanalysis, it can hardly be credited with distinctions between basic and surplus expenditure, receipts, outlay, income, and much less with an account of their various dynamic relations. But until such distinctions are drawn and their dynamic significance understood, the aggregates and relations cannot be contained implicitly in any system. (*MD:ECA* 91–92)

As we can see from this statement, Lonergan's key technical terms are 'basic' and 'surplus.' As systematically conceived, they modify terms familiar to us from analyses based on the pricing system such as expenditure, receipts, outlay, and income. The usual meanings of those words as they are used in the supply and demand framework of conventional economics are transformed by these modifiers in a manner that is both novel and

91 *MD:ECA* 139–40 (and footnotes 196, 197), 141–42.

incommensurate with ordinary economic meanings. It is not that the realities referred to by these terms are never discussed or elaborately diagnosed in conventional economics; indeed they are. But they are not mutually defined and related systematically and functionally in these other analyses the way they are in this *Essay*. For Lonergan, 'basic' and 'surplus' name the significant variables that specify the aggregates and interdependencies among them, and enable us heuristically to diagnose the breakdowns revealed by the events from 1929 to 1933. As operating within a dynamic analysis, these variables measure velocities and accelerations of flows and are applicable to a changing, evolving economic reality.

Hence, Lonergan believed that he had managed to expound the main lines of a dynamic analysis of the fundamental macroequilibria of production and exchange by means of a method of analyzing monetary circulation. The set of definitions generated by this analysis are achieved independently of concepts of value theory, of postulates regarding value, and of deductions concerning scarce objects with alternative uses. They are derived directly from the exigencies of monetary circulation itself as immediately reflective of the aggregates of initial, transitional, and final payments, which in turn are functionally related to the processes and rhythms of production.

When in 1976 Lonergan was first inspired to hope that Kalecki's work might provide a bridge to academic economics and began reading back issues of *The Economic Journal*, one of the articles on which he took extensive notes was Brian J. Loasby's 'Hypothesis and Paradigm in the Theory of the Firm.'[92] Loasby applied to issues in economics Thomas Kuhn's distinction in *The Structure of Scientific Revolutions* between scientific theories or hypotheses and paradigms. After reading the article, Lonergan began to think of himself as working out a new paradigm for economics. He did not, of course, share the relativistic presuppositions present in Kuhn's notion of paradigm. But if we understand paradigm in the general sense of defining for a science 'the type of relationships to be investigated and the methods and abstractions to be regarded as legitimate within a particular problem area,'[93] then we see that the idea of a paradigm is analogous to

---

92 *The Economic Journal* 81 (1971) 863–85.

93 Quoted in Lonergan's typed notes on p. 866 of Loasby, and referring to Kuhn, *The Structure of Scientific Revolutions* (Chicago: University of Chicago Press, 1962) 10–11.

Lonergan's own notions of model and ideal type.[94] It makes sense, then, to characterize the nature of Lonergan's work in economic theory as elaborating a new paradigm.

6   The Systematic Significance of the Fundamental Distinction between Basic and Surplus Production and Exchange: A Normative Theory of the Pure Cycle

Before considering the circulation of money involved in an advanced exchange economy the *Essay* analyzes economic activity: the aggregate of ordered and variable processes and rhythms by which human beings transform the potentialities of nature to fulfill the material conditions of human existence in a standard of living. For Lonergan the standard of living, like the rhythmic processes that produce it, is dynamic – not a static sum of available goods and services at any moment, but a flow, a 'so much every so often.' So Lonergan conceives of this flow as a velocity.

But if economic activity is aimed at the standard of living, in an exchange economy production occurs by means of and in view of payments: expenditures that become receipts, and outlays that become income. Money intended for expenditure performs a demand function; and money intended for outlay performs a supply function. Thus, outlay and expenditure, income and receipts, all function as operative in monetary circulation, because they are each functionally congruent with distinct productive processes. Payments not correlated in that way with the productive process Lonergan calls not operative but redistributive, in the sense that they do not directly operate to advance industry and commerce as initial, transitional, or final payments for newly produced goods and services. Nevertheless, the redistributive function is the locus of all money to be mobilized for general purposes, whether immediately productive or not. Lonergan sometimes compared it to calculus's constant of acceleration because in its function of general monetary mobilization it conditions and controls the accelerations in the surplus and basic circuits of payments.

Lonergan was not content to consider only a stationary economy that reproduces itself. His dynamic analysis comes to terms with growth or a process, within a relatively unchanging framework of institutions, of continuous variations in rates of production and payments that may be

---

94 On models and ideal types in Lonergan, see *Method in Theology* xii, 224, 227–28, 284–85, 287, 288, 292.

expressed in terms of velocities, accelerations, and differentials of flows. If Lonergan chided nineteenth-century political economists for lack of attention to the differentials of the flow, for him (as he expressed it in one of his early essays on history), 'the differentials of what has flowed ... integrate into the reality of the present, and that is of supreme concern to us.' The differentials that affect the aggregates commonly considered in macroanalysis are so important because 'the differentials of flow are something beyond the elements, the individuals in the flow.' [95] Throughout this dynamic, aggregate, and functional analysis, Lonergan granted great heuristic significance to the analogy from differential calculus.

Lonergan was not 'under the spell of classical mechanics with its ideal of exact prediction and with the complementary notion that probability was no more than a cloak for ignorance' (*MD:ECA* 92). He was fully cognizant of post-Einsteinian physics and modern biology that scientifically take randomness, statistics, and emergence into account (*MD:ECA* 92–93).[96] Lonergan applied theorems from calculus to delineate a model or ideal type that may prove useful for formulating hypotheses that can approximate and be verified in actual economic events. In a major article of 1943,[97] Lonergan acknowledged what he called 'the fertility of concrete plurality'[98] and the upsweep of 'vertical finality.'[99] There one sees that he was on the way towards transposing Aristotle's and Aquinas's descriptive qualification of natural regularities as holding 'for the most part' into the all-inclusive world view that in *Insight* he would name 'emergent probability.'[100] In terms of this comprehensive world view, the concrete unfolding and interplay of complex natural and human intelligibilities with their statistical uniformities give rise to probabilities of emergence and survival that are also relevant to the explanatory intelligibility of any exchange economy's normatively interrelated equilibria and disequilibria. So, in a strikingly

95 Lonergan, 'Philosophy of History' 99 (see note 5 above).
96 See Philip McShane, *Randomness, Statistics and Emergence* (Dublin: Gill & Macmillan, 1970).
97 Lonergan, 'Finality, Love, Marriage,' *Collection*, vol. 4 of Collected Works of Bernard Lonergan, ed. Frederick E. Crowe and Robert M. Doran (Toronto: University of Toronto Press, 1988) 17–52.
98 Ibid. 21–33.
99 Ibid. 18–23.
100 Lonergan, *Insight* 121–24/144–51, 259–67/284–92; as relevant to human affairs, 209–11/234–37, 226–27/252–53, 698/720.

open and risk-filled manner, Lonergan fits his dynamic analysis of monetary circulation into a general conception of economy as an ecology (*MD:ECA* 3–4, 89, 93) conditioned by a hierarchy of natural and human processes.

The kind of emergence crucial to Lonergan's fundamental systematic distinction between 'basic' and 'surplus' expenditures, receipts, outlays, and incomes is set out concretely by the historical anthropologist Christopher Dawson in *The Age of the Gods* (1928),[101] a book Lonergan often mentioned as having influenced him deeply. Dawson describes the transformation of primitive culture brought about by 'the discovery of the ox and large-scale agriculture with its long-term investments,'[102] and depicts how the productive rhythms of the traditional standard of living underwent a fundamental differentiation caused by the rise of new and different kinds of productive rhythms aimed directly at capital formation.[103]

Note that for Lonergan the key feature of this massive differentiation is not primarily or originally social (in the sense of deriving from class structures), legal, or proprietarial. Even more significantly, it is not derived from prices, values, interest, profit, or wages, although any or all of these aspects, while not essential, probably would be involved concretely in cases of such a transformation of the means of production. It is the *functional* aspect of the differentiation of productive rhythms that is of systematic importance to Lonergan (*MD:ECA* 26, 118, 144–46 note 201). What makes all the difference to macroeconomic dynamic analysis is how the purpose or function of each set of productive activities differs from that of the other. One set issues forth in the consumer goods and services of the standard of living; it is basic. The other set transforms the conditions for the future production of the standard of living by creating producer goods and services; it is surplus.[104] If the flow of the basic standard of living may be

101 Christopher Dawson, *The Age of the Gods: A Study in the Origins of Culture in Prehistoric Europe and the Ancient East* (London and New York: Sheed & Ward, 1933; first published, London: John Murray, 1928).

102 Lonergan, 'Philosophy of History' 102; see Dawson, *The Age of the Gods* 92–93.

103 Lonergan, *Insight* 209–10/235.

104 Note the difference from Marx, whose notion of surplus value has sociological and proprietarial dimensions – that is, the difference between the full value bestowed on a commodity by the laborers and what is returned to laborers in the form of wages – rather than the sheerly functional dimensions that constitute its intrinsic meaning for Lonergan.

conceived in terms of velocity, Lonergan conceives the disproportionate volumes of production entailed by capital formation's surplus production of producer goods (machinery, factories, machine tools) as an accelerator, or even as a hierarchically ordered series of accelerators of the standard of living.

Lonergan pointed out that this differentiation of economic activities into the production of consumer goods in the standard of living and the production of producer goods that transform the possibilities for future consumer-goods production is discussed by traditional economists such as S.M. Longfield (1802–1884), John Rae (1796–1872), Nassau Senior (1790–1864), Eugen von Böhm-Bawerk (1851–1914), and in the heavily disputed 'Ricardo effect.' But Lonergan credits Piero Sraffa as having clarified it most thoroughly in his famous essay, *Production of Commodities by Means of Commodities* (1960).[105] Yet even Sraffa does not use his sophisticated explanation of the 'Ricardo effect' and the 'roundabout' or 'concertina'-like phenomena associated with it in the way Lonergan does.[106]

Lonergan is alone in using this difference in economic activities to specify the significant variables in his dynamic analysis. To our knowledge, no one else considers the functional distinctions between different kinds of productive rhythms prior to, and more fundamental than, wealth, value, supply and demand, price levels and patterns, capital and labor, interest and profits, wages, and so forth. While other economists also may conceive of the standard of living's consumer-goods production as a velocity in relation to acceleration by producer-goods production, only Lonergan analyzes booms and slumps in terms of how their velocities, accelerations, and decelerations are or are not equilibrated in relation to the events, movements, and changes in two distinct monetary circuits of production and exchange as considered both in themselves and in relation to each other by means of crossover payments.

Lonergan's distinction between basic and surplus production and circulation enables him to envisage clearly those 'further equilibria that have to be maintained' in the normative framework of a pure theory of economic expansion and growth. It allows him to specify classes of payments, and to consider velocities and accelerations of each circuit of payments in relation to the other. Because the mutual relationships of acceleration and deceler-

---

105 Piero Sraffa, *Production of Commodities by Means of Commodities: Prelude to a Critique of Economic Theory* (Cambridge: Cambridge University Press, 1960).

106 On the 'Ricardo effect' see Blaug (note 42 above) 96–97, 540–46.

ation between the two distinct circuits unfold over time, the theoretical account of these relationships has to delineate normative phases in their expansions and taperings-off and disequilibria. An explanatory account of the intrinsically evolutionary processes of any industrial exchange economy's cycles of surplus (or producer-goods) and basic (or consumer-goods) production and exchange has to reveal how the different phases in the distinct cycles intermesh and coordinate in an intelligible sequence, by means of differential rates of crossover payments from basic to surplus and from surplus to basic, depending on what phase of aggregate expansion or leveling off the economy happens to be in at any given time.

In Lonergan's macroeconomic dynamic analysis, then, the heart of the normative theoretical framework that can actually explain business and trade cycles is what he calls the 'pure cycle' (*MD:ECA* §10, §24: 114). This cycle generalizes into clearly articulated relationships the ideal phases characteristic of major economic transformations as they depart from a stationary phase and move through phases first of surplus expansion and then of basic expansion, only to return to a new stationary phase. This pure cycle stands to our ordinary apprehension of economic booms and slumps as the explanatory conception of acceleration stands to our ordinary apprehension of going faster and slower. It sheds the 'new light on equilibrium' that Schumpeter was seeking. The meaning of the pure cycle is fully revealed in the course of the *Essay*. Here we offer only two brief illustrations of the implications of that model.

6.1 Profit

Before Schumpeter, in his *Theory of Economic Development*, spoke of profit as a return to entrepreneurs as innovators in the dynamic economic process whose new ideas initiate an enlargement of the surplus production of plants and equipment, the late-nineteenth-century economic tradition's development of marginal productivity regarded profit as merely a disequilibrium phenomenon that occurs only when monopoly is present. In either case, profits, either in the sense of the national accountant's labeling of the wages of management and supervisors, or in the sense of payments in excess of the opportunity costs of the factors of production, are understood as something automatic; they do not involve correct understanding and moral choice in terms of the relationships between surplus and basic circuits of money.

By and large, the main thing people agree about when it comes to profit is the role it plays in motivating entrepreneurial activity. From the liberal-capitalist perspective of 'rugged individualism' profit is good. It embodies our culture's image of the successful and 'self-made' man that has survived the replacement of the entrepreneurial model of business by the managerial model with its CEOs and boards of directors. From the socialist perspective of an equally 'rugged collectivism' it is bad, because it embodies possessive individualism and a system of differential rights in which the 'haves' exploit the 'have-nots' and the rich few keep on getting richer and the many poor keep on getting poorer.

For Lonergan profit in these senses is a descriptive and not an explanatory category. It can indeed convey a legitimate motive for economic activity; but it also has been perverted in capitalist and socialist perspectives by individual and group bias.[107] Even more perniciously, profit has been transformed by the general bias of common sense[108] from being a legitimate motive into being an economic criterion. Lonergan demonstrates how, in the case of mercantilism (*MD:ECA* 61 and note 71,), the capitalist form of commonsense bias mistakenly dealt with profit in terms of maintaining a 'favorable balance of foreign trade'; in today's corporate ethos (*MD:ECA* 119–20, 80–82) profit is misconstrued in terms of undifferentiated ideas of 'the bottom line'; again, in the modern welfare state (*MD:ECA* 171–75, 175–76) the socialist version of commonsense bias wields the 'haughty name of welfare' (*MD:ECA* 86) and sets up an irrational weighting of entitlements that spawns a permanent underclass. And so bias has in one way or another kept both capitalist and socialist outlooks from achieving a correct understanding of profit as a 'social dividend.'

According to Lonergan, profit as coopted by bias systematically excludes an intelligible account of the 'social dividend' which would be the reasonable return on entrepreneurial activity that ramifies throughout the entire society (*MD:ECA* 133–44, 144–56). For in the measure that it is unbiased, being an entrepreneur means taking initiative in improving the social and cultural order of a society in its provision of goods and services by transforming and exploiting the means of production. Accordingly, profit as the flow of an economy's resources for the sake of a major transformation and expansion of capital goods would be 'pure surplus income.' Lonergan comments:

---

107 Lonergan, *Insight* 218–22/244–47, 222–25/247–50.
108 Ibid. 225–32/250–57.

It is true that our culture cannot be accused of mistaken ideas on pure surplus income as it has been defined in this essay; for on that precise topic it has no ideas whatever. However, the phenomena here referred to by the term 'pure surplus income' are not, as is the term, a creation of our own. The phenomena are well known. (*MD:ECA* 153)

Because of the word 'surplus' in Lonergan's expression for profit, 'pure surplus income,' the meaning of the word 'profit' shifts from its sense in ordinary language to the meaning it can only have within the normative framework of Lonergan's aggregate functional analysis of the surplus and basic phases in a pure cycle of production and exchange. It takes on a systematic meaning. 'Systematic profit' arises when an economy moves from a stationary to an expansionary phase as entrepreneurs, spurred on by some major innovation, shift from simple maintenance and replacement of existing plants and equipment into a large-scale production of new plants or equipment or massive technological, commercial, or organizational improvements. Then there arises the need for the 'new fixed investment of an expansion' (*MD:ECA* 152). This phase calls for an 'anti-egalitarian' major acceleration of the surplus circuit fueled by an 'aggregate ... return upon capital investment' (*MD:ECA* 146) that will continue during the transitional phase when a basic expansion is beginning. Such 'systematic profit' is not what Lonergan calls 'constant normal profit,' which is the excess of receipts over bills payable during stationary states enabling entrepreneurs or managers to keep firms solvent and to maintain a standard of living proportionate to their contributions (*MD:ECA* 81). 'Systematic profit' is 'net aggregate savings ... functionally related to the rate of new fixed investment' (*MD:ECA* 153). It is money to be directly or indirectly invested, and is not to be spent or saved as a contribution to personal income (*MD:ECA* 81–82). As such, it is a specifically *social* dividend functionally required to taper off and reduce to zero as the basic or consumer-goods expansion follows the surplus expansion in an 'egalitarian' acceleration that increases the purchasing power of workers and the supply of consumer goods.

Instead of moralizing about profit, Lonergan's analysis of the natural intelligibility of the pure cycle reveals how profit as 'constant and normal' is related to profit as 'pure surplus income,' which is a social dividend. It is intrinsic to the intelligibility of capitalist process that there be an exigence for the 'anti-egalitarian' requirements of the major surplus expansion to yield eventually to the 'egalitarian' requirements of the major basic expansion. The movement from an anti-egalitarian flow to the egalitarian flow that naturally should follow it (*MD:ECA* 135, 117 note 150, 115 note 148, 135–37, 140 note 197, 151, 153) is not something that happens automatically; *it demands correct understanding and moral choice.* Because of the precariousness and seriousness of this passage from surplus to basic expansions, Lonergan holds that 'pure surplus income is at the nerve center of free economies' (*MD:ECA* 147).

According to Lonergan, when profit shifts from being a motive to being a criterion, however, then the inevitable and reasonable tapering off to zero of profits as pure surplus income goes against mistaken expectations. This may induce measures akin to panic on the part of capitalists, who drain the basic circuit in order to keep surplus profits and incomes accelerating – which is one of the ways the pure cycle is transformed into the booms and slumps that economies usually experience. Something like the same mistaken reasoning based on profit as a criterion and not only a motive underpins the reaction of labor unions to the tremendous increases in profits and income in the earlier phases of the surplus expansion (*MD:ECA* 138). Insofar as their demands for higher wages are out of season, they represent one group's misguided attempt to claim for itself what is actually the social dividend of a society-wide aggregate. This would be another way of misreading the demands of the pure cycle (*MD:ECA* 128–29).

Even though the pure cycle does entail decelerations and shifting disequilibria, an especially illuminating implication of the pure cycle for Lonergan's theory of economic growth is that it does not entail aggregate contractions of the sort induced by unintelligent and irresponsible reactions that bring about disastrous price spirals, panic, ruthless behavior, and so forth (*MD:ECA* 136 note 192, 137 note 193, 154–55). According to Lonergan, the trade or business cycle is distinguished from the pure cycle by the consequences due to lack of correct understanding. This ignorance fosters the two-sided blunder of exaggerating the phase of major surplus expansion and 'systematic profits' into a boom, and of reducing what from a normative viewpoint is supposed to become a basic expansion (with a higher standard of living for workers involving neither unemployment nor inflation) into a slump (recession, depression, crash). Moreover, what makes policies on the balance of foreign trade (*MD:ECA* 165–73) and deficit spending paid by taxes (*MD:ECA* 173–75) problematic for Lonergan is that they also regularly offer ways of misinterpreting the meaning of profit as a social dividend.

6.2 Interest

In chapter 23 of *The General Theory* Keynes praised the Scholastic doctrine of usury for being 'directed towards the elucidation of a formula which should allow the schedule of the marginal efficiency of capital to be high, whilst using rule and custom and the moral law to keep down the rate of interest.' His practical concern was subordinated to his theoretical appreciation of the fact that the Schoolmen had, by 'an honest intellectual effort,' distinguished with respect to interest what 'the classical theory has inextricably confused together.'[109] Lonergan too discriminates between entrepreneurial borrowers, who use liquid funds actively in production and commerce, and sterile lending for the sake of passive, nonproductive reception of interest. In the light of his theory of the 'pure cycle,' Lonergan can make Keynes's distinction between the productive entrepreneur and the functionless *rentier* in an even more radical way. So too with Keynes's critique of excessive savings by the wealthy, in terms of recommendations about interest rates. He does not do this critique by returning to classical accounts of the role of money. Instead, he specifies the aggregate conditions of the properly functioning economy in terms of the normative phases in the pure cycle. Clearly, it makes all the difference with respect to the manipulation of interest rates whether the economy is (1) in a static phase where surplus and basic circuits are bringing about a constant standard of living; or (2) in a long-term surplus expansion where surplus production maintains capital stock at a constant level, and undertakes growth of the sort involved in a five-year plan or when a major innovation entails the improvement of the national industrial equipment; or (3) in a period when surplus expansion is leveling off, and a basic expansion involving the overall improvement in a nation's standard of living is in order; or (4) in a period of return to a stationary phase at the new, higher standard of living.

Lonergan's analysis allows the Keynesian distinctions to be reconceived in a more differentiated way, because it makes available a more differentiated heuristic grasp of those 'further equilibria that have to be maintained.' For instance, such a grasp would keep a plausible concept such as an 'equilibrium rate of interest' from 'involv[ing] an indiscriminate lumping together of quite different things' (*MD:ECA* 141, 141–43, 141 note 198, 140 note 197). For it is obvious that the same high rate of interest that motivates some people to save will keep people who should be doing so from entrepreneurial borrowing; and conversely, the same low interest

109 Keynes, *General Theory* 352.

rate will inspire entrepreneurs at the same time as it discourages the saving upon which investment depends. The manipulation of interest rates by itself does not differentiate the functional needs of any given phase of the economic cycle. When a surplus (producer-goods) expansion causes more surplus expenditure and makes more overall income available for the same or a decreasing number of consumer goods, adjustment of the rate of interest will be insufficient to supply the aggregate needs of the economy at that time.

Lonergan's same objection regarding the indiscriminate lumping together of quite different things holds true, mutatis mutandis, when it comes to relating other levers, such as Kalecki's manipulation of the quantity of money, to basic and stationary phases of an economy's development.

6.3 Lonergan's Critique of 'Supply-Side' and 'Demand-Side' Economics

For Lonergan the subject matter of macroeconomics is the fundamental value of a properly functioning economy (compare *MD:ECA* 14). Independently of human psychology, his macrodynamic analysis addresses the strictly economic 'process of production and its divisions; the process of payments and its divisions; the various forms of interdependence of these flows; finally, the conditions under which they function or malfunction and their respective consequences.'[110] He was convinced that 'either men learn rules to guide them individually in the use of the economic machine, or else they surrender their liberty to be ruled along with the machine by a central planning board.'[111]

Although Lonergan formulated an anti-bureaucratic critique of socialism, he also supplied a basis for meeting in strictly economic terms the core of the socialist grievance against liberal capitalism: the failure of the societies that have undergone the major surplus expansions (named 'take-offs' by W.W. Rostow)[112] consistently and fully to follow through with the major basic expansion for which the capitalist expansion is the intelligible preparation (*MD:ECA* 79–80).

By developing a pure theory of aggregate producer-goods and con-

---

110 Taken from Lonergan's brief course description 'Macroeconomics and the Dialectic of History,' Spring 1978.

111 Lonergan, 'An Outline of Circulation Analysis' 110.

112 W.W. Rostow, *The Stages of Economic Growth: A Non-Communist Manifesto* (Cambridge: Cambridge University Press, 1961; first published 1960); see numerous references in the index, under Take-off.

sumer-goods expenditures and receipts, outlay and income, Lonergan has supplied a framework for disclosing to individuals the *group* intelligibility at stake in economic exchanges. Contrary to 'supply-side' economics he diagnoses the failure of capitalist managers to understand that profit as pure surplus income is not the property rewarded to individuals, but a social dividend. When capitalist expansions thereby are exaggerated into booms that can only end in slumps, perfectly good, but less powerful and smaller, businesses lose out along with the masses of people (*MD:ECA* 80–86).

This critique cuts both ways. Against liberal capitalism it shows why 'the bottom line' as it is usually understood cannot be a criterion for economic practice. Contrary to 'demand-siders' it also diagnoses how similar misinterpretations of the forced savings caused by the price spread in major surplus expansions could mislead doctrinaire trade unionists to be precipitous in demanding for their group wage increases out of the social dividend. Lonergan's analysis shows both what it means that profit is a matter of decreasing returns for entrepreneurs, and why this need not be a counsel of despair. He also shows that it is unreasonable, before the major basic expansion is under way, to use suddenly available increased consumer income to purchase more and more of the proportionately fewer goods and services, because the long-term effect will be to prohibit the abundance of cheaper goods and services that the phase of major basic expansion would otherwise bring about in the future.

Lonergan reinterprets in a differentiated way all the nostrums of traditional economics that 'savings equal investments' (*MD:ECA* 70, 133), and 'consumers always pay.' He rethinks the meaning of the favorable balance of trade, grounding a nonideological critique of imperialism (80–86, 169–72). He exposes what is problematic about the habits of multinational corporations. He sets forth the meaning of deficit spending, revealing just what it can and cannot do, and showing why, as a long-term policy, it is so degrading for human beings (85–86, 173–75).

7   Lonergan's Critique of Secularist Ideologies: The Need for a Theological Viewpoint

Lonergan held that the overall lack of ingenuity and inquisitiveness on the part of both liberal capitalism and socialism causes the general stagnation of an unintelligible social situation grounded in dramatic, egoistic, group, and general biases. A healthy and vibrant economy demands that a critical mass of people be committed to the authenticity of attentiveness, intelligence, reasonableness, and responsibility. Both liberalism and socialism are secularist solutions to the problem of human living. For Lonergan they are themselves products of what he calls a major surrender of intelligence at the speculative level.[113] They are collective 'cover stories' or 'rationalizations' that trivialize the human problem of evil.

As secularist strategies for solving the radical problem of individual and social autonomy without God (*MD:ECA* 94–95), liberalism and socialism fail to reach the root of the crises in modern exchange economies, namely, moral impotence.[114] Lonergan made his article 'Healing and Creating in History'[115] (part 2 of the present edition) required reading for his 'Macroeconomics and the Dialectic of History' course. In this article he writes that overcoming political and economic problems democratically calls for a supernatural *healing* of human beings. Ultimately God's unmerited liberating of human liberty is at stake.

In contrast, liberals try to solve the problems of individual and social autonomy by speaking about 'interest': pursuing one's own interest, enlightened self-interest, the public interest, and so on. The term 'interest' was selected by liberalism so that public discourse about politics and economics might avoid the limitations associated with the term 'opinion,' which the Enlightenment made synonymous with religious beliefs (read: fanatical superstitions) about the common good, and with the term 'passions,' which also carries the connotation of arbitrariness. The implication of the term 'interest' is that pursuing one's interest is more in accord with the public interest than acting in the name of the common good.

Even liberals have acknowledged that 'interest' needs to be 'enlightened' or 'rightly understood,' and so the Enlightenment project of humanistic self-affirmation originally coined the amoral slogan of liberal democracy, 'enlightened self-interest.' This has tended to mean calculating how looking out for someone else's interest might be to one's advantage. According to Lonergan, it has not meant the surmounting of biases that is required for overcoming social and cultural decline.

The project of modern 'enlightened' philosophy was to apply reason

---

113 Lonergan, *Insight* 230–32/255–57.
114 On 'moral impotence' see ibid. 627–30/650–53.
115 Lonergan, 'Healing and Creating in History,' *A Third Collection* (New York: Paulist, and London: Geoffrey Chapman, 1985) 100–109. Originally a lecture at Thomas More Institute, Montreal, 13 May 1975, and published there (1975) in *Bernard Lonergan: 3 Lectures* 55–68.

unassisted by anything but scientific method to the empirical workings of humanity's self-regarding passions in order to engineer (administrate, manage) the social conditions of freedom.

The idea of engineering human welfare is repugnant to Lonergan, for 'managing people is not treating them as persons. To treat them as persons one must know and one must invite them to know.'[116] Making the survival of democracy possible by 'effectively augmenting the enlightenment of ... enlightened self-interest' cannot be identified merely with the Enlightenment's project of steering public opinion from unenlightened to enlightened self-interest. Instead, Lonergan envisaged a vast and long-term educational effort. He insisted that rational control of the economy 'can be democratic only in the measure in which economic science succeeds in uttering not counsel to rulers but precepts to mankind, not specific remedies and plans to increase the power of bureaucracies, but universal laws which men themselves administrate in the personal conduct of their lives.'

Lonergan's deeply Christian anthropology sets his approach to democracy apart from the secularism of both liberalism and socialism. He had no doubt that God is at work in human history bringing about a divine solution to the problem of evil. But as a theologian he also thought that this supernatural solution can only be fully transformative of human history with our free cooperation in the form of human *creativity*.

Such creativity entails understanding the economic mechanism as both independent of and subordinate to the political domain. In his classes Lonergan often expressed his dissatisfaction with social ethicists' tendency to be content with 'vague moral imperatives' instead of figuring out how moral precepts can be derived from the immanent intelligibility of economic processes. So he often asked, Where were the Christian counterparts to the 'crazy old man' Karl Marx, sitting in the British Museum voraciously reading and relentlessly studying about political economy?

For Lonergan, the proper understanding of economic dynamisms also needs to be set in the context of the 'dynamics of history' that encompass not only growing understanding and knowledge, but the objective surd of sin, and the redemptive potentialities of God's grace (*MD:ECA* 94–95). Lest the problem of evil be trivialized, enlightened self-interest has to be radically transformed from the calculating selfishness of even Tocqueville's 'self-interest rightly understood' into a rightly ordered self-love open and receptive to the gift of God's love.

116 Lonergan, 'Cognitional Structure,' *Collection* 205–21, at 220–21.

Lonergan was deeply convinced that God is working redemptively in history to heal human hearts and to give people that antecedent willingness that makes compliance with the twofold command of love for God and neighbor humanly achievable. This conviction also led him to expect people in the contemporary world eventually to meet the critical need for an adequate explication of a pure cycle of economic growth that has its normative goal in the attainment of a new, higher stationary phase of prosperity. For how else can economic agents know objectively where they stand in order freely to adapt their preference schedules and modify their expectations to match the successive phases of the pure cycle?

But the educational task towards a democratic economy is massive. Just how massive is suggested by the following statement from the present essay:

> Now to change one's standard of living in any notable fashion is to live in a different fashion. It presupposes a grasp of new ideas. If the ideas are to be above the level of currently successful advertising, serious education must be undertaken. Finally, coming to grasp what serious education really is and, nonetheless, coming to accept that challenge constitutes the greatest challenge to the modern economy (*MD:ECA* 119).

FREDERICK G. LAWRENCE

Acknowledgments

The editors would like to express their deep appreciation to Frederick E. Crowe, s.j., and Robert M. Doran, s.j., editors-in-chief of the Collected Works of Bernard Lonergan, for entrusting us with this task, and for doing all within their power to help bring it to a successful conclusion.

Thanks are due to Nicholas Graham of Toronto for original research made available to the Lonergan Centers in Toronto and Boston. Professor Philip McShane deserves a special votum of gratitude not only for helping to put the present editors, with many others, on the right track at the earlier stages of grasping Lonergan's economic thought, but also for double-checking our work at the end – as well as for his own pioneering writing in this field.[1]

Also contributing in many ways to our understanding have been Dr Eileen deNeeve of the Thomas More Institute for Research in Adult Lib-

---

1 See 'An Improbable Christian Vision and the Economic Rhythms of the Second Million Years' and 'Lonergan's Economics: Comparisons and Contrasts,' in *Lonergan's Challenge to the University and the Economy* (Washington, DC: University Press of America, 1980) 92–111, 112–28, with notes 182–97, 197–200; 'Features of Generalized Empirical Method and the Actual Context of Economics,' in *Creativity and Method: Essays in Honor of Bernard Lonergan, S.J.*, ed. Matthew L. Lamb (Milwaukee, WI: Marquette University Press, 1981) 543–71; *Wealth of Self and Wealth of Nations: Self-Axis of the Great Ascent* (Hicksville, NY: Exposition Press, 1975); and *Economics for Every One: Das Jus Kapital* (Edmonton, AB: Commonwealth Publications, 1995).

eral Studies, Montreal, and Lonergan Fellow at Boston College, who wrote a thesis at Concordia University on Kalecki as well as (to our knowledge) the first doctoral dissertation on Lonergan's macroeconomic analysis;[2] and William Mathews, s.j., of Milltown Institute, Dublin, who has done extensive research for an intellectual biography of Lonergan that at the time of writing is near completion.[3] We would also acknowledge a collaborator from afar, Australian economist S. Peter Burley, who had long since seen the need for this project, and has encouraged us to meet it.[4]

We would also like to thank our colleagues from the Economics Department at Boston College, Professor Francis McLaughlin and Professor Harold Peterson, who have been unstintingly generous with their time, patience, and support of their non-economist friends.

For their help in the final phases of making this volume a reality, our gratitude is due to Matthew Mullane, Joseph Tadie, Lauren Weis, and Andrew Hamilton.

Finally, with deep appreciation, we acknowledge Professor Joseph Flanagan, s.j., long-time Chair of the Philosophy Department and Director of the Lonergan Institute at Boston College, for his vision and for his unflagging friendship and encouragement.

2 Eileen O'Brien deNeeve, 'Bernard Lonergan's 'Circulation Analysis' and Macroeconomics,' thesis for the Ph.D. degree, McGill University, Montreal, 1990.

3 'Lonergan's Economics,' *METHOD: Journal of Lonergan Studies* 3:1 (March 1985) 9–30.

4 'A Summary of Lonergan's Economic Diagram,' *Riverview Reflections* (Katoomba, Australia: Bennett & Son, 1985) 1–10 [now also *Australian Lonergan Workshop*, ed. William J. Danaher (Lanham, MD: University Press of America, 1993) 3–11]; 'A von Neumann Representation of Lonergan's Production Model,' *Economic Systems Research* 1:3 (1989) 317–30 [now also *Australian Lonergan Workshop* (see above) 103–22]; 'Von Neumann Models with Money,' Ninth International Congress on Input-Output Techniques, Keszthely, Hungary, 4–9 September 1989; 'Lonergan as a Neo-Schumpeterian,' *Australian Lonergan Workshop* 249–57.

MACROECONOMIC DYNAMICS:

AN ESSAY IN CIRCULATION ANALYSIS

Preface[1]

[1980] Contemporary physics has established a distinction between classical and statistical laws. Roughly, classical laws reveal that if A then B, provided other things are equal, while statistical laws tell us how often that proviso is met.

A series of classical laws forms a chain when the consequent of each preceding law in the series is the condition of the next following law in the series. Such a series becomes a scheme of recurrence when the consequent of the last is the condition of the first. For example, if A then B; if B then C; if C then D ...; if X then A.

Chains of laws and schemes of recurrence are abstract possibilities that become actualities in accord with statistical laws. Relevant to any scheme at a given time may be its probability of emerging or its probability of surviving once it has emerged.

An ecology is an interrelated and interconnected set of schemes of recurrence. Ecologies too have their probabilities of emergence and survival. A series of ecologies can form chains of sequential dependence, with prior ecologies grounding the probability of the emergence of the next.

---

1 The 'final' version of Lonergan's *Essay* has no introductory section. The three previous versions (1980, 1981, and 1982) all begin with the same 'Introduction,' the text of which is included as the first part of the present 'Preface.' In all the earlier versions (1944, 1978, and 1979) the first page of the *Essay* is an 'Outline of the Argument,' which is added at the end of this 'Preface' as 'Summary of the Argument.'

Low probabilities become higher as numbers increase and time intervals are longer. Since in our universe numbers are vast and time intervals are enormous, even very low probabilities are likely to be realized.[2]

Human communities devise their own schemes of recurrence: the commonly understood and commonly accepted ways and means of cooperating. Among them are the firms that keep producing goods and rendering services and no less the households that purchase the goods produced and the services rendered. Such is the economy, which is a structure resting on the ecologies of nature and underpinning social and cultural structures.

Studies of the economy divide into macroeconomics and microeconomics. Microeconomics is concerned with the firms and the household. Macroeconomics is concerned with dynamic structures: the interrelations of aggregate rates of production and of payment, of their equilibria and disequilibria, of expansions and contractions, of inflation and unemployment.

This study of macroeconomics differs from others in two closely connected respects. First of all, its account of the productive process prescinds from exchange and so is equally applicable to the Russian[3] and the American economies. Both have their velocities and their changes of velocity, and as they speed up or slow down, their rhythm will be either concordant or discordant with the expected rhythm in rates of monetary aggregates. When they are concordant, it would seem that an overall equilibrium is satisfied. When they are discordant, it would seem that the interpretation by theorists or by businessmen is not true to the signs of the times. In other words, the productive process itself contains implicit criteria, and if these criteria are unknown or ignored, things may go from bad to worse. And as we all know, such an eventuality has already occurred.

Our title[4] regards not only macroeconomics but also the dialectic of his-

2 At this point Lonergan's text has a reference to *Insight: A Study of Human Understanding* (first published in 1957; 2nd rev. ed., London: Longmans, Green and Co., and New York: Philosophical Library, 1958; Collected Works edition, Toronto: University of Toronto Press, 1992); references to *Insight* will give first the 1958 and then the 1992 page numbers (e.g., 626/649); in the present instance the relevant pages are 115–39/138–61.

3 In this passage (written in 1980), Lonergan is referring to the former Soviet Union as the premier example of a communist, state-planned economy.

4 Lonergan is here referring to the title of his course, 'Macroeconomics and the Dialectic of History,' for which the *Essay* was assigned reading.

tory. By dialectic I understand a process that is at once concrete, dynamic, and contradictory. The concrete and dynamic component is supplied by human individuals. The contradiction emerges from the fact that in their choices they may or may not attend to the relevant data, they may try to understand or neglect understanding, they may be reasonable or unreasonable in their judgments, they may be responsible or irresponsible in their decisions, they may be in love with their parents, helpmates, and children, with the human community, with God, and on the other hand, they may opt for hatred in one or more of these respects.

This dialectic connects immediately with the macroeconomic analysis. There, there are discernible criteria immanent in the productive process. But the dialectic arises from the contradiction that arises when the criteria are adverted to or not, understood or not, affirmed or denied, observed responsibly or disregarded, by a community of love or a community of egoists.

Summary of the Argument

[1944] The present inquiry is concerned with relations between the productive process and the monetary circulation. It will be shown (1) that the acceleration of the process postulates modifications in the circulation, (2) that there exist 'systematic,' as opposed to windfall, profits, (3) that systematic profits increase in the earlier stages of long-term accelerations but revert to zero in later stages – a phenomenon underlying the variations in the marginal efficiency of capital of Keynesian General Theory, (4) that the increase and decrease of systematic profits necessitate corresponding changes in subordinate rates of spending – a correlation underlying the significance of the Keynesian propensity to consume, (5) that either or both a favorable balance of trade and domestic deficit spending create another type of systematic profits, (6) that while they last they mitigate the necessity of complete adjustment of the propensity to consume to the accelerations of the process, (7) that they cannot last indefinitely, (8) that the longer they last, the greater becomes the intractability of ultimate problems. From the premises and conclusions of this analysis it then will be argued (9) that prices cannot be regarded as ultimate norms guiding strategic economic decisions, (10) that the function of prices is merely to provide a mechanism for overcoming the divergence of strategically indifferent decisions or preferences, and (11) that, since not all decisions and preferences possess this indifference, the exchange economy is confronted with the dilemma either of eliminating itself by suppressing the freedom of exchange or of certain classes of exchanges, or else of effectively augmenting the enlightenment of the enlightened self-interest that guides exchanges.

PART ONE

_____

1　Analysis

|1983| Five brief considerations will locate both the topic and the purpose of this section. The first is a reflection of Joseph Schumpeter's on the lack of analysis in a certain stage of business-cycle theory. The second is an illustration of analysis drawn from the development of modern chemistry. The third is the technique of implicit definition needed to cope with shifts in meaning that arise in a developing science. The fourth and fifth are negative: analysis is not deductivist, and it is not guesswork.

In his *History of Economic Analysis* Joseph A. Schumpeter wrote:

> By the end of the period [that runs from 1870 to 1914 and later],[5] the lists of the features or symptoms that characterize cyclical phases – which different economists did draw up or would have drawn up – looked much alike. And not only that: by the end of the period most workers agreed – or tacitly took for granted – that the fundamental fact about cyclical fluctuations was the characteristic fluctuation in the production of plant and equipment. Now, how is this? We seem to be discovering a lot of common ground that should have assured much parallelism of effort and much agreement in results ... On the contrary, we seem to behold nothing but disagreement and antagonistic effort ... The contradiction is only apparent however. Agreement on

5 The bracketed clause is Lonergan's addition to this quotation.

the list of features, even if it had been complete, does not spell agreement as to their relations with one another, and it is the interpretation of these relations and not the list per se which individuates an analytic scheme or business-cycle 'theory.' Even agreement to the effect that it is the activity in the plant-and-equipment ('capital goods') industries which is the outstanding feature in cyclical fluctuations does not go far toward ensuring agreement in results since it leaves the decisive question of interpretation wide open.[6]

In this passage three distinct elements may be discerned: (1) the activities involved in producing new plant and equipment, (2) the relations between the products of these activities, and (3) the interpretation that makes a meaningful whole of these relations. On the basis of these distinctions Schumpeter was contending that a business-cycle theory is to be found in the interpretation of the whole.

Our second consideration provides a clear-cut illustration of such an interpretation. In chemistry one distinguishes analysis and synthesis: analysis begins from the mixtures and compounds of ordinary experience and advances towards the discovery of a periodic table of elements (atoms) out of which the mixtures and compounds can be reconstructed and into which they can be resolved. It was Mendeleev (1834–1907) that was the first to formulate the notion of a periodic table, and the existence of such a reality was regarded as established when, within the sixteen following years, there were found to exist three hitherto unknown elements which Mendeleev had predicted on the basis of his table. Finally, Niels Bohr (1885–1962) deduced from the subatomic structure of the atoms the necessity of the periodicity of the table.

In chemical analysis, then, we find the already mentioned three components: (1) an enormous array of repeatable investigations and experiments which constitute the concrete fact of the analytic process from mixtures and compounds to elements or atoms; (2) within this array there is an array of relations which, one by one, chemists discovered as connections linking the elements to one another and to their compounds and mixtures; and (3) the interpretation, the achievement of human understanding, the command of the whole process that enables a chemist to advance from his understanding of atomic numbers and atomic weights to the rela-

6 Joseph A. Schumpeter, *History of Economic Analysis* (New York: Oxford University Press, 1954) 1125 (Lonergan's reference).

tionships between atoms and to the possibility or impossibility of proposed compounds, and so on. Beginners, of course, can offer instances of such interpretation, but for full information one must go to the expert in the relevant section of chemical science; and what might be full information today tomorrow may prove incomplete. As knowledge of chemistry began from very small beginnings and continued to grow, so, by the laws of probability, we may expect such growth to continue in the future.

Our third consideration comes out of the second. Precisely because analysis is an ongoing process, it is subject to revision. In the measure that revision is radical, it involves new concepts and even new definitions. In this fashion the fact of revision displaces the old reliance on essential definitions and gives way to a search for significant basic variables. For *variables*, because it is process that is under investigation; for *significant* variables, because only significance contributes to the relevant acts of understanding; finally, for *basic* variables, because others depend on them, and they depend on one another. In other words, basic variables form a closed circle, in which terms are fixed by their relations, relations fix the terms, and the whole is justified by the degree in which it and its implications are verified.

To conclude, analysis begins from matters of fact, say, the conspicuous recurrence of changes in plant and equipment and the concomitance of such changes with the business cycle. Next, analysis turns from such instances of concomitance to lists of both successful and unsuccessful changes. Finally, from a study of such instances, by a process of trial and error, analysis aims to arrive at an ever fuller understanding of business cycles.

In the fourth place, when I said that analysis is not deductivist, I had no intention of excluding the clarifying use of logic that defines terms, distinguishes premises and conclusions, and so puts in order what one proposes and why. My intention was to exclude the apodictic demonstration in which first premises are not only true and certain but also necessary so that conclusions are similarly true, certain, and necessary. Such a position accounts both for the scepticism of the late Middle Ages and the subsequent rationalisms whether realist (Descartes, Spinoza, Leibniz) or, with a new conception of logic, idealist (Fichte and Hegel). I should say that all investigation begins from data, develops through cumulative insights, and aims at a consequent judgment. The difference between natural and human science is that the data for the former are basically sensible, while the data for the latter add human meanings. It is the addition to the sensible data of human meaning that enabled August Boeckh to define *Philolo-gie* as the reconstruction of the constructions of the human spirit.[7] In other words, *Philologie* correctly understands the constructions of the human spirit insofar as it correctly reconstructs what the constructing was intended to mean.

The process to this goal has been well described by Joseph Schumpeter.[8] His *History of Economic Analysis* is divided into five parts, of which the first is forty-seven pages of introduction. The need for forty-seven pages followed from his conception of a History of Economic Analysis: it is for him the history of the efforts men have made in order to understand economic phenomena. But though he boldly states his objective to be a history of human intellectual efforts in order to understand economic phenomena, he can also wonder how many will find this topic to their taste.

> Whatever the problems that, to snare the unwary, lurk below the surface of the history of any science, its historian is in other cases at least sure enough of his subject to be able to start right away. This is not so in our case. Here, the very ideas of economic analysis, of intellectual effort, of science, are 'quenched in smoke,' and the very rules or principles that are to guide the historian's pen are open to doubt and, what is worse, to misunderstanding.[9]

> Cannot the old stuff be safely left to the care of a few specialists who love it for its own sake?
> There is much to be said for this attitude. It is certainly better to scrap outworn modes of thought than to stick to them indefinitely. Nevertheless, we stand to profit from visits to the lumber room provided we do not stay there too long ...

---

7 See Bernard Lonergan, *Method in Theology* (London: Darton, Longman & Todd, and New York: Herder and Herder, 1972; Toronto: University of Toronto Press, 1990, 1994, 1996) 209–10 (Lonergan's reference.)

8 At this point the 1983 version of the *Essay* quotes a passage from Schumpeter's *History of Economic Analysis*. A longer quotation that includes the same passage appears, together with three sentences of Lonergan's, on a separate, unnumbered page, headed 'The Idea of a History of Economic Analysis,' between §§2 and 3. In order to avoid repetition, the contents of that page have been inserted here. See also note 10.

9 Schumpeter, *History* 3 (Lonergan's reference).

... whatever the field, the problems and methods that are in use at any given time embody the achievements and carry the scars of work that has been done in the past under entirely different conditions. The significance and validity of both problems and methods cannot be fully grasped without a knowledge of the previous problems and methods to which they are the (tentative) response.[10] Scientific analysis is not simply a logically consistent process that starts with some primitive notions and then adds to the stock in a straight-line fashion. It is not simply progressive discovery of an objective reality – as is, for example, discovery in the basin of the Congo. Rather it is an incessant struggle with creations of our own and our predecessors' minds and it 'progresses,' if at all, in a criss-cross fashion, not as logic, but as the impact of new ideas or observations or needs, and also as the bents and temperaments of new men, dictate. Therefore, any treatise that attempts to render 'the present state of science' really renders methods, problems, and results that are historically conditioned and are meaningful only with reference to the historical background from which they spring. To put the same thing somewhat differently: the state of any science at any given time implies its past history and cannot be satisfactorily conveyed without making this implicit history explicit.[11]

In brief, science develops: it comes to understand what previously was not understood; logic unfolds: it states explicitly what already has been said implicitly.

Finally, while we frequently hear or read that science attains its goal when it can predict, I think it important to add the post-Keynesian contention that the past cannot be changed and that the future is uncertain. In particular I would insist that analysis may attain its goal without being able to predict, and on the other hand, successful predictions may be attained, say, by a Ptolemy, without any analysis of the real grounds that makes the prediction successful. Indeed, the present study will offer an analysis of the macroeconomy that accounts for its successes and failures without attempting the historical and statistical research that would be necessary if any pre-

---

10 In the numbered pages of Lonergan's 'final' typescript, his quotation of Schumpeter (see note 8 above) begins with the next sentence and continues through the words '... historical background from which they spring.'
11 Schumpeter, *History* 4 (Lonergan's reference).

cise prediction were to be made. How is this possible? It is possible because knowledge of facts is one thing, and understanding known facts is another. The facts of the macroeconomy are already well known. What is lacking is a clear and precise understanding of the mechanism behind such obvious facts as the relations between expansion and contraction of the economy, employment and unemployment, inflation and deflation, and many other things that are just common knowledge.

2   Economic Process

Economic process is a shifting network of exchanges in which firms supply households with goods and services while members of households seek work and receive income from firms. Within any given country the network may expand as resourceful individuals at their own risk add to the routes of trade, to the goods produced, or to the services rendered. But besides the trading internal to a country there also is trading with foreign countries, and while in both cases the exchanges are ruled by supply and demand, the ruling operates differently.

Within a country exchanges occur as long as sellers prefer the price they receive and buyers prefer the goods or services they obtain. Moreover, when the numbers of buyers and sellers are large enough, prices paid and received will tend towards a single price that clears the market. But in foreign trade, equilibrium is reached inasmuch as each country buys abroad no more than it sells, and sells abroad no more than it buys. For if it were to sell more than it bought, it would force down the prices of its own products; and if it bought more than it sold, it would devaluate its own currency. So in internal trade, supply and demand determine the price of each product. But in foreign trade, any country's excessive selling tends to cheapen its own products; and excessive buying tends to devalue its own currency.

Now in such matters, first there occur the objective relationships, secondly occurs observation of them, thirdly there is the series of ever less unsuccessful attempts to deal with them, and finally emerge the economists who eventually eliminate their differences of opinion and establish a reasoned view. But we must cut this matter short and be content with mentioning an earlier policy, mercantilism, and a later practice, arbitrage.

Mercantilism was a government policy that required merchants to sell more abroad than they bought. Unfortunately, not all countries could put such a policy into practice, for the sum of instances in which a favorable balance could be secured was possible only if there was no remainder of unfavorable balances. For the unfavorable balance meant either that one's currency was continuously devaluated or else that the price one could obtain for one's exports continuously declined or, more probably, enough of each of these to balance one's foreign accounts.

While the logic of this situation was intolerable, there were enough backward areas in which its implications were not understood, enough independent countries too weak to resist being victimized, enough stronger countries that could enter into trade agreements, build empires, or declare wars. But this process of trial and error also gave rise to the financial capitals of the world, where currencies were traded against currencies, and the traders, to be successful, had to be adept at purchasing quantities of undervalued currencies by paying with overvalued currencies. Such trading at its fine point became known as arbitrage, and it had the happy effect of transferring to those engaged in foreign trade the burdens hitherto imposed by mercantilist convictions. For once the money market existed, merchants could know that too much or too little of their products was being sold abroad when their prices fell or rose; and similarly they could infer that they were buying too much or too little abroad when their own currency there was undervalued or overvalued. But none of these consequences could be accepted as a consistent policy by those engaged in foreign trade, and so the merchants themselves and their bankers would provide an automatic mechanism that would liberate them from the burdens involved in mercantilism.

Supply and demand, then, provide an automatic mechanism controlling both the quantities bought and sold and the prices at which the exchanges occur. But the control operates differently in the domestic market and in the foreign markets. In the domestic market the control operates separately on the prices and quantities involved in each class of exchanges. In the foreign market it is the value of a currency that in all classes of exchanges goes up or down; and similarly it is the goods and services of a given country that begin to sell more briskly or more sluggishly when too little or too much is being imported from that country.

The existence of automatic mechanisms that ward off unhappy consequences led liberal thinkers to affirm that there must be some automatic mechanism that would safeguard the equilibrium of the domestic economy. But after the Great Depression (1929–1933), John Maynard Keynes's *General Theory of Employment, Interest and Money*[12] argued successfully that

12 John Maynard Keynes, *The General Theory of Employment, Interest and Money*. Lonergan's text refers to the original edition (London: Macmillan, 1936).

this equilibrium might be merely a prolonged depression, since deficit spending was not to be cured by any automatic mechanism.

It is this conclusion that has given rise to the division of economics into two parts, microeconomics and macroeconomics; and it will be the intention of this paper to work out an analytic basis for the well-being of the macroeconomy, the proper functioning of the economy as a whole.

3   Significant Basic Variables

Variables are quantities subject to change; constants are not. A rate means 'so much every so often': it is a quantity that is neither all at once nor continuous but over a period of time. A change of rate may be positive, negative, or zero: so it means either 'so much more every so often,' or 'so much less every so often,' or 'about the same as before.'

It will simplify our expression if we use the word 'velocity' instead of 'rate' in the sense of 'so much every so often,' and the terms 'positive acceleration,' 'negative acceleration,' and 'zero acceleration' in the sense of positive, negative, or zero change of rate.

Positive acceleration is illustrated by the expanding economy, by ongoing prosperity, by the boom. Negative acceleration is the recession, the depression, the crash. Zero acceleration is the stationary state which includes fluctuations in which swings cancel with roundabouts.

Note that the foregoing variables are significant inasmuch as together they present the bare bones of the business cycle. For economic developments are finite, and so no economic development will accelerate indefinitely. They operate against an increasing resistance, to justify Juglar's celebrated pronouncement: 'the only cause of depression is prosperity.'[13] Similarly, negative accelerations are limited; they are not the neutron bomb. An economy will be gravely crippled by a crash; it will be reduced to a stationary state at a very low level; and so it was through the desolation of the early thirties and the noneconomic frenzy of the Second World War that the West began to recover its former prosperity.

Moreover, in his third postulate Nassau William Senior (1790–1864) spoke of products that are used as a means of indefinitely increasing further production.[14] Such products are familiar to us as 'producer goods.'

13 As quoted by Schumpeter, *History* 1124.
14 See ibid. 638 (Lonergan's reference).

For instance, shoe factories and their equipment are supplied not to consumers but to producers of shoes. As long as they are maintained in working order, they may be used to produce more shoes. In that sense there is no definite limit to their utility.

Now the makers of shoe factories and the makers of their equipment have their means of production, and so the third postulate implies that they will be able to produce further shoe factories and further equipment indefinitely. There may be, then, not just a single but a double acceleration of the production of shoes: for from each factory will come a stream of shoes, and from each producer of factories and each producer of the equipment needed in factories there will come streams of factories and of equipment. The result will be a stream of streams of new shoes.

In brief, the acceleration of production becomes institutionalized in capitalist production, and it is this that confers on it a reputation for abundance and variety. It remains that every degree of industrial development has its limitations. A capacity for indefinitely increasing the supply of shoes does not imply a capacity for indefinitely increasing the supply of leather for shoes, and as the price of leather goes up, canvas uppers with composite soles or wooden soles become more common. Similarly, the machines that make spindles for making cotton into thread, and the looms that make the thread into cloth, and the sewing machines that make cloth into clothing, all can be multiplied more readily than the acreage on which cotton can be planted, cultivated, and harvested. So cotton can come to be in short supply, and as its price rises, substitutes are sought.

Let us now turn from production to exchange. Capitalist production is production for sale. Products that fail to be sold, despite the ingenuity of modern marketing, are regarded as just waste. It follows that acceleration in production demands a proportionate acceleration in selling and buying. And as we have already distinguished the production of producer goods from the production of consumer goods, so now we must distinguish two distinct markets and advert to the influence each exerts upon the other.

First, then, there is a wave-like structure that places the accelerated production of producer goods in advance of the consequent acceleration of the production of consumer goods. Next, the wages paid workers for their part in the accelerated production of producer goods will increase the effective demand for consumer goods, but as yet there will be no increase in the supply of consumer goods. Thirdly, there will be a tendency for consumer prices to rise, and this tendency will be all the stronger, the more roundabout is the source of the additional producer goods and so the greater the delay in their beginning to add to the supply of consumer goods.

However, once the supply of consumer goods begins to increase, another threat looms over the horizon. Where before effective demand was strong and supply was short, now supply is strong but the effectiveness of demand will weaken as soon as the acceleration of the production of producer goods begins to taper off, the bill for wages begins to decrease, and the desire for consumer goods lacks to some extent the backing of ready money.

The ineffectiveness of consumer demand rises in significance as the expanding production of producer goods becomes broader and deeper. The broader it becomes, the wider will be its influence. The profounder the transformation it effects, the greater the disruption that may result. So we distinguish the minor disturbance of a recession, the major upset of a depression, and the paralysis brought on by a serious impairment of financial institutions.

Besides production and exchange, there is a third source of economic variation, finance.[15]

4   Circulation Analysis

|1980| An analysis of the circulation of payments meeting the flow of goods and services is concerned with the undertow that afflicts developing and deteriorating economies. It aims at imparting an understanding of economic change that can master both the distortion of developments by one-sided conceptions and the disaster of collapse that can change a recession into a breakdown.

Such an analysis is primarily interested in the phenomena set forth in W.W. Rostow's *Stages of Economic Growth*[16] and *Politics and the Stages of Growth:*[17] at different times different economies chance to be prepared for

15 Early in 1983 Lonergan stated in conversations that he had some new ideas on this 'third source of economic variation,' but he appears to have left nothing in writing on the point.

16 W.W. Rostow, *The Stages of Economic Growth: A Non-Communist Manifesto* (Cambridge: Cambridge University Press, 1960; 3rd ed., 1990).

17 W.W. Rostow, *Politics and the Stages of Growth* (Cambridge: At the University Press, 1971).

a takeoff; through this takeoff they advance towards commercial and industrial maturity; and through maturity they attain an enormous intensification of consumer goods and services.

What the analysis reveals is a mechanism distinct though not separable from the price mechanism which spontaneously coordinates a vast and ever shifting manifold of otherwise independent choices from demand and of decisions from supply. It is distinct from the price mechanism, for it determines the channels within which the price mechanism works. It is not separable from the price mechanism, for a channel is irrelevant when nothing flows through it.

I have spoken of the analysis as revealing channels and bringing to light an undertow. My meaning may become clearer by referring to the distinction sometimes made between general equilibrium (Walras, Wicksell) and partial equilibrium (Marshall). The channels of circulation replace the overall dominance claimed for general equilibrium theory,[18] but they reveal the conditions under which partial equilibria can exist.

More positively, the channels account for booms and slumps, for inflation and deflation, for changed rates of profit, for the attraction found in a favorable balance of foreign trade, the relief given by deficit spending, and the variant provided by multinational corporations and their opposition to the welfare state.

5   Procedure

The procedure of circulation analysis involves a minimum of description and classification, a maximum of interconnections and functional relations. [Perforce, some description and classification are necessary; but they are highly selective, and they contain the apparent arbitrariness inherent in all analysis.][19] For analytic thinking uses classes based on described similarities only as a springboard to reach terms defined by the correlations in which they stand. To take the simplest illustration, only a few of the natural numbers in the infinitely extended number series are classes derived from described similarity. By definition the whole series is a progression in which each successive term is defined as one more than its predecessor. It

---

18 Nicholas Kaldor, 'The Irrelevance of Equilibrium Economics,' *The Economic Journal* 82 (1972) 1237–55, at 1245.

19 The bracketed sentence appears in the 1978 version, where the section heading is 'Method' rather than 'Procedure.'

is this procedure that gives arithmetic its endless possibilities of accurate deduction; and as has been well argued, it is an analogous procedure that underlies the construction of successful theory.

On this model, circulation analysis raises a large superstructure of terms and theorems upon a summary classification and a few brief analyses of typical phenomena. Classes of payment quickly become rates of payment standing in the mutual conditioning of a circulation. To this mutual and, so to speak, internal conditioning there is immediately added a distinction between different types of circulation and their mutual conditioning through transfers from each to the other. This twofold conditioning in the monetary order is correlated with the conditioning constituted by productive rhythms of goods and services, so that positive, zero, and negative changes in rates of payment are concomitant with various dynamic configurations in the productive process.[20] There results a closely knit frame of reference that can envisage any total movement of an economy as a function of a sequence of changes in rates of payment, and that define the conditions of desirable movements as well as exhibit the causes of breakdowns. Finally, through such a frame of reference one can formulate the mechanism to which such a classical precept as thrift and enterprise is only partially adapted; and through it again one can formulate the fuller adaptation that has to be attained.

It follows that this analytic procedure differs notably from the procedures of the descriptive or the statistical economist.[21] By the nature of his task the descriptive economist is led to use, as far as possible, the language of ordinary speech in buying and selling. He is content with resemblances that strike the eye. He aims to move through easy stages of generalization to a nuanced picture of what, in the main, takes place. On the other hand, the statistical economist has a procedure of his own. He will take advantage

20 In the 1978 version, the preceding three sentences read: 'Classes of payments quickly become rates of payment standing in the mutual conditioning of a circulation; to this mutual and, so to speak, internal conditioning there is immediately added the external conditioning that arises out of transfers of money from one circulation to another; in turn this twofold conditioning in the monetary order is correlated with the conditioning constituted by productive rhythms of goods and services, and from the foregoing dynamic configuration of conditions during a limited interval of time, there is deduced a catalogue of possible types of change in the configuration over a series of intervals.'

21 In the 1978 version, Lonergan adds that 'to set up such a systematic unit of terms and theorems' is a 'procedure with norms and criteria of its own.'

of a specialized terminology, but as far as he is concerned, the only justification for a terminology is a proximate possibility of measurements. Further, he has no objection to generalization, but his generalizations, like those of positive science, await the verdict of verification.

Now as statistical procedure differs from descriptive, so analytic differs from both. Out of the endless classificatory possibilities analysis selects not the one sanctioned by ordinary speech nor again the one sanctioned by facility of measurement but the one that most rapidly yields terms which can be defined by the relations in which they stand to one another. To discover such terms is a lengthy and tedious process of trial and error. To justify them, one cannot reproduce the sequence of blind efforts that ultimately chanced upon them. One can only appeal to the success, be it great or small, with which they serve to account systematically for the phenomena under investigation.

There is a further corollary. Learned readers will be frequently bothered by the question, Why is the author off on this odd track? Indeed, the more learned they are, the more they will be troubled. But the only explanation I can offer at the start is a general one. A satisfactory explanation of anything involves many steps. The most expeditious procedure is to postpone the steps that presuppose other steps, and to begin with those that have minimal presuppositions. Only at the end of the labor can one grasp the explanation itself and then, looking back, see why each step was taken along the way.

6   The Productive Process

|1944| The term 'productive process' is to be used broadly. It denotes not merely 'making things' but the extraction or cultivation of raw materials, their transportation and assembly, the planning and designing of products, processing and distribution. It includes not only activities upon material objects but also services of all kinds, not only labor but also management, and not only production management but also sales management. In brief, it is the totality of activities bridging the gap between the potentialities of nature, whether physical, chemical, vegetable, animal, or human nature,[22] and, on the other hand, the actuality of a standard of

22 Lonergan's use here of the phrase 'potentialities of human nature' presupposes the details of his philosophical intentionality analysis. In brief, that analysis holds that the specifically human potentiality is grounded in a structure of

living. Such activities vary with the conditions of physical geography and with the cultural, political, and technical development of the population. They range from the simple and fixed routines of primitive hunters and fishers to the highly complex and mobile routines of modern Western civilization. Yet in every case there is one effect: the potentialities of nature become a standard of living. And in every case this effect is attained in the same way: it is attained not once and for all but only by a continuous succession of activities, by a rhythmic repetition of constant or mobile routines, by a process.

The productive process is, then, the aggregate of activities proceeding from the potentialities of nature and terminating in a standard of living. Always it is the current process, and so it is distinguished both from the natural resources, which it presupposes, and from the durable effects of past production. To draw sharp lines of demarcation is not possible immedi-

---

consciousness. Further, that structure is differentiated into four levels: experience, intelligence, reasonableness, and responsibleness. Again, each level is characterized, but not exclusively defined, by its principal act: experiencing, understanding (insight), judging, and deciding. Further, the levels and acts are linked by questions which prompt transitions from one act to the next: experiencing is inquired into, and such inquiries seek understanding; reflective questions ask about the correctness of acts of understanding and seek judgments; questions about what should be done follow upon accurate judgments of what the facts are and find their culmination in decisions and achievements. Again, such questions are grounded in an unrestricted desire to know and love.

Hence 'human potentiality' as such is this structure of human consciousness, concrete, present, and operating in each and every human being. As 'potential,' it is the concrete and actual condition of the possibility for all human decisions, whether individual or social. That is, 'human potential' designates whatever can result from decisions based upon judgments about what the situation is and what should be done, which in turn are based upon insights into experiences. Given the unrestrictedness of the desire which is the ground of all such questions and acts, such human potential turns out to be remarkably vast.

For fuller exposition, see Lonergan, *Insight*, especially chapters 1, 9–12, 15, and 18; more briefly, 'Cognitional Structure,' *Collection*, Collected Works of Bernard Lonergan, vol. 4 (Toronto: University of Toronto Press, 1988) 205–21 (original publication, New York: Herder and Herder, 1967: 221–39); and *Method in Theology*, chapters 1 and 2.

ately, but it will be possible later. Meanwhile it will be sufficient to advert to the fact that the current process is always a rate of activity,[23] that this rate of activity differs from the potentialities of nature, from which it proceeds, and that it differs from its finished products, which, *ex hypothesi*, are no longer in process but already produced. No doubt the three are closely related, but relation presupposes distinction, and before relations can be grasped adequately, the distinctions must be grasped. Goods that have been completed are not goods in process; services that have been rendered are not services being rendered. Again, goods in process are not the natural resources from which they are derived; and services being rendered are not the natural potentialities from which they are derived. There can be resources and potentialities without goods or services being derived from them; and while they are in process of being derived, the goods are not yet produced and the services not yet rendered.

Thus the productive process is a purely dynamic entity. We began by saying how broadly the term was to be taken. But it is also necessary to insist how narrowly. It is not wealth, but wealth in process. It is none of the potentialities of nature, whether physical, chemical, vegetable, animal, or human. It is none of its own effects, if by effects are understood what has been completed. It is neither the existence nor the use of durable consumer goods, of clothing, houses, furnishings, domestic utensils, personal belongings, or indeed any item of private or public property that can be listed as a consumer good and has passed beyond the process to become an element of the community's standard of living. On the other hand, with regard to producer goods a distinction has to be drawn: they are in the process as means of production; they are in the process in the sense that labor is in the process or that management is in the process, namely, their use forms part of the process; but once they are completed they no longer are under process, any more than labor or management is under process and being produced. A ship under construction is part of the process; but once the ship is completed and begins to transport ocean freight, it is not the ship but only the use of the ship that is part of the process. The same

---

23 Lonergan continually emphasized that his circulation analysis is primarily concerned with rates; quantities are relegated to secondary importance. Indeed, it is the set of problems associated with changes of rates – with dynamic accelerations in the economy – that was his central concern. For his remarks on the theoretical (analytical) theory of accelerations, see *Insight* 21–23/46–47, and especially 25/49–50. See also notes 26, 27, and 29 below.

distinction is to be made with regard to every other item of producer goods: factories and machinery, railways and power units, warehouses and offices are in the productive process only while being produced; once they are produced, they themselves have passed beyond the process to enter the category of static wealth, even though their use remains as a factor of production.

Thus the productive process, which proceeds from the potentialities of nature, terminates in a standard of living in two distinct ways. It terminates in a standard of living inasmuch as the goods and services it renders become elements in a standard of living. But it may also terminate indirectly in a standard of living inasmuch as the goods and services it renders complement the potentialities of nature to make the process capable of effecting a higher standard of living. Consumer goods and services enter directly into a standard of living. Producer goods and services enter indirectly into a standard of living: directly they are improvements upon nature that facilitate the productive process and increase its power and efficacy; and only indirectly, through this increased power and efficacy, do they affect the standard of living by improving and increasing the supply of consumer goods and services.

Additional Note to Section 6[24]

|1982| Lowe, *The Path of Economic Growth* (Cambridge University Press, 1976) 32.

Plantations	–	cotton
Cotton gins	–	clean cotton
Spindles	–	cotton thread
Looms	–	cotton cloth
Sewing machines	–	cotton dresses
Extraction machinery	–	coal; iron ore
Blast furnaces	–	pig iron
Steel mills	–	steel
Machine tools	–	gins, spindles, looms, sewing machines

24 In the 1982 and 1983 versions of the *Essay,* the following table was included on a separate page. While attributed to Lowe, Lonergan's table shows certain differences.

7   Division of the Productive Process

|1944| The foregoing section isolated the productive process as a purely dynamic entity, and drew a distinction between consumer goods that enter the standard of living and producer goods that raise the standard of living. That distinction must now be examined more fully. It is to be shown that the correspondence between elements in the productive process and elements in the standard of living may be a point-to-point, or a point-to-line, or a point-to-surface, or even some higher correspondence.

There exists, then, a point-to-point correspondence between bushels of wheat and loaves of bread, between head of cattle and pounds of meat, between bales of cotton and cotton dresses, between tons of steel and motorcars. In each case the elements in the standard of living are algebraic functions of the first degree[25] with respect to elements in the productive process. These functions are not immutable. There can be more or less wheat in a loaf of bread, more or fewer pounds of meat from a head of cattle, more or fewer cotton dresses from a bale of cotton, more or fewer motorcars from a ton of steel. One can, for instance, spin the cotton more loosely, weave it more broadly, cut it more skillfully, shorten skirts, eliminate sleeves, and perhaps find other devices to make more dresses out of fewer bales of cotton. But such efforts only serve to emphasize the existence of an inexorable law of limitation. No matter how one makes the dresses, one cannot get more cotton in the dresses than one had in the bales. No matter how one arranges the points, the point-to-point correspondence remains. For in the totality of such instances there is an identity of elements: the very material elements that were in the productive process

---

25 By 'algebraic functions of the first degree' is meant functions involving no exponential powers of the variables other than 1 – that is, no x^2, no x^3, no $x^{1/2}$ ($= \sqrt{x}$) – and no transcendental functions of x such as log x, e^x, sine x, and so on. To give a simple example, if the number of loaves of bread is represented by the variable y, and the number of bushels of wheat by the variable x, then a relevant algebraic function might be $y = bx \pm c$, where b represents the number of loaves of bread which can be obtained from one bushel of wheat under current technological means, and c represents any fixed loss or gain which is independent of the number of bushels (if, for instance, government regulations were to require the testing of c loaves per production period, these loaves would not be available for consumption).

Lonergan first wrote this section in 1944. A parallel point seems to have been made in 1976 by Lowe in *The Path of Economic Growth* 27–47.

enter into the standard of living; and the affirmation of a point-to-point correspondence is no more than the affirmation of the permanence of this material identity.

However, not all material objects in the productive process are limited to a point-to-point correspondence with elements in the standard of living. When a primitive hunter makes a spear, he makes it to kill not one wild animal, nor ten, nor fifty, but just as many as he possibly can get. Similarly, the primitive fisher makes his net not for one but for an indeterminate series of catches of fish. The shipbuilder constructs ships not for one but for an indeterminate number of voyages. And in our industrial age machines are built and factories rise not for each batch of manufactured products but for an indeterminate series of batches. There is a new piece of leather, but not a new shoe factory, for every new pair of shoes. There is a new lot of metals, but not a new plant, for every new motorcar. In each of these instances the point-to-point correspondence is escaped because it is not the product but some ulterior effect of the product that enters into the standard of living. Spears, nets, ships, factories, machines end up as means of production. They enter the standard of living, not in themselves, but in their effects of pounds of meat and fish, ocean voyages, shoes, and motorcars. Such a correspondence may be named point-to-line: elements in the productive process correspond not to single elements in the standard of living but to indeterminate series of the latter.

Higher correspondences are possible. The machines that make shoes are made by machine tools. Since the former are in a point-to-line correspondence with elements in the standard of living, the latter by that very fact are in a point-to-surface correspondence. Again, the machines used in shipbuilding are made by machine tools: the ships are in a point-to-line correspondence with elements in the standard of living; the machines making ships are in a point-to-surface correspondence; the machine tools making the machines used in making ships are in a point-to-volume correspondence.

Now there exist the same types of correspondence between elements of activity or services in the productive process and elements in the standard of living. The matter is clear when the services are, as it were, incorporated in a material product. All the services involved in growing wheat, storing it, transporting it, milling it, making bread, distributing bread are proportionate to the supply of bread. They are repeated as often as wheat is grown and bread supplied. No doubt, they are variable functions of the wheat-to-bread process: more or less activity, a greater or less efficiency, may be involved. But the correspondence remains point-to-point, for there is no possibility of these services being done once and then the wheat-to-bread process being repeated an indeterminate number of times. Even if robots were employed, the robots would have to go through the motions every time wheat grew and was processed into bread. In like manner the activities and services involved in making ships are repeated as often as ships are made but not as often as ships are used. Their correspondence remains point-to-line. And the same holds for the activities and services incorporated in the making of machine tools. Their correspondence is point-to-surface, or point-to-volume, or at times even higher; they are repeated when the making of machine tools is repeated; they are not repeated when the use of machine tools is repeated; and much less are they repeated when the use of the products of the machine tools is repeated.

However, not all activities and services are coincident with the process of material objects to take their correspondence from that of the objects. It remains that the same general types of correspondence may be discerned. There is a point-to-point correspondence between movements of trains and passenger-miles, not indeed in the sense that there is some fixed ratio between train-miles and passenger-miles, but in the sense that the train has to move as often and as far as passengers move. From instance to instance, a train may have more or fewer passengers, to vary the ratio between train-miles and passenger-miles; but the ratio is always some definite ratio; it is something determinate in the present of each instance. In fact, it is but another form of the flexibility of the point-to-point correspondence: as there may be more or less cotton in a cotton dress, as there may be greater or less efficiency in the operations coincident with growing wheat and making bread, so there may be greater or less efficiency in the transportation of passengers. The flexibility does not eliminate but rather emphasizes the point-to-point correspondence.

Train journeys illustrate one type of service that is not incorporated in material objects. Another ambiguous type is the maintenance of capital equipment. Strictly one may regard maintenance, like replacements, as a prolongation of the process of production of the capital equipment. On the other hand, one might prefer to consider it as a condition of the use of the equipment, and so to classify it along with the power that drives the equipment, the labor that operates it, the management that directs the operations. In fact, maintenance is an accountant's unity, and it comprises quite different realities.[26] There are types of maintenance that are part and parcel of use; there are others that arise whether or not the equipment is in use; and it should seem best to distinguish, at least in a theoretical discussion, according to concrete circumstance, and sometimes count maintenance in the lower correspondence in which the equipment is used, sometimes in the higher correspondence in which the equipment is made.

So much, then, for the division of the productive process. In the previous section it was defined as a purely dynamic entity, a movement taking place between the potentialities of nature and products. In the present section, there has been attempted a dynamic division of that dynamic entity. Elements in the process are in point-to-point, or point-to-line, or point-to-surface, or even some higher correspondence with elements in the standard of living. Some general reflections are now in order.

The division is not based upon proprietary differences. It is not a difference of firms, for the same firm may be engaged at once in different correspondences with the standard of living. Again, it is not a division based upon the properties of things: the same raw materials may be made into consumer goods or capital goods; and the capital goods may be point-to-line or point-to-surface or a higher correspondence; they may have one correspondence at one time and another at another. Similarly, general services such as light, heat, power, transportation may be employed in any correspondence, and in different proportions in the several correspondences at different times. The division is, then, neither proprietary nor technical. It is a functional[27] division of the structure of the productive pro-

26 An 'accountant's unity': that is, a category used in accounting. For Lonergan, accounting generally denotes an enterprise within common sense which uses descriptive, as contrasted with explanatory, terms (on these terms see *Insight* 37–38/61–62, 178–79/201–3, 247–48/272–73; also note 27 below). Insofar as that is true, the accountant's unity is not an adequate index for the normative, explanatory analysis of the productive process.

27 'Functional' is for Lonergan a technical term pertaining to the realm of explanation, analysis, theory; it does not mean 'who does what' in some common-sense realm of activity.

Lonergan illustrates his basic meaning of 'explanation' by referring to D. Hilbert's method of implicit definition:

'Let us say, then, that for every basic insight there is a circle of terms and relations, such that the terms fix the relations, the relations fix the terms, and the insight fixes both ...

cess: it reveals the possibilities of the process as a dynamic system, though to bring out the full implications of such a system will require not only the next two sections, on stages of the process, but also later sections on cycles.[28]

There remains, however, a more immediate question. The point-to-line and higher correspondences are based upon the indeterminacy of the relation between certain products and the ultimate products that enter into the standard of living. Now such indeterminacy does not seem to be a fact. Granted that there is not a new shoe factory for every new pair of shoes, still every factory has a calculable life, and the same holds for every piece of machinery; in advance one can estimate, and in historical retrospection one could know, exactly how many pairs of shoes are to be produced or were to be produced by the given equipment. Hence the whole division breaks down. There is no real difference between point-to-point, point-to-line, and the higher correspondences.

The objection is shot from a double-barreled gun: the indeterminacy is not a fact, first, because at some date, in a more or less remote future,

---

'Thus, the meaning of both point and straight line is fixed by the relation that two and only two points determine a straight line.

'In terms of the foregoing analysis, one may say that implicit definition consists in explanatory definition without nominal definition' (*Insight* 12/36–37).

Lonergan went on to identify the contemporary notion of a 'function' as one of the most basic kinds of explanatory, implicit definition – one that specifies 'things in their relations to one another' (*Insight* 37–38/61–62). In Lonergan's circulation analysis, the basic terms are rates – rates of productive activities and rates of payments. The objective of the analysis is to discover the underlying intelligible and indeed dynamic (accelerative) network of functional, mutually conditioning, and interdependent relationships of these rates to one another.

28 This sentence has been altered by the editors. As Lonergan originally wrote it, the sentence refers to 'the next section' and 'a later section.' It has been altered to take account of two changes Lonergan later made in the *Essay*: (1) In the 1944 version there is a single section, entitled 'The Basic and Surplus Stages of the Productive Process,' which sets out the distinction, quite central to Lonergan's argument, between these stages; in 1982 he divided this section, adding what is now the heading of §9 below and altering the heading of §8. (2) In the 1944 version the section following the one on basic and surplus stages was divided into three subsections; in 1982 Lonergan separated these into what here are §§10, 11 (to which he gave a new title), and 12.

determinate information is possible, and second, because here and now a very accurate estimate is possible. It should seem that the indeterminacy is very much a present fact. One has to await the future to have exact information. And while estimates in the present may be esteemed accurate, the future has no intention of being ruled by them: owners do not junk equipment simply because it has outlasted the most reliable estimates; nor are bankrupts kept in business because their expectations, though mistaken, are proved to have been perfectly reasonable. The analysis that insists on the indeterminacy is the analysis that insists on the present fact: estimates and expectations are proofs of the present indeterminacy and attempts to get round it; and, to come to the main point, an analysis based on such estimates and expectations can never arrive at a criticism of them; it would move in a vicious circle. It is to avoid that circle that we have divided the process in terms of indeterminate point-to-line and point-to-surface and higher correspondences.

8   The Basic Stage of the Productive Process

In the sixth section the productive process was isolated as a dynamism proceeding from the potentialities of nature and terminating in a standard of living. In the seventh section the dynamism itself was subjected to analysis: different types of correspondence were found to exist between elements in the process and elements in the standard of living. The purpose of the present, eighth, section is in the main to collect results.

Let us assume as known what is meant by the term 'standard of living.' Let the term 'emergent standard of living' be defined as the aggregate of rates at which goods and services pass from the productive process into the standard of living. Then each of these rates will be a 'so much every so often'; for instance, so much bread a year, so much meat a year, so much clothing a year, so many motorcars a year, so many passenger-miles a year, and so forth throughout the whole catalogue of elements entering into the standard of living. It follows that the emergent standard of living, the aggregate of such rates, is a variable with respect to intervals of time; for instance, in a comparison of successive years, one may find two types of difference: the catalogue of elements may change, some items being dropped and other new items added; further, the rates with respect to the same items may change, becoming greater or less than in the previous year. Thus the emergent standard of living is an aggregate of rates that are both qualitatively and quantitatively variable with respect to successive intervals of time.

Next, let the basic stage of the productive process be defined as the aggregate of rates of production of goods and services in process and in a point-to-point correspondence with elements in the emergent standard of living. As explained in section 6, goods and services are in process when they are neither the mere potentialities of nature nor on the other hand finished products. As explained in section 7, goods and services are in a point-to-point correspondence with elements in the standard of living when they are some determinate, though not immutable or unvarying, algebraic function of the first degree with respect to elements in the standard of living. Finally, just as the aggregate of rates constituting the emergent standard of living is an aggregate of instances of 'so much every so often,' so also is the aggregate of rates of production in the basic stage of the process; and again, as the emergent standard of living, so also the basic stage of the process is an aggregate of rates that are qualitatively and quantitatively variable with respect to successive intervals of time.

It is to be noted that the emergent standard of living and the basic stage of the process are not identical aggregates of rates. The basic stage of the process is, in its pure form, an aggregate of rates of labor, of managerial activity, of the use of capital equipment for the sake of the goods and services that enter the standard of living.[29] Let us say that some ultimate product, whether service or material object, is q_i; that j enterprises contributed

29 Beginning with the next sentence, and continuing through the end of the *Essay*, Lonergan's notation has been altered to avoid confusion. A brief account of reasons for this editorial policy follows.

In successive versions of his *Essay* Lonergan made use of various notational devices for emphasizing the central importance of the fact that his analysis concerns *rates*, or as he later wrote (perhaps influenced by Lowe's *The Path of Economic Growth*), *flows*. In the 1944 version, he frequently designated *quantities* by simple upper-case letters, and rates or flows by upper-case letters prefixed either by a lower-case d (usually in the case of rates of nonmonetary quantites, for example, numbers of products per interval) or an upper-case D (usually in the case of rates of payments). However, he also used both d and D to denote differentials of the calculus, so that, for instance, DE' meant a rate of basic expenditure, and D^2E' meant a rate of a rate (that is, an acceleration) of basic expenditure, while simultaneously D^2E' meant a first-order differential of DE'. Later he attempted to clarify by substituting, in most cases, the letter f for d or D, to designate rates or flows. Elsewhere, however, he used the lower-case f, followed by one or two primes (′ or ″) in a more conventional way, namely, to indicate the first and second derivatives of mathematical functions (see §11,

each a respective q_{ij} to the emergence of q_i; that in each of these enterprises k factors of production, such as labor, management, capital equipment in use, contributed each a respective q_{ijk} to the emergence of q_i; then the ultimate product q_i is a double summation of the contributions of the factors of production q_{ijk}. For the ultimate product is the summation of the contributions of the several enterprises to the ultimate product; and the contribution of each enterprise is a summation of the contributions of each of its factors of production; so that there is some sense in which

$$q_i = \Sigma\Sigma \; q_{ijk} \tag{1}$$

the summations being taken, first, with respect to all instances of k and, secondly, with respect to all instances of j. But if the ultimate product q_i is related by a double summation to the contributions of factors of production q_{ijk}, then the total flow of ultimate products[30] Q_i is also related by a double summation to the rates of the contributions of the factors of production Q_{ijk}, where both Q_i and Q_{ijk} are instances of the form 'so much or so many every so often.'

Since the form of the relation between them is a double summation, the emergent standard of living and the basic stage of the process are not iden-

---

'A Technical Restatement,' below). In order to avoid confusion, and to bring Lonergan's notation into line with notational conventions of the fields of mathematics and economics, the following scheme has been adopted by the editors throughout the remainder of the text.

Rates or *flows* are generally designated by upper-case letters (primed or unprimed), and upper-case letters (primed or unprimed) always designate rates or flows, unless otherwise specifically noted.

Quantities are generally designated by lower-case letters (primed or unprimed), using the same letter as for the rate or flow, where pertinent. At times lower-case letters are also used, following Lonergan's own practice, to designate *fractions*; but these and other exceptions to the scheme will be specifically noted.

Thus in the present section, for example, what appears in the text as q_i (the ultimate product) was originally Q_i, while the text's Q_i (the *flow* of ultimate products) was originally dQ_i and later fQ_i. Note that while this shift in notation is intended to minimize confusion, the importance of a distinct symbolism for rates or flows cannot be overstated.

30 The expression 'total flow of ultimate products' was introduced in the 1978 version, to substitute for 1944's 'rate of emergence of.'

tical aggregates of rates. On the other hand, precisely because the relation is a double summation, they are equivalent aggregates of rates. However, this statement requires three qualifications. First, mistakes are made in the productive process: there are activities that are useless in the sense that they do not contribute to any of the goods and services that enter the standard of living; materials are wasted; production is begun but not completed; operations are performed wrongly and have to be begun over again. Second, there is an extremely complex and somewhat variable pattern of lags between the time of the contribution made by the factor of production and the time of the emergence of the ultimate product; to select the time limits of the elements q_{ijk} relevant to a given q_i would be a Herculean task that would have to be repeated on every occasion on which there was a variation in the pattern of the lags; however, though a Herculean task, it would not be an impossible task, since such time limits are objectively determinate in the present and past,[31] for every contribution to q_i which now exists did take place during a determinate period of time. The third qualification is with regard to the meaning of the equivalence: the symbolic expression (1) is not a mathematical equation and it cannot be, until a common measure is found for ultimate products and contributions to ultimate products; such a common measure is not had until the measure of exchange value is introduced; for the present, then, the equivalence in question is not a mathematical equality but a form of correlation, a double summation, that can become a mathematical equality.

Hence, both the emergent standard of living and the basic stage of the productive process are aggregates of rates that are quantitatively and qualitatively variable with respect to successive intervals of time; and further, when allowance is made for lags and for mistakes in production, the relation between these two aggregates of rates is a double summation.

9   The Surplus Stage[32]

The basic stage is only part of the current productive process. Besides it, there is a series of surplus stages. Each of these surplus stages is an aggre-

---

31 Lonergan originally wrote, '... it would not be an impossible task, in the sense that such time limits are not objectively determinate in the present and past ...'
32 In the 1944 version this section continues the previous one with no break. The section heading used here first appeared in the 1982 version.

gate of rates of production of goods and services in process and in a point-to-line, or point-to-surface, or higher correspondence with elements in the standard of living. As before, each of these rates is a 'so much or so many every so often'; again, each is qualitatively and quantitatively variable with respect to successive intervals of time; and finally, the relation between an ultimate product q_i of any surplus stage and the contributions of factors of production in that stage with respect to that product, q_{ijk}, is again a double summation in which allowance must be made for lags and for mistakes in production.

However, there is this difference between the basic stage and the surplus stages. The ultimate products of the basic stage, whether goods or services, enter into the standard of living. The ultimate products of the surplus stages, whether goods or services, do not enter into the standard of living. From being under process themselves they pass into use in a lower stage of the process: they become means of production or the replacement or the maintenance of means of production, where production is understood in the broad sense already defined.[33] Thus, as the emergent standard of living is consumer to the basic stage of the process, so the basic stage in turn is consumer to the lowest of the surplus stages, and each lower surplus stage is consumer to the next higher surplus stage. In other words, producer goods and services are goods and services consumed by producers. Not passengers but railway companies consume rolling stock and rails. Passengers consume transportation. And similarly in similar cases.

But if the ultimate products of the surplus stages do not enter into the standard of living, nonetheless they are related to it. To determine that relation a distinction has to be drawn between short-term and long-term accelerations of the productive process. A short-term acceleration is an increase in rates of production due to a fuller use of existing capital equipment, to a greater efficiency of labor and management, to a decrease in stocks of goods. A long-term acceleration is an increase in rates of production due to the introduction of more capital equipment and/or more efficient capital equipment. The latter is termed a long-term acceleration because it changes the basis on which the short-term acceleration works: the short-term acceleration makes the best of existing equipment; the long-term improves and increases the equipment which a corresponding short-term acceleration will use in the fullest and most efficient manner.

Now, as is apparent from the definitions, the several stages of the process

33 See §6, 'The Productive Process.'

may have, independently, short-term accelerations. But long-term accelerations take place in virtue of the dependence of each lower stage on the next higher stage. More, and more efficient, capital equipment is had in the basic stage by procuring more, and more efficient, equipment from the lowest of the surplus stages. If the demand in the basic stage is strong enough, the lowest of the surplus stages will have to go into a long-term acceleration to obtain for itself more, and more efficient, capital equipment. Similarly, the next stage may need a long-term acceleration to meet its demand, and so on until the highest of the surplus stages is reached; and there only a short-term acceleration is possible. Thus the structure of the productive process is a series of stages, where each stage is an aggregate of rates of production, and each lower stage receives from the next higher stage the means of long-term acceleration of its rates.

The phenomena of a generalized long-term acceleration of the whole productive process are well known. They may occur in a backward economy that is copying the achievements of an advanced economy, and then one gets a series of five-year plans. They may occur in an economy that is pioneering advance for the rest of the world, and then one gets an industrial revolution. In either case there is a transformation of the capital equipment of the economy. There are continuous migrations of labor as it is displaced by more efficient equipment and turns to operating more equipment. There is first a period in which the consumption of materials and the quantity of labor mount with no corresponding increase in the standard of living; and after this period of transformation, of equipping industry and commerce anew, there follows a period of exploitation[34] in

---

34 Lonergan's meaning of 'exploitation' in this sentence moves in just the opposite direction from Marx's usual meaning, but the overall thrust of Lonergan's point heads towards a Marxian revolutionary desideratum.

   Exploitation for Marx generally refers to the systemic relations of production that regularly cause the expropriation of the surplus part of the labor value produced by the workers so that it becomes the profits of the capitalists, while the workers' standard of living collectively approaches the mere subsistence level. That Lonergan was quite aware of Marx's position is shown from a supplement handed out to his class in 1979: 'We, on the other hand, have to distinguish basic and surplus [prices and quantities], P' and P'', Q' and Q''. For unless surplus is conceived as a distinct circuit with its own final market, the Marxists object that the basic final market is demanding payment not only for basic goods and services but also for surplus as well; hence

which the fruits of the long-term acceleration finally reach the last[35] stage
of the process and the standard of living rises to a new level. Thus a wave or
cycle[36] is inherent in the very nature of long-term accelerations of the productive process.

To waves or cycles the argument returns later. The one point to be
observed at present is that long-term accelerations are limited. With
respect to a given field of natural resources and population, and on the
supposition of a given level of cultural, political, and technical development, there is a maximum rate of production for the process. The ground
of the limitation is that both the greater complexity of more efficient
equipment and the greater quantity of more equipment postulate proportionate rates of replacement and maintenance. The process accelerates
against an increasing resistance, so that every element of acceleration
reduces the room for further accelerations. In the limit the whole effort of
the surplus stages is devoted to replacement and maintenance of capital
equipment, and then the only possibility of further acceleration is to
depart from the assumption of a given level of cultural, political, and technical development. For with better men, a better organization of men, and

---

the accusation [that] profit is robbing workers of part of the labor value of
their contribution.'

In the present context of Lonergan's presentation of the surplus stage of
the pure cycle of production, the point is that the new basis for overall production of the standard of living of the total economy brought about by the
significant addition of more and/or new plant and equipment is to be
exploited in the widening and deepening of basic production that raises the
standards of living of everyone, but especially of the workers (or, as he used to
say in class, 'of the widows and orphans'). The whole point of Lonergan's analysis, then, is to emphasize what he also makes clear in the 1979 page mentioned above: 'And now with the circuits distinguished, the crossover makes it
manifest that it supplements the wages paid in the basic circuit, so that profits
are not robbery and there is no need for the gifts of bank credit to supplement
workers' basic wages.' (For a fuller quotation, see note 87 below.)

35 The 1944 version has 'basic.' In 1978 and 1980 'basic' is crossed out, and
nothing replaces it, but in 1982 it is again crossed out and now replaced by
'last.'

36 Here and at several other places later in the *Essay*, Lonergan in 1982 added
the words 'wave or' to 'cycle,' and 'waves or' to 'cycles,' probably to make sure
that the cycles he is discussing would not be thought of as being static in
any way.

better practical ideas, it becomes possible through the short-term accelerations to introduce more efficient equipment, displace labor, devote the displaced labor to a greater quantity of equipment, and so recommence the wave or cycle of long-term advance.

10   Cycles of the Productive Process

The wave or cycle that is inherent in the very nature of a long-term acceleration of the productive process is not to be confused with the familiar trade cycle. The latter is a succession of booms and of slumps, of positive and then negative accelerations of the process. But the cycle with which we are here concerned is a pure cycle. It includes no slump, no negative acceleration.[37] It is entirely a forward movement which, however, involves a wave or cycle inasmuch as in successive periods of time the surplus stage of the process is accelerating more rapidly and, again later, less rapidly than the basic stage. When suitable classes and rates of payment have been defined, it will be possible to show that under certain conditions of human inadaptation this pure cycle results in a trade cycle. However, that implication is not absolute but conditioned, not something inevitable in any case but only something that follows when human adaptation is lacking.

These further consequences are not to the present point. For the present issue is whether the pure cycle is itself inevitable on the supposition of long-term acceleration. Would it not be possible to have a long-term acceleration and yet 'smooth out' the pure cycle? Or must one say that, in view of the dynamic structure of the productive process, pure cycles become inevitable if long-term accelerations are attempted? A discussion of this issue turns upon two main points. What is involved in a long-term acceleration of the productive process? What is involved in a pure cycle? These will be discussed in turn.[38]

There are three reasons for expecting a long-term acceleration to be a massive affair. In the first place, it is a matter of long-term planning: the utility of capital formation emerges only over long periods; hence long-term planning is involved in capital formation, and since one is settling one's fate for years to come, it is generally worth while to do so in the best manner possible. In the second place, the introduction of more, or more efficient, units of production is not to be expected to take place in

37 For further explanation, see §24 and especially figure 24-6.
38 See below, §§15 and 16 on acceleration, and §24 on the pure cycle.

random fashion: the supply of a single product depends upon the activities of many units, so that it is worth while for many units to develop when it is worth while for any one of a series to develop; on the other hand, increased demand does not concentrate upon some one product but divides over several products, so that if there is an increased demand for one, there will be an increased demand for many; and as the increased demand for one justifies development in a series of productive units, so the increased demand for many justifies development in a series of series of units. There is a third consideration of a more abstract character. The emergence both of new ideas and of the concrete conditions necessary for their practical implementation forms matrices of interdependence: any objective change gives rise to series of new possibilities, and the realization of any of these possibilities has similar consequences; but not all changes are equally pregnant, so that economic history is a succession of time periods in which alternatively the conditions for great change are being slowly accumulated and, later, the great changes themselves are being brought to birth.

|1982| (As to smoothing out the trade cycle, I have no doubt that that is possible. But I see that possibility in repudiating the notion of automatic progress, in eliminating our mistaken expectations, in forgetting the delusions of grandeur to which we have succumbed in the past and even in the present.)[39]

11   A Technical Restatement[40]

|1944| It will be well to state systematically the foregoing conclusion that cycles are inherent in the very nature of a long-term acceleration of the

---

39 This paragraph first appears (without parenthesis marks) in the 1982 version, typed at the bottom of the last page of what is now §10; it does not replace anything, and why Lonergan added it is not entirely clear – perhaps simply as a concession to what might be expected to follow at this point in his argument. In any case, the paragraph is not referring to the smoothing out of the *pure* cycle mentioned in the preceding paragraph; what it does allude to does not, in fact, become evident until the end of the *Essay*. See also the Editors' Introduction above.

40 In the 1944 version this section appears as the second subdivision of the seventh section and bears the title 'Cycles in the Productive Process.' The title used here first appears in the 1978 version.

productive process. Consider the following four series of continuous functions[41] of time, namely,

$$f_1'(t), f_2'(t), f_3'(t), \dots$$
$$f_1''(t), f_2''(t), f_3''(t), \dots$$
$$A_1, A_2, A_3, \dots$$
$$B_2, B_3, \dots$$

The suffixes 1, 2, 3, … refer respectively to the basic stage of the productive process, the lowest of the surplus stages, the next to lowest of the surplus stages, and so forth. Expressions of the type $f_n'(t)$ measure the rate of production on the nth level, while the derived functions $f_n''(t)$ measure the acceleration of the rate of production. Again, the functions A_n measure the short-term acceleration of the rate of production on the nth level, so that the long-term acceleration is $f_n''(t) - A_n$. Finally, the functions B_n measure the rate of production that is effecting merely replacements and maintenance on the next lower stage, so that the rate of production effecting long-term acceleration on the next lowest stage is given by $f_n'(t) - B_n$.

Now let a, $b - a$, $c - b$, … be time lags, and let k_2, k_3, … be multipliers that connect the rate of production effecting long-term acceleration and the rate of acceleration so effected. Then, since this effect emerges with a time lag, one has

$$k_2[f_2'(t-a) - B_2] = f_1''(t) - A_1$$
$$k_3[f_3'(t-b) - B_3] = f_2''(t-a) - A_2$$
$$k_4[f_4'(t-c) - B_4] = f_3''(t-b) - A_3.$$

The equations are simply symbolical expressions of the analysis to the effect that any stage may accelerate in either of two ways: by a short-term acceleration in the stage itself when A_n becomes greater than zero and so $f_n''(t)$ increases equally; or in virtue of the fact that on the next higher stage the rate of production is greater than a rate of mere replacement and maintenance and so is bringing about, with a time lag, a long-term acceleration of the next lower stage.

---

41 Notice that in what follows Lonergan uses f' to designate the first derivative with respect to time, and f'' to designate the second derivative with respect to time. Lonergan's usage here has been retained, in exception to the convention adopted in note 29 above.

The advantage of such symbolical expression is that its brevity makes its implications more obvious. Thus it is evident that any level of the process can accelerate on its own in short-term fashion, but if such acceleration occurs on any level but the lowest, then, since a small increase in $f_n''(t)$ is identical with a great increase in $f_n'(t)$, there will have to be great increases in replacements and maintenance, in B_n, if there is not to be, with a time lag, a great long-term acceleration of the next lowest stage. If such an acceleration occurs, the same argument re-occurs to give a still greater long-term acceleration on the next lower stage. Hence, if on any level of the process except the lowest there occurs a short-term acceleration, then unless this rate of production is totally absorbed by increasing rates of replacement and maintenance, there is released a series of expansive movements in which each successive movement measures the acceleration of the next. It is as though an airplane were so difficult to accelerate that its accelerator were not a simple lever but a wheel turned over by a motor; and this motor in turn had its accelerator run by another motor; and so on.

This dynamic structure has now to be connected with the idea of cycles. Let us distinguish two totally different types. There is the familiar trade cycle which is characterized by a succession of positive and negative accelerations of the productive process; there are booms and then there are slumps. Quite different from this trade cycle one may conceive a pure cycle or wave that has no necessary implications of negative acceleration. A pure cycle of the productive process is a matter, simply, of the surplus stage accelerating more rapidly than the basic, then of the basic stage accelerating more rapidly than the surplus.[42]

12   Classes of Payments[43]

In any economy with a degree of development beyond that of primitive fruit-gathering, it is possible to verify the existence of a productive process with one or more surplus stages, a basic stage, and an emergent standard of living. Equally may one verify the facts that as the emergent standard of living is consumer to the basic stage, so the basic stage is consumer to the lowest surplus stage, and similarly up the hierarchy of stages. Again, in each case this rate of consumption stands, with due allowances, as a double

42 See 'Additional Note to Section 24: The Pure Cycle,' p. 120 below.
43 In the 1944 version this section, with the same title, was a subdivision of the seventh section.

summation of the activities constituting the product to be consumed. Finally, while each higher stage is for the long-term acceleration of the next lower stage, the basic stage is for the standard of living, and the standard of living for its own sake.

These differences and correlations have now to be projected into their monetary correlatives to set up classes of payments. Thus a restrictive supposition is introduced into the argument. The productive process is now to be envisaged as occurring in an exchange economy.[44] It will be supposed to be an economy of notable size, complexity, and development, with property, exchange, prices, supply and demand, money. However, to obviate considerations irrelevant for the moment, it will be convenient to suppose that foreign trade and foreign payments do not exist; and this supposition is to be maintained until notice to the contrary is given.

The supposition of an exchange economy is a supposition of a relation to sales. Thus, along with the productive process of the exchange economy in a given geographic area, there may exist other productive processes. Any individual may set up his own Robinson Crusoe economy in which he is both monopolist seller and monopsonist buyer in transactions which occur only in his mind. One may go to a barber or shave oneself. One may live in maximum dependence upon the goods and services of the exchange process, or one may pursue an ideal of autarky[45] on a farm. There results from such decisions a difference in the size of the exchange economy, and this difference in size is constituted by setting up another complete or partial economy distinct from the main exchange process or, on the other hand, by eliminating such withdrawals.

It follows that the productive process of the exchange economy is a process of production for sale. Already it was remarked that the productive process included sales management as well as production management. The remark has now to be completed. The productive process includes not

---

44 The explanatory terms and relations developed thus far have a transcultural and transhistorical invariance: they pertain to any level of human cooperation involved in producing a standard of living. Prior to this point, nothing Lonergan has said depends in any way on money or specificities deriving from its usages. From this point onward, however, he adds to the invariant analysis terms and relations which are specific to economies where some medium of exchange, money, also plays a fundamental role.

45 'Autarky': self-sufficiency, from *arkein*, 'suffice'; not, that is, autarchy in the sense of absolute rule.

only sales management but the sales themselves. What is produced and not sold either does not appertain to the exchange economy at all or else it is an unfinished product. Inversely, in any section or stage of the productive process, goods and services are completed only if they are sold and only when they are sold. For in the exchange economy production is not a matter of art, of doing or making things for the excellence of the doing or the making; it is a matter of economics, of doing and making things that other people want and want badly enough to pay for.[46]

This gives a fundamental division of exchanges into operative and redistributive. Some exchanges are operative: they are part and parcel of the productive process; they mark the completion of an element at some section or stage of the process; they not merely mark that completion but constitute it; for without the exchange the element remains an unfinished product. Because they are intrinsic to the process and partial constituents of the process, operative exchanges form a network that is congruent with the proprietary network flung over the process itself. Thus they recur with the recurrence of its routines. In general, they are proportionate to the volume of these routines, to set up the immanent manifestation of their success and the only immediate common measure of their magnitude. Finally, there is a correlation of operative exchanges based upon the technical correlations involved in the physical productive process.

While this description of operative exchange is derived from a deduc-

---

46 It would be unfair to ascribe to Lonergan, on the basis of these sentences, a modern, secularist utilitarianism of the type whose foundations were laid by Hobbes, Locke, and Smith. Lonergan's whole life work makes clear that he does not identify the general idea of value, which has a transcendental range (see *Method in Theology* 34–36, 101–103), with economic value. Indeed, as is clear from this context and others, Lonergan is making a distinction based on not eliminating or reducing noneconomic values. This distinction has to do with the fact that, given property rights as the means of correlating particular persons with particular objects, and given money as the medium of exchange, the modern industrial dynamic configuration of surplus and basic production will function on the basis of decisions to exchange in such a way as to concentrate upon production as *for* sale, thus turning economic value into exchange value. Indeed, Lonergan's concern for the dynamic mechanism of macroequilibria is for the sake of intelligently *subordinating* economic to other social, cultural, personal, and religious values. (See *Method in Theology* 31–32, on the hierarchy of values, where it becomes apparent that economics has to do with the material substratum that conditions the realization of higher values.)

tion of the idea of production for sale, the meaning of the description may be made clearer by an example. Consider in broad outline the production of shoes. It involves in an exchange economy payments by consumers to shopkeepers, payments by shopkeepers to wholesalers, payments by wholesalers to manufacturers, payments by manufacturers to tanners, to spinners, to makers of nails, payments by each of these to their sources of supply. It also involves a host of other categories of payments, but our purpose is not a study of the shoe industry but an illustration of the idea of operative payments. Now the payments listed above are part and parcel of the production of shoes in an exchange economy. They occur at proprietary frontiers. They are repeated at regular intervals as long as the process is maintained. They increase and decrease with the volume of the shoe trade. They are the index of its prosperity as also of its misery. They provide the one common measure of all its elements, a measure that is intrinsic to the element as completed. Finally, they are correlated with one another along lines of interconnection that are congruent with the correlations involved by a process from leather, cotton, and iron into shoes.

Redistributive exchanges form a remainder class. They are all nonoperative exchanges. Like operative exchanges they transfer ownership; but unlike them, they are not constitutive elements of the current productive process. They are with respect to the natural resources that are presupposed by current production. They are with respect to the durable products of past production, provided these have not reentered the current process as happens in some cases of the secondhand trade. Finally, they may be with respect to money, that is, they include exchanges in which money is not only what is paid but also what is paid for. No doubt, redistributive exchanges may be related intimately to operative exchanges; no doubt, this relationship is at times highly significant; but, without metaphysical digressions, it perhaps may be taken for granted that it is one thing to be related to another type of exchange, and that it is something quite different to be an instance of that other type. Again, borderline cases exist in which one has to attend closely to the definitions if one is to apply them correctly; but that is a misfortune that is common to every effort to place data in the categories of a classification; and it will be more convenient to postpone a study of a few such problems until operative exchanges have been identified more fully by their division into basic and surplus, and by the division of both basic and surplus into initial, transitional, and final payments.

Operative exchanges are intrinsic to the current productive process;

but that process divides into basic and surplus stages; hence operative exchanges also divide into basic and surplus. For every element under process becomes a completed product only when it is sold. Again, every element under process stands in a point-to-point, or a point-to-line, or some higher correspondence with the emergent standard of living. There are, then, operative payments completing basic elements, and these may be termed basic operative payments. There are also operative payments completing surplus elements, and these may be termed surplus operative payments. The division of operative payments into basic and surplus is but a corollary of the division of the productive process into basic and surplus stages.

Further, it has been argued that the products, whether goods or services, of any stage of the process stand as a double summation of the activities of that stage. There is a first summation with respect to factors of production within a given entrepreneurial unit. There is a second summation with respect to the contributions of several entrepreneurial units towards the same product. This formal structure of any stage of the process gives the division of payments of that stage into initial, transitional, and final. Initial operative payments are to the factors of production within a given entrepreneurial unit; they reward each contribution to the process and are with respect to that contribution; they are wages and salaries, rents and royalties, interest and dividends, allotments to depreciation, to sinking funds, to undistributed profits. Initial payments are the payments of the first summation. Now the second summation may emerge, not all at once, but gradually: sources of raw materials are paid by dealers, dealers are paid by manufacturers, manufacturers are paid by wholesalers, wholesalers by retailers; again, any one of these may pay the contributions of transportation companies, of public utilities, and so forth. But in any such case, the second summation is only in process. Payments that regard the second summation in process are termed transitional. They are from one entrepreneurial unit to another as operating in the same stage of the process. In any particular case, the entrepreneurial unit might be fully self-sufficient and on its stage of the process reach from raw materials to final buyer; then transitional payments are a zero class; for then the second summation takes place not gradually but all at once. Lastly, whether the second summation takes place gradually or all at once, it must be completed; else we are outside the supposition of an exchange economy; production becomes like art, for itself and not for sale. The payments with respect to the completed second summation are termed final payments. They are final in the sense that they are the last payments that are operative with respect to that product. They are final in the sense that any subsequent resale involves not an operative but a redistributive payment. They are final in the sense that they define the limit of the current process; for once these payments are made, the product is no longer under process but a product of past production.

So much then for the classes of payments. With respect to any exchange one has to ask, Is it a constitutive element of current production, recurrent with the recurrence of productive routines, in correlation with other similar payments along lines defined by the physical and technical dependence of products upon their sources? If the answer is negative, the payment is redistributive. If the answer is affirmative, the payment is operative, and further questions arise. Is the element, economically completed by this payment, in a point-to-point correspondence with elements in the emergent standard of living? If the answer is affirmative, the payment is a basic operative payment. If the answer is negative, the payment is a surplus operative payment. In either case, further questions arise. The lines defined by the physical and technical dependence of products on their sources have the structural form of a double summation. If the given basic or surplus operative payment is an item that is added in the first summation, a cost in the broadest sense but in its primary form, then the payment is initial. Next, if the payment occurs as the second summation gradually adds together the results of the first summation, then the payment is transitional. Lastly, if the payment occurs in the completed second summation, the payment is final.

The divisions of the process into basic and surplus stages, and the formal structure of the stages as double summations of activities, have been discussed previously. The troublesome borderline cases arise from the fundamental distinction between operative and redistributive payments, and, as is to be expected, they occur at the frontier of final operative payments. Four types of instances are discussed: the resale of durable basic products, the resale of durable surplus products, such resales when there is an organized secondhand trade, and financial operations.

First, the resale of durable basic products where no secondhand trade is involved gives a redistributive payment. Mr Jones has a private home constructed for his personal use. He pays the construction company for it. His payment is the final operative payment on that product. If he did not pay, the company would have the home on its hands, an unfinished product in the sense of an unsold product. When he does pay, his payment is submitted to the analysis of a double summation: the construction company is given the means of carrying on its own internal, and so initial, payments, and further, by transitional payments it gives other companies the means of carrying on their internal and so initial payments. Next, Jones sells the home to Brown. This may occur after forty years or it may occur immediately. In either case Brown's payment is redistributive. It changes titles to ownership. However relevant to current production – for otherwise Brown might have had a house of his own built – Brown's payment is not a constituent of current production.

Second, the case is exactly the same if Jones had a factory built instead of a home. The final operative payment on the factory is the payment made by Jones. Any subsequent resale involves not an operative but a redistributive payment. Objection, however, may be made to calling Jones's payment final. Does he not intend to get his money back? Does not the consumer pay? But the question is not whether the consumer pays for the factory in some virtual sense. The only question is whether the consumer comes to own the factory. Evidently, the consumer does not. There is no question of the consumer owning the factory, because there is no question of the consumer buying the factory. What the consumer buys are products made in the factory. Again, the question is not whether Jones intends or hopes to get his money back. No doubt, he has such intentions and hopes; but they are not intentions and hopes of anything so elementary as getting the money back by reselling the factory; they are the more sophisticated intentions and hopes of getting the money back, and more, and still remaining owner of the factory. The final operative payment made upon the factory was made by Jones when he bought it from the construction company. That payment completed an element in current production. But the production Jones will carry on in the factory, though current, will not be production of the factory but of something else. The profits Jones garners or fails to garner will be operative payments, not in the process that built the factory, but in the process in which the factory is used. Finally, should Jones happen to sell the factory to Brown, that event occurs neither in the process that built the factory nor in the process in which the factory is used; it involves a redistributive payment outside the process.

In the third place, it will be best to consider financial operations, that is, any exchange in which a sum of money is paid for a sum of money to be received. Now either the two sums of money are equal, or else one is greater than the other. If the two are equal, the transaction is purely redistributive. If one is greater than the other, then, generally speaking, the difference is the payment for a service of some specific type; rendering such services is as much a part of current production as rendering any other service, while the payment will be divided up, perhaps among different entrepreneurial units, and commonly in initial payments of wages, salaries, rents, dividends, reserve funds, and so forth. In other words, financial operations are partly redistributive payments and partly payments for services rendered; thus in banking, payments of principal are redistributive, but payments of interest are operative, with interest paid to the banks as a final operative payment and interest paid by the banks to depositors an initial operative payment; again, in insurance the payment of policies is redistributive, but the payment of premiums on policies is partly redistributive and partly operative; it is redistributive to the extent it balances the payment of policies; and it is operative to the extent it pays insurance companies for their services.

There remains the secondhand trade. As a trade with recurrent routines of varying volume, it is part of current production of services; but what is traded belongs to past production or, as is the case with the indestructible properties of the soil, never was a human product. Thus, with regard to the secondhand trade, one again must distinguish between payments for the object traded and payments for the services of the trader: the former are redistributive; the latter are operative. The analysis applies of course not only to old watches and jewelry, books and motorcars, but equally well to real estate, and, except in the first instance of investment, to the resale of stocks and shares. Investment itself is a complex payment, but its analysis may be left until later. However, there is a special instance of the secondhand trade in which an old product is brought back into the process as a raw material or semifinished product; in such a case the payment causing reentry into the process is redistributive but subsequent payments are operative.

13   Rates of Payment and Transfer[47]

|1978| A baker's dozen of classes of payments have been defined by the relation of the payments to the productive process. The argument now moves from classes of payments to rates or flows of payments, and from the

47 In the 1978 version, this was the eighth section of the *Essay*. It replaced a section of the 1944 version, relevant portions of which have been reincorporated here as indicated when they occur.

rates or flows to their circulatory interdependence. Just as there is a dynamic structure of the productive process, so also there is a dynamic structure of the monetary circulation. The classes of payments provide the link between the two: the classes are based upon the dynamic structure of the process; the rates or flows, constructed from the classes, aim at an analysis of the circulation.

Eight rates or flows of payments form the main points of reference in the monetary circulation. They will be denoted by the symbols E', E'', R', R'', O', O'', I', I''. In each case we would emphasize the fact that we are speaking, not of some static quantity, but of a flow, a rate, a 'so much every so often.'[48] Upper-case letters stand, respectively, for expenditure, receipts, outlay, and income. The suffixed primes (' and ") serve to distinguish basic and surplus expenditure, basic and surplus receipts, basic and surplus outlay, and basic and surplus income. So the outlay of entrepreneurs becomes the income of workers and suppliers, their income becomes basic and surplus expenditure, and the expenditure becomes the receipts of the entrepreneurs.

All rates refer to some standard interval of time: a day, a week, a month, a quarter, a half year, a year, as the subject matter of the issue may permit or demand.

The [rates or] flows E' and R' are the two aspects of final basic operative payments: E' is the expenditure of consumers purchasing the emergent standard of living of the given interval; R' is the receipt of this expenditure by the final agents of basic supply.

The [rates or] flows E'' and R'' are the two aspects of final surplus operative payments. E'' is the expenditure of producers purchasing surplus prod-

---

48 This sentence has been altered. As explained in note 29 above, rates of payment are designated in the 1944 version by the symbols DE', DE'', and so on; in later versions, from 1978–1983, the symbols used are fE', fE'', and so on. Hence in these versions the sentence reads: 'The prefix, f, in each case is used to emphasize the fact that we are speaking, not of some static quantity, but of a flow, a rate, a "so much every so often."'

According to the editors' convention, E', E'', and so on now designate rates of payments. That is, $E' = \Delta e'/\Delta t$ or de'/dt, depending on the context, and similarly with E'' and the other symbols (e' = a total quantity of money exchanged in this category). Moreover, the primes (') and double primes (") in this instance do not designate derivatives of either quantities or rates, as the following sentences make clear.

ucts: [1944][49] it includes the payments of basic producers to the final agents of the lowest stage of surplus supply; the payments of producers in the lowest stage of surplus supply to the final agents of [the] next to lowest stage of surplus supply; and so on up the dynamic ladder of the productive process. On the other hand, R'' is the receipt of such expenditure by the final agents of surplus supply, no matter what level of surplus supply they may represent.

Next, both R' and R'' stand as double summations to activities in basic and surplus industry, respectively. The analysis leaps across the double summations to the initial elements. O' is the aggregate of initial basic payments during the given interval; O'' is the aggregate of initial surplus payments during the same interval. These rates may be named basic outlay and surplus outlay, respectively; they are payments of wages and salaries, rents and royalties, interest and dividends, and allocations to depreciation, sinking funds, undistributed profits; they are the rewards of the ultimate factors of production in the basic stage and in the surplus stage, respectively, of the productive process.

Now while R' is identical with E', and R'' is identical with E'', not only is O' not identical with R' nor O'' with R'', but it usually happens that it is greater or less. One is not to think of O' as the distribution of R' among the factors of production. O' is simultaneous with R', an aggregate calculated with respect to the same time interval as R'. A present O' is an aggregate of initial payments that at a series of future dates will reach their place in a double summation to become elements in some R'; similarly, a present R' is a double summation with respect to initial payments occurring at a series of past dates. The same is true of R'' and O''.

|1978| Now [as we have seen,] just as in the production process one distinguishes initial, transitional, and final contributions to the ongoing flows of basic and surplus goods and services, so the receipts R' and R'', while initially received by the final seller, are distributed in the opposite direction through the transitional to the initial contributors.

It can, of course, happen that this distribution gives to each initial contributor the equivalent of his outlay on the previous turnover and thereby encourages entrepreneurs to keep the economy in a steady state. But there are any number of reasons why O' or O'' of the next turnover may turn out

49 The remainder of this paragraph, together with the two paragraphs that follow it, was omitted in the 1978 version and has been reincorporated by the editors.

to differ from its predecessor; and for that reason there will follow similar differences in [basic income] I' or [surplus income] I''.

A brief exploration of this complexity leads to the introduction of the notion of the monetary function. [Thus the argument takes a further step towards defining a circulation of money.][50] For the circulation of money is not a rotational movement of money. Rather it is a circular series of relationships of dependence of some flows of payments on other flows. Money moves only at the instant of payment or transfer. Most of the time it is quiescent. It may be totally quiescent, as when it is held in reserve for no determinate purpose whatever. But it may also be dynamically quiescent, and then it is held in reserve for some definite purpose.

Money held in reserve for a defined purpose will be said to be in a monetary function. Five such functions are distinguished: basic demand, basic supply, surplus demand, surplus supply, and a fifth redistributive function. Money held in reserve for basic expenditure [and so on its way to entering E'] will be said to be in the basic demand function. Money held in reserve for surplus expenditure [and so on its way to entering E''][51] will be said to be in the surplus demand function. Again, money on its way from R' to O', from final basic operative payments to initial basic outlay,[52] will be said to be in the basic supply function. Similarly, money on its way from R'' to O'' will be said to be in the surplus supply function. Finally, money held in reserve for any of a number of redistributive purposes will be said to be in the redistributive function.

Now initial payments are income. [They may be supposed to be, at least for an instant, in the basic or surplus demand functions,] so that in every case [one may write, without affecting the generality of the analysis,]

$$O' + O'' = I' + I'' \tag{2}$$

[where I' are the initial payments entering basic demand, and I'' are the initial payments entering surplus demand during the given interval of time.][53]

50 The bracketed sentence has been restored from the 1944 version.

51 The bracketed phrase, together with the parallel phrase in the preceding sentence, has been restored from the 1944 version, with the usual change in symbols.

52 The 1944 version, instead of 'initial basic outlay,' has 'initial basic operative payments.' There is no fundamental difference in meaning.

53 The three bracketed sections of this sentence have been restored from the 1944 version.

Basic and surplus outlay together equal basic and surplus income together. However, [let us now introduce two crossover ratios:][54] not a little of the income derived from surplus production is destined to be spent on the standard of living, and so there is some fraction, say c'', of O'', that moves to the basic demand function.[55] Similarly, there are large salaries and large profits to be had, at least at times, by contributors to the standard of living, and so there can be some fraction, say i', of O', that heads to the surplus demand function. |1982| Again, there is a fraction of O'', say i'', that goes to surplus demand, and a fraction of O', say c', that goes to basic demand. Finally, there may be fractions of O' and O'', say s' and s'', intended to improve one's balance in the redistributive function RD. Hence [we are led to replace the ambiguity of equation (2) by the precision of equations (3) and (4):][56]

$$I'' = i'O' + i''O'' + s''O'' \tag{3}$$

$$I' = c'O' + c''O'' + s'O' \tag{4}^{57}$$

In these equations the crossover is represented by the inclusion in I'' of $i'O'$ and in I' of $c''O''$. Let G represent the crossover difference in favor of basic demand, so that

$$G = c''O'' - i'O' \tag{5}$$

---

54 The material in brackets has been restored from the 1944 version.

55 Note that Lonergan's use of the symbols c, i, and s, which are fractions rather than quantities, does not follow the convention set out in note 29 above. From here to the end of the present section, there were notable major changes between 1978 and 1983, which are considered in the 'Appendix: History of the Diagram, 1944–1998' below.

56 The bracketed clause is from the 1978 version.

57 Equations (3) and (4) present special difficulties in fulfilling the editorial goals of restoring as much as possible of Lonergan's own writing, while at the same time maintaining a consistent notation (see notes 29 and 48). Here the source of difficulty lies in the complexity of the changes Lonergan made in the present section of the *Essay* between 1978 and 1983. Strictly speaking, $s'O'$ and $s''O''$ head, not for the basic demand function (I') and the surplus demand function (I''), respectively, but instead for the redistributive function (see §14, 'Diagram of Rates of Flow'). What actually enters the basic demand function and the surplus demand function are complex aggregates of rates of payments, $(D' - s'I')$ and $(D'' - s''I'')$, respectively. In general these complex aggregates of rates of payments stand in complex relationships to $s'O'$ and

and the condition of equilibrium will be

$$G = 0 \qquad\qquad (6)$$

On the common assumption that all savings are invested, $s'O'$ and $s''O''$ may be neglected unless a contrary opinion is entertained.[58] Finally, on adding both sides of (5) to both sides of (3) and then subtracting both from both of (4), we get

$$I'' + G = c''O'' + i''O'' = O'' \qquad\qquad (7)$$

$s''O''$ as mediated by the activities of the redistributive function. Equations (3) and (4) tacitly assume a less general set of conditions, namely, that the entirety of $s'O'$ passes through the redistributive function, as if transparently and without alteration, directly into basic demand function I'; likewise for $s''O''$ passing into surplus demand function I''. That is, the assumption in equations (3) and (4) is that the redistributive function does no more than redistribute some fraction ($= s'$) of O' from certain basic enterprises to other basic enterprises and thence to their workers, and similarly redistribute some portion ($= s''$) of O'' from certain surplus enterprises to others. (These two equations, as Lonergan formulated them in his 1944 version, did not introduce such simplifications.)

The limitations of this less than general set of assumptions quickly vanish, however, since Lonergan immediately introduces a yet more restrictive assumption – see the sentence that follows equation (6) – namely, that $s'O' = s''O'' = 0$. As soon as Lonergan has completed his analysis under this more restrictive assumption, he reverts to the more general case (see §15 and following), and never actually makes any use whatever of the tacit assumptions in equations (3) and (4).

For further details, see 'Appendix: History of the Diagram, 1944–1998.'

58 A 'contrary opinion' – namely, that $(S' - s'I')$, $(S'' - s''I'')$, $(D' - s'I')$, and $(D'' - s''I'')$ will *not* all be zero – is hinted at towards the end of §15, 'Circuit Acceleration (I),' where Lonergan concludes that there is only the remotest chance of accelerating without new money coming into the circuits. It follows from this conclusion, therefore, that the 'contrary opinion' is implicit in all subsequent sections where accelerations are assumed; for example in §§16 and 18–22. Explicitly, however, the 'contrary opinion' first appears in §27, 'The Cycle of Pure Surplus Income'; it also appears in §§29–31 on various forms of superposed circuits.

$$I' - G = c'O' + i'O' = O' \tag{8}$$

and thereby revert to the outlays from which we began.[59]

[1978] Movements between four monetary functions have now been named and defined. They form two circuits connected by a crossover. There is a basic circuit of basic expenditure E', becoming basic receipts R', which move towards basic outlay O', which with allowance made for the crossover difference G, becomes basic income I'. Similarly, there is a surplus circuit of surplus expenditure E'', becoming surplus receipts R'', which move towards surplus outlay O'', and with allowance made for the crossover difference G, becomes surplus income I''.

Now we shall study the redistributive function (for the time being) only in relation to these two circuits. Basically these relations are changes of quantities of money in the circuits. In any given interval let M' be [the money] added to the basic circuit and M'' be the money added to the surplus circuit. In the same interval let additions from the redistributive function to basic supply be S' and to basic demand be D', while additions to surplus supply are S'' and to surplus demand are D''. Hence, on taking the crossover into account, we get[60]

$$M' = (S' - s'O') + (D' - s'I') + G \tag{9}$$

$$M'' = (S'' - s''O'') + (D'' - s''I'') - G \tag{10}$$

where any of the flows involved may be positive or negative. [1944] G has been defined already. $(S' - s'O')$, $(S'' - s''O'')$, $(D' - s'I')$, $(D'' - s''I'')$ are

---

59 The arrangement of the next three paragraphs calls for a fuller explanation than usual. The editors first restored material written for the 1978 version but omitted in the final version. This material was itself a condensation of Lonergan's more extended argument in 1944; accordingly, the corresponding 1944 material was then added. The sequence of these three paragraphs thus follows that of the 1944 version, but the wording of the first two follows the 1978 version.

60 The following two equations have been altered and renumbered so as to conform with the 1983 version. For the earlier versions of this material and explanatory commentary, see 'Appendix: History of the Diagram, 1944–1998' below.

quantities of money per interval transferred from the redistributive function to basic supply, surplus supply, basic demand, surplus demand, respectively. These quantities per interval are net quantities, that is, the net result of all transferences in either direction. $(S' - s'O')$ and $(S'' - s''O'')$ are the quantities added to, or if negative subtracted from, the quantity of money moving from basic receipts to basic outlay (R' to O') and from surplus receipts to surplus outlay (R'' to O''), respectively, during the interval.[61] $(D' - s'I')$ and $(D'' - s''I'')$ are the quantities added to, or if negative subtracted from, the quantity of money moving from basic income to basic expenditure (I' to E') and from surplus income to surplus expenditure (I'' to E''), respectively, during the interval. Hence equation (9) states that the total quantity of money added to the basic circuit during the interval, that is, M', is equal to the quantity added from the redistributive function to basic supply, $(S' - s'O')$, plus the quantity added from the redistributive function to basic demand, $(D' - s'I')$, plus the quantity added from the other circuit by the crossover difference G. Similarly, equation (10) states that the total quantity of money added to the surplus circuit during the interval, that is, M'', is equal to the quantity added from the redistributive function to surplus supply, $(S'' - s''O'')$, plus that added from the redistributive function to surplus demand, $(D'' - s''I'')$, minus the quantity contributed to the other circuit by the crossover difference G. Any of these seven quantities[62] per interval may be negative; and when they are negative, 'added' is to be replaced by 'subtracted' in the above statement.

[1978] It is to be observed that there is no simple correlation between quantities of money added to the circuits or subtracted from them and, on the other hand, the rates of flow in the circuits. For the rates of flow in the circuits are not just quantities of money but quantities multiplied by velocity. Hence without suppositions regarding velocities in the circuits, no conclusions can be drawn about rates of flow in the circuits. Inversely, with

61 Although Lonergan illustrates $(S' - s'O')$ and $(S'' - s''O'')$ with 'a quantity of money,' seemingly violating the point that these are rates, it must be noted that these quantities of money are 'moving ... during the [respective] interval,' that is, quantities *per unit interval* – rates.

62 The seven quantities: G, M', M'', $(S' - s'I')$, $(S'' - s''I'')$, $(D' - s'I')$, and $(D'' - s'I'')$. Even though M' and M'' include some of the other quantities, the point Lonergan is making – that any of these may be negative – can still be applied to any of the seven independently.

velocities undetermined, changes in rates of payments yield no conclusions about changes in quantities.

|1982| On the basis of the foregoing definitions and relations we shall set up a diagram of the economic circulation. But it will be well at once to draw attention to J.A. Schumpeter's insistence on the merits of a diagram as a tool.[63]

First, there is the tremendous simplification it effects. From millions of exchanges one advances to precise aggregates, relatively few in number, and hence easy to follow up and handle.

Next come the possibilities of advancing to numerical theory. In this respect, despite profound differences in their respective achievements, the contemporary work of Leontieff may be viewed as a revival of François Quesnay's *tableau économique*.

Most important is the fact that this procedure was the first to make explicit the concept of economic equilibrium. All science begins from particular correlations, but the key discovery is the interdependence of the whole. While it is true that a *tableau* or diagram cannot establish the uniqueness of a system or rigorously ground its universal relevance, it remains that the diagram has compensating features that a system of simultaneous equations may imply but does not manifest.

[1978] This section may be resumed by explaining the diagram of transfers between monetary functions. In figure 14-1 the reader will notice five circles representing the monetary functions:[64] RD the redistributive, O' basic supply, O'' surplus supply, I' basic demand, and I'' surplus demand. In a given interval the action from the redistributive function changes (positively or negatively) the quantities of money available in the other four functions by $(S' - s'O')$, $(D' - s'I')$, $(S'' - s''O'')$, $(D'' - s''I'')$, respectively. In the same interval basic supply makes basic initial payments O', with $c'O'$ going to basic demand and $i'O'$ going to surplus demand. Similarly, surplus supply makes basic surplus initial payments O'', with $c''O''$ going to basic demand and $i''O''$ going to surplus demand. The circuit is completed with basic expenditure E' going to basic supply, and surplus expenditure E'' going to surplus supply.

The other flows in the analysis are given by the equations:

---

63 Schumpeter, *History* 240–43, on the Cantillon-Quesnay *tableau*.

64 The notation that follows has been altered to conform with the final version of the diagram.

$$
\begin{aligned}
R' &= E' \\
R'' &= E'' \\
I' &= O' + M' \\
I'' &= O'' + M'' \\
G &= c''O'' - i'O' \\
M' &= (S' - s'O') + (D' - s'I') + G \\
M'' &= (S'' - s''O'') + (D'' - s''I'') - G \quad\quad (11)^{65}
\end{aligned}
$$

|1982| I would add that the aims and limitations of macroeconomics [that is, the circulation analysis presented here] make the use of a diagram particularly helpful, at least from the viewpoint of the present essay. For its basic terms are defined by their functional relations. The maintaining of a *standard of living* is attributed to a *basic process*, an ongoing sequence of instances of *so much every so often*. The maintenance and the acceleration (positive or negative) of this basic process is brought about by a sequence of surplus stages, in which *each lower stage* is maintained and accelerated by the *next higher*. Finally, transactions that do no more than transfer titles to ownership are concentrated in a redistributive function, whence may be derived changes in the stock of money dictated by the accelerations (positive or negative) in the basic and surplus stages of the process.

So there is to be discerned a threefold process, in which a basic stage is maintained and accelerated by a series of surplus stages, while the needed additions to or subtractions from the stock of money in these processes is derived from the redistributive area.

A first task thereafter will be to correlate the need for more or less money in the productive processes with the magnitudes and frequencies of their turnovers. On that basis it will be possible to distinguish stable and unstable combinations and sequences of rates in the three main areas and so gain some insight into the longstanding recurrence of crises in the modern expanding economy.

65 The material of the previous two paragraphs, beginning with 'This section may be resumed,' has been added from the 1978 version, where it immediately follows a paragraph beginning 'It is to be observed that there is no simple correlation ...,' likewise reinserted above. The list of equations (11) has been altered to conform with Lonergan's usage in the 1983 version.

14   Diagram of Rates of Flow[66]

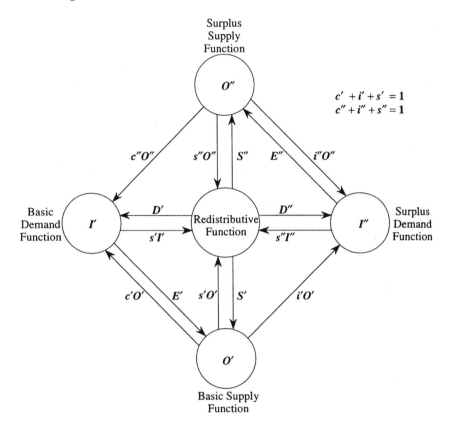

Per interval, surplus demand [function], I'', pays E'' for current surplus products, and receives dividends $i''O''$ from surplus production [i.e., surplus supply function] and $i'O'$ from basic production [i.e., basic supply function].

Per interval, basic demand [function, I',] pays E' for current basic products and for its services receives $c''O''$ from surplus supply [function] and $c'O'$ from basic supply [function].

Vertical arrows represent transactions between the redistributional area and surplus and basic supply [functions]; horizontal arrows the dealings of demand [functions] with the redistributional area.

Figure 14-1 Diagram of Rates of Flow

66 For the relation of Lonergan's diagram as it appears here to previous versions, see 'Appendix: History of the Diagram, 1994–1998.'

15   Circuit Acceleration (1)

|1982| The foregoing section defined two circuits of outlay, income, expenditure, receipts, a pair of crossovers, and four pairs of transfers between the redistributive function and the demand and supply functions. The present section is concerned to watch the circuits in motion, and more particularly to inquire into the conditions of their acceleration. The inquiry involves three steps: first, one asks what is the possibility of circuit acceleration when the crossovers balance and each of the four pairs of transfers cancel, so that the quantity of money in each of the circuits remains constant [that is, when $(S' - s'O')$, $(S'' - s''O'')$, $(D' - s'I')$, $(D'' - s''I'')$, and G are each zero]; secondly, we ask what is the possibility of circuit acceleration when the crossovers balance, transfers to the demand functions balance, but transfers to the supply functions do not [that is, when $(S' - s'O')$, $(s'' - s''O'')$ are positive or negative but $(D' - s'I')$, $(D'' - s''I'')$ and G remain zero]; thirdly, one asks what happens if the crossovers or the transfers to demand do not cancel [that is, when none of these is zero].[67]

[1] On the first and largest assumption the quantity of money in each circuit remains constant, interval by interval, over an indefinite series of intervals. The possibility of acceleration, accordingly, can arise only from changes in the velocity of money. However, not any change in velocity is relevant: a change in the rapidity with which money changes hands is in itself impotent to effect a circuit acceleration; what is needed is a change in the circuit velocity of money, in the rapidity with which money performs a circuit of work moving, say, from expenditure through receipts, outlay, income back to expenditure. This difference is important. For, while the rapidity with which money changes hands is a highly indeterminate concept, the rapidity with which it performs a circuit of work may be correlated exactly with the turnover frequency of commerce and industry.

To clarify the notion of turnover frequency, let us define the unit of enterprise as any integrated and determinate contribution to the basic stage or to the surplus stage of the productive process. A contribution is said to be integrated when it is not the effect of labor alone, or |1944| capital alone, or management alone, but of all three taken together. A contribution is considered determinate when it answers the specification to be found, say, in a catalogue, an order, a contract, and, further, the functional

---

67 The bracketed additions correspond with Lonergan's text in the 1944 version, but have been altered to conform with his usage in the 1983 version.

distinction is drawn between basic and surplus. Thus a contribution is any good or service sold at any transitional or any final market by any entrepreneur; it is exclusively the contribution of that entrepreneur, even though what is sold includes the contributions of earlier entrepreneurs in the production series; finally, though exclusively the contribution of the entrepreneur in question, it is not specified by the personality of the entrepreneur (who may conduct simultaneously several units of enterprise) but by the description found in a catalogue, order, or contract, along with the added determination of basic or surplus.

Now every unit of enterprise involves a turnover magnitude and a turnover frequency. The statement would be merely a truism if it meant no more than that the rates of payments received and made by the unit of enterprise involved quantities and velocities of money; for obviously all rates of payment are products of quantity and velocity. But the statement is not a truism, for it involves a correlation between the quantities and velocities of rates of payment [and] the quantities and velocities of goods and services.

The existence of this correlation may be seen readily enough. To double, say, rates of payment, one may either double the sums of money in each payment in the rate or one may double the frequency with which each payment is made. Similarly, to double a rate of production, one may double the number of items handled at once by a unit of enterprise or one may double the frequency with which this number is produced and sold. There are, then, alternatives between quantity and velocity in both rates of payment and rates of production. But the quantity alternative in the rates of payment is conjoined with the quantity alternative in the rate of production, and the frequency alternative in the rate of payment is conjoined with the frequency alternative in the rate of production. The two cases of quantity-velocity are not only parallel but also correlated.

The point may be illustrated by simple examples. Suppose a shipbuilder to have four ships under construction at once, and to finish a ship every two hundred days. Let demand be doubled. Then the builder may put eight ships under construction at once or he may study Henry Kaiser's methods and learn to complete a ship in one hundred days. In either case his rate of production is doubled, and, we may suppose, his rates of payments received and made are doubled, that is, the selling price of each ship remains the same, and payments made include profits. But the doubling of the rates of payments takes place in different ways. If he has eight ships instead of four under construction at once, then the magnitude of payments in the rates is doubled: every two hundred days his payments received amount to the value of eight ships, and his payments made amount to the value of eight ships, where before the payments received and made with the same frequency amounted to the value of only four ships. If, on the other hand, he has only four ships under construction but completes a ship in one hundred days, the magnitude of his payments received and made amounts to the value of four ships, but their frequency is doubled since these payments take place every hundred days instead of every two hundred days.

Now it might be thought that this distinction between turnover magnitude and turnover frequency was valid in such discontinuous production as shipbuilding but broke down as production approximated to continuity. It happens, however, that while production may approximate to continuity, sales do not, and that the period relevant to turnover frequency is not simply the production period but the period of production and sales. The perfect example of productive continuity is the supply of electric power, in which the generation, the distribution, and the consumption of the product are practically simultaneous. However, a power company cannot collect payments due as rapidly as it can supply electrical impulses. While conditions of production do not limit the frequency of its turnovers, conditions of collection provide a very palpable limit. A power company might decide to receive smaller payments more frequently, but then it would have to hire more men to read meters and a larger office staff to send out bills; further, this greater cost of collection would not yield a higher turnover frequency unless people responded and paid their bills at shorter intervals.

Similarly, in every unit of enterprise there is some determinate turnover magnitude and turnover frequency. The magnitude of the turnover depends upon the number of items handled at once and the selling price of each item. The frequency of the turnover depends upon the period of production plus any time lag involved in sales or collection. In general, each unit of enterprise first estimates demand, which determines both rate of payments received and rate of supply; in the second place, it estimates turnover frequency from its conditions of production and of sale and, *caeteris paribus*, selects a more rapid rather than a less rapid frequency; in the third place, it finds its turnover magnitude determined by the other two factors. The estimate of demand comes first, because there is no use producing without selling. The estimate of frequency comes second, because a more rapid frequency is, in the main, an advantage but one can never have as rapid a frequency as one pleases. Finally, turnover magnitude is left to be determined by the other two factors, because turnover magnitude is the easiest to control of the three.

Now, if in each unit of enterprise the magnitude and frequency of payments depend upon the magnitude and frequency of turnovers, it follows that with respect to the aggregate of basic units and again with respect to the aggregate of surplus units we have quantities and circuit velocities of money determined by turnover magnitudes and frequencies. Hence to say that the circuits accelerate in virtue of greater, or less, circuit velocities of money is to postulate an aggregate change in turnover frequencies. Either production periods are shortening, or lengthening, or the lag of sales or collection is shortening, or lengthening. The question before us, then, is the possibility of changes in turnover frequency when there are no changes in the aggregate quantities of money available in the circuits.

First, one may expect a general increase in turnover frequencies in the brisk selling of a boom, and similarly one may expect a general decrease in turnover frequency in the lagging sales ushering in a slump. But whether one may expect either a boom or a slump without changes in the aggregate quantity of money available in the circuits, that is another question; and to it we shall give an answer that is negative. In the second place, there is the increment in turnover frequency due to reduced, or increased, production periods. Now there are variations in production periods to meet variations in demand, for at times it is simpler to vary the production period than the used capacity; but one may expect such variations to cancel; they may be as much one way as another; they provide more a means of adaptation than a general principle of acceleration. In the main, variations in production periods result from the application of new ideas: these may introduce more efficient machinery, more efficient organization, more efficient labor, more efficient selling. The effect of such changes may be very great. But they are all long-term changes. In the short run they occur in random units of enterprise. Further, under the limitation we are considering, namely, unchanged quantities of money in the circuits, the acceleration possible from these increased frequencies is limited by the irregularity of their incidence. All units of enterprise contributing in a series to one final product have to keep in step. Unless all the units in the series simultaneously increase frequency from reduced turnover periods, there cannot be a general acceleration due exclusively to increased frequency; the units with increased frequency have to reduce their turnover magnitudes to allow other units in the series without increased frequency to accelerate by increased turnover magnitudes.

This brings us to the conclusion of the first step of the inquiry. |1982| On the assumption that the quantity of money in each of the circuits remains constant [that is, that $(S' - s'O') = (S'' - s''O'') = (D' - s'I') = (D'' - s''I'') = G = 0$][68] there is the possibility of circuit acceleration but only of one that is quite limited. For with quantities [of money] unchanged the only possibility of acceleration lies in increasing or decreasing velocities of circulation. This change in circuit velocities involves a change in turnover frequencies, and these depend not only on the supply functions but also on [the] demand functions, since a frequency depends not only on production but also on sales.[69] Now turnover frequencies are the least controllable of the factors in the process of production and sales. Each unit of enterprise already tends to be at its greatest turnover frequency and to depend on the emergence of more |1944| efficient methods for increments of frequency. Further, units in a series have to keep their rates of production adjusted, and since increments in frequency occur at random, the supposition of constant aggregate quantities of money cuts down the acceleration effect of increased frequencies by making necessary simultaneous reductions of turnover magnitude in the units with greater frequency. Finally, while booms and slumps effect a general increase or decrease of frequencies by shortening or lengthening the lag of sales, still one must have the booms or slumps before one can have the frequency changes that result from them.

[2] If now one turns to the second step in the inquiry, the question is, |1982| What is the possibility of circuit acceleration when G is zero, D' and $s'I'$ are equal and opposite, and the same holds for D'' and $s''I''$ $[0 = (D' - s'I') = (D'' - s''I'') = G]$, so that transfers to surplus supply $[S'' - s''O'']$ or to basic $[S' - s'O']$ or to both may be positive. [Now there is a sense in which this supposition is contrary to the common assumption of investment equaling savings, but a discussion of that issue had best be reserved until we have given a definition of savings and of investment.][70]

---

68 The bracketed equation is from the 1944 version, with the symbols altered to conform with Lonergan's later notation.
69 In the 1944 version the preceding sentence reads: 'This change in circuit velocities involves a change in turnover frequencies which, of course, are determined not merely by the supply functions but, since they depend on sales and are lengthened by a lag of sales, no less upon the demand functions.'
70 This sentence has been restored from the 1944 version. The definitions Lonergan refers to are introduced in §16, 'Circuit Acceleration (II),' especially p. 70.

Clearly there follows [from this supposition] the possibility of recurrent aggregate increments in the quantity of money available in the circuits, and the need for such increments is supported by the long history of monetary practice. Mercantilism is among the earliest products of economic thinking; it arose when inquiries into the prosperity of some and the poverty of other communes of the Italian Renaissance led to the view that prosperity depended on an abundance of gold; so for centuries cities strove to buy abroad less than they sold; and by the time mercantilism became discredited, other means had been found to meet the issue. Idle money had been decried, laws against usury attacked.[71] Bills of |1944| exchange and discounting houses flourished. Banking developed. There followed the fundamental increase in means of payment by the introduction of a gold standard and fiduciary issue. And in our own day we have witnessed the elimination of gold, even as a constitutional monarch, and the substitution of a managed money, that is, a money managed according to the requirements of industry and commerce and not according to rules of thumb and a gold reserve. Now unless the operative circuits have an appetite for ever greater means of payment, this whole development appears meaningless. On the other hand, the supposition that circuit acceleration to some extent postulates increments in the quantities of money in the circuits accounts both for mercantilism and for the substitution of more elegant techniques in place of mercantilism. Further, it points to excess transfers to supply, to $(S' - s'O')$ and $(S'' - s''O'')$, as the mode in which increments in quantities of money enter the circuits.

The effect of excess transfers from the redistributive function to the supply function, of $(S' - s'O')$ and $(S'' - s''O'')$, is twofold. Primarily it is a matter of aggregate increments in monetary circulating capital; secondarily it is a

---

71 In the 1944 version the corresponding passage reads: 'Mercantilism is among the earliest of the products of economic thinking; it arose when inquiries into the prosperity of some and poverty of other principalities and republics of the early Italian Renaissance led to the conclusion that prosperity depended upon an abundance of gold; for centuries nations endeavored to buy abroad less than they sold [so] that they might have a favorable balance of gold payments. Further, by the time mercantilism became discredited, other means had been found to provide the circuits with greater quantities of money. Idle money had been decried. Laws against interest and usury had been attacked successfully.'

matter of absorbing windfall losses and profits.[72] As to the primary effect, the function of monetary circulating capital is to bridge the gap between payments made and payments received; as goods and services are in process, the unit of enterprise makes payments to earlier units in the production series and to its own factors; only when goods and services are sold are payments received. Now this gap increases with increments in turnover magnitude: the greater the number of items the unit of enterprise handles at once and the greater the price per item handled, the greater the need of monetary circulating capital. Thus, at a first approximation $(S' - s'O')$ and $(S'' - s''O'')$ are positive when turnover magnitudes in the aggregate are increasing, and they are negative when turnover magnitudes in the aggregate are decreasing. There is, however, a second approximation to be made. Payments received are subject to windfall losses and profits, and these may not be passed on to decreased or increased initial payments made. For the entrepreneur may prefer to allow windfall losses and profits to average out to zero over a series of intervals; then fluctuations in payments received are smoothed out by transfers from or to a reserve fund in the redistributive function, so that payments made vary only with changes in the scale of operations or in prices; in this fashion windfall losses are covered by positive elements in $(S' - s'O')$ and $(S'' - s''O'')$, while windfall profits yield negative elements in $(S' - s'O')$ and $(S'' - s''O'')$.[73] Evidently enough, this second effect of transfers to supply, insofar as it exists, should be small in the aggregate of basic units and in the aggregate of surplus units unless, as perhaps in a boom or slump, windfall effects tend to be generalized either as profits or as losses.

72 Lonergan did not always adjust the symbols in the text to keep pace with his 1981 changes in the diagram (§ 14). In keeping with the new diagram, the editors have substituted $(S' - s'O')$ and $(S'' - s''O'')$ where Lonergan had only S' and S'', respectively. The presence of two factors in each of these substituted expressions suggests a strong connection with the two functions: S' and S'' with aggregate increments; $s'O'$ and $s''O''$ with windfall losses and profits. Not having modified the symbolism, however, Lonergan himself did not explicitly make this connection.

73 When he ceased working on the manuscript, Lonergan had not modified the symbols S' and S'' to match the more differentiated analysis set out in his diagram. Both symbols have been changed to bring them into conformity with more thoroughly revised portions of the manuscript, on the conviction that this is what Lonergan would have done eventually.

Now on the supposition of increasing quantities of money in the circuits due to positive values of $(S' - s'O')$ and $(S'' - s''O'')$, there follows an acceleration of turnover magnitudes proportionate to the magnitude of $(S' - s'O')$ and $(S'' - s''O'')$, and to this may be added any acceleration of turnover frequency that occurs. Interval by interval the rates of basic outlay, basic income, basic expenditure, and basic receipts are stepping up; similarly, interval by interval the rates of surplus outlay, surplus income, surplus expenditure, and surplus receipts move upwards. Inversely, when $(S' - s'O')$ and $(S'' - s''O'')$ are negative there is a similar deceleration of the circuits; turnover magnitudes are decreasing proportionately to the magnitude of the negative values of $(S' - s'O')$ and $(S'' - s''O'')$; and these decreasing magnitudes will tend to effect decreasing frequencies both because of lagging sales and because |1982| units of enterprise cannot be run at their optimum capacity.

[3] So much for the first two steps of the inquiry. With the crossover difference zero and with exchanges from the redistributional function to the supply functions and the demand functions canceling, circuit accelerations are possible in virtue of changing turnover frequency but they are extremely limited because the available quantity of money does not change. On the other hand, with transfers to supply positive (or negative), positive (or negative) accelerations in turnover magnitude become possible; and these may easily be accompanied [by] corresponding changes in turnover frequency. But there now arises the question, What happens when the transfers to demand are positive (or negative) or the crossover difference is not zero?

The immediate answer can only postpone the issue by defining different cases. First, there is the case of the superposed circuit when transfers to surplus demand are opposite in sign to transfers to basic demand; such a superposed circuit may be generated when foreign trade does not balance or government indulges in deficit spending.[74]

---

74 The two preceding paragraphs replace the following passage from the 1944 version, in which the notation has been altered to conform with Lonergan's latest usage. The discussion referred to in the final clause appears in §§ 29–31 of the present edition.

  'So much for the first two steps of the inquiry. With all five rates of transfer, $(S' - s'O')$, $(S'' - s''O'')$, $(D' - s'I')$, $(D'' - s''I'')$, G each at zero, circuit accelerations are possible in virtue of changing turnover frequency but limited because aggregate turnover magnitudes remain constant. With only $(D' - s'I')$,

Second, with G at zero, positive or negative transfers to basic demand $[D' - s'I']$ and consequent similar transfers to surplus demand $[D'' - s''I'']$ belong to the theory of booms and slumps. They involve changes in [aggregate basic or aggregate surplus] demand, with entrepreneurs receiving back more (or less) than they paid out in outlay [which includes profits of all kinds]. The immediate effect is on the price levels at the final markets, and to these changes [in price], enterprise as a whole responds to release an upward (or downward) movement of the whole economy. But the initial increased transfers to demand [that is, $(D' - s'I')$ and $(D'' - s''I'')$ are not zero][75] are not simply to be supposed. For that would be postulating without explaining the boom or slump.

Third, when G is not zero, then one circuit is being drained to augment the quantity of money in the other circuit. This increment |1944| in quantity of money appears at the final markets, so that its immediate effect is upon prices, except insofar as it is offset by equal and opposite action by $(D' - s'I')$ and $(D'' - s''I'')$. Again one has to deal with cyclic phenomena and not the general case of circuit acceleration.

Thus the general theory of circuit acceleration is that it takes place in a constrained and limited way when quantities of money in the circuits are constant, but without let or hindrance when quantities of money are variable. Further, the normal entry and exit of quantities of money to the circuits or from them is by the transfers from the redistributive to the supply functions. Finally, provided $(D' - s'I')$, $(D'' - s''I'')$, G vary only slightly from zero, so that their action is absorbed by stocks of goods at the final markets, they exercise a stimulating effect in favor of a positive or a negative circuit

---

$(D'' - s''I'')$, G each at zero, there are accelerations in aggregate turnover magnitudes, and these may easily be accompanied and reinforced by similar accelerations in turnover frequency. There remains the question, What happens when $(D' - s'I')$, $(D'' - s''I'')$, G are not zero?

'The immediate answer aims at no more than postponing the issue by defining different cases. First, there is the case of the superimposed circuit, when in addition to the basic and surplus circuits there is a third circuit involving the redistributive function; this phenomenon arises when, say, $(D' - s'I')$ and $(D'' - s''I'')$ are opposite in sign; it will be discussed when we treat the circulatory effects of a favorable balance of foreign trade or deficit government spending.'

75 All the words in square brackets in this paragraph were inserted editorially.

acceleration; otherwise their action pertains either to the superimposed circuits of favorable balances of foreign trade and deficit government spending, or else to the cyclic phenomena of booms and slumps.

|1978| The foregoing account of circuit acceleration has been based on the diagram of transfers between monetary functions. It has been simply macroeconomic, and so needs to be supplemented with a microeconomic analysis that will clarify certain details of the general picture.[76] [This will be done in two steps, the first in the following appendix to the present section, the second in section 16.]

Appendix to Section 15[77]

[1944] On the assumption that all units of enterprise begin turnover 1 simultaneously and end turnover n simultaneously, it is possible to construct a simple mathematical model of circuit acceleration. One may write

$$R' = \sum_{i'} \sum_{1}^{n} f_{ij}$$

$$O' = \sum_{i'} \sum_{1}^{n} o_{ij}$$

$$(S' - s'O') = \sum_{i'} \sum_{1}^{n} s_{ij} \ ^{78}$$

where the unit of enterprise i, in turnover j, increases its monetary circulating capital by s_{ij}, makes initial payments o_{ij}, and receives final payments f_{ij}, and each double summation is taken in each unit of enterprise from turn-

76 Beginning with the 1978 version, the two preceding sentences stand at the beginning of what Lonergan entitles an appendix to the section on circuit acceleration. This appendix (not to be confused with the appendix to §15, immediately following this paragraph) appears in the present edition as §16, 'Circuit Acceleration (II).'

77 In the 1944 version, this section appears as an appendix to the ninth section ('Circuit Acceleration'). The versions of 1978 and later omit it. Alterations have been made to bring its notation into line with Lonergan's latest practice.

78 The third equation has been altered to conform with Lonergan's later notation.

over 1 to turnover n and then with respect to all basic units of enterprise i'.[79]

Now f_{ij} is zero in all units of enterprise that do not deal immediately with final buyers. Let[80] T_{ij} be transitional payments received and t_{ij} be transitional payments made by the unit of enterprise i, in turnover j. Further, let j' denote the turnover immediately preceding turnover j. Then, since the increment in monetary circulating capital may be equated to the excess of payments made in turnover j, over payments received in turnover j', one has

$$f_{ij'} + T_{ij'} = o_{ij} + t_{ij} - s_{ij}$$

Submitting this equation to a double summation, one has

$$\sum_{i'} \sum_{0}^{n-1} (f_{ij} + T_{ij}) = \sum_{i'} \sum_{1}^{n} (o_{ij} + t_{ij} - s_{ij})$$

where the difference between turnovers j' and j is covered by the difference of the limits. However, the limit on the left-hand side may be assimilated to that on the right-hand side by introducing[81] $\Delta R'$ and $\Delta T'$ defined by the equations

79 Note that the symbol i' in the preceding sentence is not identical with the symbol i' of Lonergan's diagram of rates of flow. The latter is always the meaning with which the symbol i' is used with the two exceptions of the present appendix and §17 below. Note also that if Lonergan had written out his equations in full, using a uniform convention for abbreviations, the first equation would probably have been written

$$R' = \sum_{i=1}^{i'} \sum_{j=1}^{n} f_{ij}$$

and the second and third equations written analogously.

80 Note here an exception to the general use (explained in note 29 above) of capital letters to represent rates and lower-case letters to represent quantities. The exception was made, retaining Lonergan's 1944 notation, in order to preserve the correspondence, suggested by his use of the symbols T and t, between the two classifications of transitional payments.

81 Although later versions of the *Essay* use a lower-case d for differentials only, the 1944 version uses it for differences. Where difference is meant, as in the following discussion, the symbol Δ has been substituted.

$$\Delta R' = \sum_{i'} (f_{in} - f_{i0}) \quad \text{(so that } \sum_{1}^{n} \sum f_{ij} - \sum_{0}^{n-1} \sum f_{ij} = \Delta R')$$

$$\Delta T' = \sum_{i'} (T_{in} - T_{i0})$$

where, since turnover 0 [zero] is the last turnover of the previous interval, $\Delta R'$ is the difference in the turnover magnitude of basic final payments at the beginning and at the end of the interval; and $\Delta T'$ is the similar difference in the turnover magnitude of basic transitional payments. Further, since, in the aggregate, transitional payments made are identical with transitional payments received, one has

$$0 = \sum_{i'} \sum_{1}^{n} (T_{ij} - t_{ij})$$

so that all summations may be eliminated and one may write

$$(S' - s'O') = \Delta T' + (O' - R') + \Delta R'$$

and by changing single primes (′) to double primes (″), one has a parallel equation for the surplus circuit.

With G at zero and D' at zero, $(O' - R')$ can be no more than a lag, and as will appear later, this lag unfortunately tends to be zero. Again, $\Delta T'$ and $\Delta R'$ will be of the same sign: final payments are not increasing when transitional payments are decreasing, nor vice versa. Thus excess transfers to or from supply, $(S' - s'O')$, tend to equal the sum of the increments of aggregate turnover magnitudes in final payments and in transitional payments. Of these two, the increment in transitional payments will be the larger, since for each sale at the final market there commonly is a sale at a number of transitional markets.

In the summations, turnover magnitudes appear directly but turnover frequencies only indirectly, inasmuch as the number of turnovers n per interval increases in the case of any given unit of enterprise. An increase of the number of turnovers per interval would have a great effect on R' and O', since it increases the number of instances of f_{ij} and o_{ij} to be summated. But it need have no effect on $(S' - s'O')$, since s_{ij} may be positive or negative and so cancel in the aggregate of instances. Finally, increasing turnover frequency, of itself, has no effect on $\Delta R'$ or $\Delta T'$, since these terms represent the difference between two turnover magnitudes, and increasing frequency only puts further apart the two magnitudes compared.

Thus, in pure theory O' and R' might accelerate to any extent while $(S' - s'O')$, $\Delta R'$, $\Delta T'$ each remained at zero. It would be a pure frequency acceleration. The contention of the preceding pages was that such pure frequency acceleration has conditions that are difficult to realize, and that the history of the development of money points to a preponderant role of increasing turnover magnitude in circuit accelerations.

16   Circuit Acceleration (II)[82]

|1978| In any unit of enterprise i, in turnover j, the receipts from the previous turnover k may be written r_{ik}.[83]

Part of these receipts may be due as transitional payments to prior units of enterprise. Let them be written t_{ij}.

If the remainder is judged insufficient, it may be supplemented by drawing on reserves (in the form of cash or of credit) in the redistributional area, to the amount s_{ij}.

On the other hand, if the remainder is judged excessive, reserves may be strengthened by the amount $-s_{ij}$.

It follows that the outlay of the unit i, in turnover j, namely, o_{ij}, will be given by the equation

$$o_{ij} = r_{ik} - t_{ij} + s_{ij}$$

Moreover, if there is some number of intervals, n, over which different units of enterprise have different numbers of turnovers completed, yet all begin a new turnover at the start of the first interval and all complete a last turnover at the end of the nth interval, then total outlay over n intervals will be given by

82 In the final version of the *Essay*, this section is an appendix (see note 76 above). Between 1978 and 1983 Lonergan made minor revisions by hand, which have been incorporated here.

83 This notation corresponds with $(f_{ij} + T_{ij})$ in the preceding appendix.

$$\sum_{i'}^{n} O' + O'' = \sum_{i'}\sum_{1}^{x} o_{ij}$$

where the summations for each enterprise i have to be calculated for its x turnovers and then these results summed for total outlay.

To be noted above all in the foregoing analysis is its indeterminacy. Each unit of enterprise is limited by the success of its previous turnover, by its indebtedness to earlier enterprises, by its reserves of cash or its command of credit. But within these limits its undertaking may be expanded, contracted, or kept constant.

Further to be noted is that there are two reasons for the complexity of the summation of outlays. The one already given was that turnover frequencies varied from firm to firm. But the full reason is the fact that the distinction between O' and O'' is extrinsic: it is made not by the authors of outlay but by its recipients, for whom it is income.

Now part of total income will go to basic demand, for all recipients have a standard of living to maintain. At the same time, when surplus supply is large, the whole of surplus income cannot go to basic demand without causing an inflationary increase in basic prices. In fact, the dynamic equilibrium of the system requires the crossovers to balance: as much money as comes to basic demand from surplus outlay, so much has to go to surplus demand from basic outlay. On that condition continuity is assured: both surplus supply and basic supply will be able to repeat their previous performance without drawing upon reserves. On the other hand, when the crossovers do not balance, then one circuit is being drained of its resources by the other; and if the lack of balance is sustained, then the firms on the losing side will contract and eventually go out of business.

Our distinction between basic and surplus demand implies a distinction between ineffective basic and ineffective surplus demand. Moreover, either type may result from the inequality of crossovers. When the crossover from basic supply is deficient, surplus demand will tend to be ineffective; when the crossover from surplus supply is defective, basic demand will tend to be ineffective.

However, as supply can expand by drawing upon reserves (cash or credit) in the redistributional area, so too ineffective demand can be remedied in the same fashion. In cash, such reserves will be savings. In credit, they will arise from the creditor's prospects of being repaid, either by the future performance of the debtor or by the penalties that may be exacted if payment fails to occur. But neither cash nor credit will avail against a sustained inequality of the crossovers.

It is a common saying that savings equal investment.[84] On the present showing it would be more accurate to say that the crossovers should balance, that a sustained lack of balance portends ruin, and that ruin can be warded off (at least for a while) by transfers from the redistributional area. These may be effected by drawing on savings, by obtaining credit, by maintaining a favorable balance of foreign trade, by deficit government spending, and by redistributing income through an income tax.

The advantage of such greater accuracy is that it does not suggest an immediate correlation between savings and investment. Provided the crossovers balance, surplus income equals surplus supply. Savings are required, not to maintain a rate of production already attained, but only to increase the rate of production already attained. In other words, savings are the accelerator of the monetary circulation. Or, as Kalecki put it, not each individual capitalist but capitalists as a group get what they spend.

In fact, savings are much more important than is suggested by the equation of savings and investment. The function of savings is to underpin the whole redistributional area of the economy. Savings are sums of money that as yet have not been spent. They are built up by savings banks, insurance companies, pension funds. They are mobilized by the agencies that float new issues of stocks and bonds, that grant credit to firms, that extend credit to consumers.

17   Measuring Change in the Productive Process (1)[85]

[1944] In sections 12 through 16, classes and rates of payment were defined to make possible a statement of conditions of acceleration of the monetary circuits. Evidently it is desirable to complete this list of condi-

---

84 It is likely that in this new technical sense, S' and S'' are investment, while $s'O'$ and $s''O''$ are savings, although Lonergan himself did not note this correspondence.

85 This section begins with a paragraph from 1944, but most of the material it includes first appeared in the 1980 version. There it replaces a 1978 section, likewise entitled 'Measuring Change in the Productive Process,' which itself is a replacement for the 1944 section on 'The Theoretical Possibility of Measurement of the Productive Process.'

tions by bringing in a consideration of the underlying acceleration of the productive process itself. But before this can be done, at least a method of defining the measurement of such acceleration must be provided. It is not necessary that any actual measurement be undertaken, or even that a method which statisticians would find practicable be assigned. But it is necessary that we have a clear and definite idea of what we are discussing when we speak of an acceleration of the productive process.[86]

|1980| An exchange occurs within the productive process when a sum of money is paid for a quantity of goods and/or services rendered. But macroeconomics is concerned, not with single exchanges but with aggregates, and naturally the concern varies with variations in the analysis that reveals which aggregates are significant.

Now we agree with the commonly acknowledged significance of the distinction between the price level P and the real income Q. We also acknowledge the significance of the gross national product Y, where Y is equal to the product PQ. But our distinction between basic and surplus production leads [us] to distinguish between the basic and surplus price levels P' and P'', the basic and surplus real incomes Q' and Q'', and the basic and surplus gross products Y' and Y''.[87]

---

86 The preceding paragraph has been restored from the beginning of the 1944 section on 'The Theoretical Possibility of Measurement of the Productive Process.' The rest of that section appears in the present edition in §23. Because it has been necessary to renumber sections, the first sentence of the paragraph has been altered; Lonergan originally wrote, 'In the three preceding sections ...'

87 In 1979, at which time Lonergan was using Robert J. Gordon, *Macroeconomics*, 1st ed. (Boston: Little, Brown and Co., 1978) as an introductory text, he distributed a two-page supplement to the section on measuring change in the productive process, showing more clearly both his agreements and his disagreements with commonly accepted ways of relating prices and quantities. The relevant passage from that supplement is as follows:

'Gordon has a very simple way of deriving P and Q, viz.,

$$\text{GNP} = PQ = Y; \quad Q = Y/P$$

'We, on the other hand, have to distinguish basic and surplus, P' and P'', Q' and Q''. For unless surplus is conceived as a distinct circuit with its own final market, the Marxists object that the basic final market is demanding payment not only for basic goods and services but also for surplus as well; hence the accusation [that] profit is robbing workers of part of the labor value of their

Further, while we acknowledge the significance of selecting a base year and considering its price level the standard of comparison (100), our analysis leads us to find significance in differences between successive price levels. In particular, we are concerned with the correlation between variations in surplus income and variations in the basic price spread. As we hope to show, a surplus expansion gives rise to an increasing basic price spread, while a surplus contraction leads to a contracting basic price spread. The former encourages tendencies towards a boom; the latter involves a recession that can turn into a depression.

It is true that the distinction between basic and surplus is functional, and that a number of activities may at one time be surplus and at another basic. So labor, services, power, transportation, materials can be known as contributions to the basic or surplus function only through further determinations and even special inquiries. But though accurate statistics are not to be expected to be available in the short run, still the analysis itself will provide rather convincing indicators, and as expertise develops the new tricks of a new trade, there well may be discovered methods of attaining a sufficient accuracy for practical purposes.

In any case the immediate task is to state as accurately as possible the general character of the unknowns to which, we hope, investigators will endeavor to approximate. [In other words, can one define two numbers, say P and Q, such that P varies with a set of numbers $p_1, p_2, p_3, \ldots$ and Q varies with another set of numbers $q_1, q_2, q_3, \ldots$?

---

contribution. Again, the proponents of social credit argue that the wages paid workers in the basic process are unequal to purchase the products of the basic process, and so should be supplemented by monthly gifts of bank credit to raise purchasing power to the level of prices which charge not only for basic products but also for the services of the surplus circuit.

'The solution, in its most comprehensible form, is to distinguish basic and surplus GNP, Y' and Y''. Then, as before,

$$Y' = P'Q'; \qquad Y'/P' = Q'$$
$$Y'' = P''Q''; \qquad Y''/P'' = Q''$$

'And now with the circuits distinguished, the crossover makes it manifest that it supplements the wages paid in the basic circuit, so that profits are not robbery and there is no need for the gifts of bank credit to supplement workers' basic wages.'

A universally valid answer to this question may be had when P and Q are not mere numbers but vectors in an n-dimensional manifold.][88] So let us have recourse to an n-dimensional configuration space, where n is the number of objects offered in exchange, so that for every difference in objects there is a distinct dimension.[89]

[1944] Let P and Q be the vectors from the origin to the points $(p_1, p_2, p_3, ...)$ and $(q_1, q_2, q_3, ...)$ respectively. Then any variation in the price pattern, that is, in any ratio of the type p_i/p_j, will appear as a variation in the angle between the projection of P on the plane ij and the axis j. Similarly, any variation in the quantity pattern will appear as a parallel variation in an angle made by a projection of Q. But besides such variation in price pattern or in quantity pattern there may be general increases or decreases in prices or in quantities. The latter appear as positive or negative increments in the absolute magnitudes of the vectors, for

$$P^2 = \sum p_i^2 \tag{12}$$

$$Q^2 = \sum q_i^2 \tag{13}$$

that is, the length of the vector P is the square root of the sum of all prices squared, and the length of the vector Q is the square root of the sum of all quantities squared.[90] Thus, one may suppose two n-dimensional spheres of

88 The two bracketed sentences have been restored from the 1944 version.

89 In the 1978 version, the section on measuring change in the productive process began with the following paragraphs, which are relevant here:

'We have seen that doubling turnover frequency may double production without any increase in the quantity of money in circulation. And in our age of inflation we are all familiar with the fact that price levels may change without change in the quantity or quality of the goods and services supplied. Accordingly we are entitled to distinguish price indices, P' and P'', and quantity indices, Q' and Q'', in the basic and surplus circuits, respectively.

'Now there are many ways in which one can approximate to the values of P' and Q', P'' and Q'', but in a theoretical discussion one would like to know just what quantity one is approximating to. To this end I have found it helpful to have recourse to an n-dimensional configuration space where n is the number of objects offered for sale, so that for every difference in objects there is a distinct dimension.'

90 In contemporary notation, $|P|^2$ would replace Lonergan's P^2, and $|Q|^2$ would replace his Q^2.

radii P and Q, respectively. The vector from the origin to any point in the first 'quadrant' of the surface of such spheres represents a determinate price pattern or quantity pattern. On the other hand, variation in P and Q is variation in the size of the spheres.[91]

|1980| Let objects in a class i', during successive intervals j and k, be sold at basic prices p'_{ij} and p'_{ik}, and in quantities q'_{ij} and q'_{ik}; similarly, let objects in a class i'', during successive intervals, be sold at surplus prices p''_{ij} and p''_{ik}, and in quantities q''_{ij} and q''_{ik}.

Let us represent the basic and surplus price and quantity indices in the first and second of the successive intervals by P'_j, Q'_j, P''_j, Q''_j and P'_k, Q'_k, P''_k, Q''_k, where

$$P'^2_j = \Sigma\, p'^2_{ij}\ \text{for all instances of } i'$$

$$Q'^2_j = \Sigma\, q'^2_{ij}\ \text{for all instances of } i'$$

and parallel expressions are to be written out for the surplus price and quantity indices in the interval j, and for both the basic and surplus price and quantity indices in the interval k. In brief, the basic price index in any interval is the line joining the origin of the configuration space to the extremity of the nth item, and the basic quantity index is the line joining the origin of the configuration space to the extremity of the nth basic quantity; and similar lines will represent the surplus price and quantity indices in the interval j, and the basic and surplus price and quantity indices in the interval k.

Moreover, basic final sales in the interval j will be represented by the dot product of $P'_j \cdot Q'_j$:

$$\Sigma\, p'_{ij}q'_{ij} = P'_j \cdot Q'_j = P'_j Q'_j \cos A'$$

where A' is the angle between P'_j and Q'_j; and clearly similar expressions hold for final sales in surplus production in the interval j, and for final sales in both basic and surplus production in the interval k.

We now have expressions in successive intervals j and k for basic and for surplus price and quantity indices, both when price and quantity are considered separately and when price is multiplied by quantity. What we now

91 This paragraph has been restored from the 1944 version. For its context in that version, see § 23.

need are expressions for the difference between successive intervals, and such differences we propose to represent by abbreviations. So let

P'_{kj} stand for $P'_k - P'_j$
Q'_{kj} stand for $Q'_k - Q'_j$
$P'_{kj} Q'_{kj}$ stand for $P'_k \cdot Q'_k - P'_j \cdot Q'_j$

and similar expressions for surplus differences are to be had by replacing single primes (') by double primes (").

Plainly, these differences may be positive, zero, or negative. When the basic products are positive or zero or negative, then the basic circuit will be expanding, stationary, or contracting, and similarly when the surplus products are positive, zero, or negative, then the surplus circuit will be expanding, or stationary, or contracting. Moreover, when either circuit is expanding or contracting, the change may be due to the differences of price or to the differences of quantity or to both.

Admittedly, we have not yet arrived at measurements but only at heuristic expressions that indicate the ideal towards which development may approximate. Such heuristic expressions are not algorithms such as procedures for long division or for taking square roots. Rather they resemble the problems in algebra that ask us to find the number or the pair of numbers such that ... The first step then is, Let the required number be x, Let the required pair of numbers be x and y. The first step is not the solution, but commonly it is a necessary clarification and can lead to further clarifications.

Many, no doubt, will urge that they would prefer something less abstruse than an n-dimensional configuration space. But I would note that the configuration space, precisely because of its complexity, can represent all the qualitative differences from one interval to the next and thereby promote the modesty that befits appeals to price and quantity indices.

18   Phases in the Productive Process[92]

The Theory of Economic Development by Joseph A. Schumpeter begins and ends with the stationary state. It is a state in which the economy reproduces its processes at a constant rate. Innovations and developments may have

92 In 1981 or 1982, Lonergan added at the top of the first page of this section a comment to the effect that the 'phases' it discusses are to be thought of as ideal types or heuristic structures; see *Method in Theology* 227–28.

occurred in the past, but they have ceased to occur. People are content to function on the basis of their inheritance, and they appear capable of doing so indefinitely.

Still, there may come a time when innovations and developments once more occur. This may happen in a variety of manners, but the simplest assumption is that it begins in the basic circuit. It consists in a greater abundance of consumer goods and services, and it is achieved by taking up slack; the unemployed become employed, and there is put to use capital plant and equipment that had been functioning under capacity. We may term it the *minor basic expansion.* It might but need not rapidly reach its full potential, for it can begin in this or that line of endeavor, gradually spread to the whole basic process, and only be forced to end when employment is full and all productive capacity is in use.

But the greater the minor basic expansion, the more likely becomes a *minor surplus expansion.* It is minor, for it consists simply in taking up slack, employing the unemployed or the underemployed, and using surplus plant and equipment closer to full capacity. It is surplus in the minimal sense that its efforts are confined to widening and deepening basic enterprises: it makes them more numerous, and it equips them with more efficient plant and machinery.

Besides the minor there is also the *major surplus expansion.* Its possibility is that the surplus process operates on many levels. Where basic goods and services stand in a point-to-point correspondence with elements in the standard of living, surplus goods and services may stand in any of a series of higher correspondences, such as point-to-line, or point-to-surface, or point-to-volume, or point-to-four-dimensional-continuum, and so on. In other words, the surplus process produces not only the basic process's means of production but also its own, and it may do so in any of many degrees of roundaboutness.

So technology advanced from tools made of fiber or wood or stone, to tools made of bronze or iron or steel, to the machine tools used in constructing machines. So extraction machinery reduces the labor and accelerates the process of obtaining coal and iron ore from mines; blast furnaces transform iron ore into pig iron; steel mills advance pig iron to the steel that yields the machine tools for any of a large variety of purposes. To take a single example, it yields the cotton gins for cleaning raw cotton, the spindles for spinning it into thread, the looms for making thread into cloth, and the sewing machines that change cloth into clothing.[93]

93 See 'Additional Note to Section 6' above.

Such is the major surplus expansion, and its natural goal is a major basic expansion. It remains that the latter occurs only with a lag, and the length of that lag will vary with the number of stages in the surplus development and the longer the period needed to get each of the stages running smoothly and keeping step with the other stages.

But besides the technical causes of a lag there also can be financial causes, and into these we now must enter, though only from a macroeconomic viewpoint. From that viewpoint equilibrium is conceived, not in terms of every case of supply being balanced by an equal demand, but in terms of balancing cash flows that continue to balance. Such continuity is to be understood broadly as a stable equilibrium. It admits deviations that tend to be offset by equal and opposite deviations. It excludes deviations that accumulate on one side and decumulate on the other.

A basic condition of macroequilibrium is the balancing of the cross-overs, of the flow from the surplus circuit into the basic circuit and the opposite flow from the basic circuit into the surplus, [of $c''O''$ equaling $i'O'$,][94] of the crossover difference G being zero. For plainly any sustained inequality would drain the basic circuit in favor of the surplus, or the surplus in favor of the basic, and so destroy the circulation as a whole.

Next, such macroequilibrium may be static or dynamic. When it is static, the crossovers are constant; they are neither increasing equally nor decreasing equally; and so there results the stationary state. On the other hand, when the crossovers are increasing equally or decreasing equally, there is a dynamic macroequilibrium which may be an expansion or a contraction.

In the minor expansions, inventories are decumulating, to be replenished by using unused capacity and by increasing the labor force. In the minor basic expansion the basic rates of income and outlay are increasing but the surplus rates are little changed. In the minor surplus expansion the surplus rates of outlay and income are increasing without any widening or deepening of surplus capital plant or equipment, while the basic rates of outlay and income are increasing in virtue of the widening and/or deepening of basic capital plant and equipment.

In the major surplus expansion one has to distinguish (1) an initial phase, (2) a transitional phase, and (3) a closing phase. In the initial phase the surplus process is widening or deepening itself but as yet this development has not begun to affect the basic process. In the transitional phase, the surplus process continues to develop, but the basic process ends its lag

94 In the 1982 version, the bracketed clause has been struck out; as reinserted here, it has been altered to conform with Lonergan's latest notation.

and begins to profit from the self-development of the surplus process. In the closing phase, the surplus process of self-development begins to taper off, but the acquired development continues to sustain an ongoing widening and deepening of basic enterprises.

Now we have seen that any acceleration in the circuits calls for an increase either in the velocity of the circular flow or in the quantity of money that is circulating. But changes in velocity suppose changes in the rate of turnovers or, equivalently, in shortening the time needed to process each batch of the product: for example, if it takes twenty million dollars to produce one ship in four years, the velocity is twenty million per four years; if one can produce the same ship in half the time, one doubles the velocity of the money one uses. The possibility of such changes, however, is limited, and commonly it is by increasing the quantity of money in the circuits that an acceleration of the circuits is effected. Finally, it is the need of a greater quantity of money for an acceleration of the circuits, for increasing the volume of production at current prices, that accounts for the development of banking, for the discounting of bills of exchange, for the transition from gold as a medium of exchange to a gold standard (that is, to an issue of paper money that can in any particular case be exchanged for a given quantity of gold, even though there never is enough gold held in reserve to buy with gold all the paper money issued), and finally the omission of the gold standard (that is, money consists in the issued paper and in the credits individuals and firms have in the bookkeeping of the legally authorized banking fraternity).

Now, even in the stationary state there are (for example, seasonal) fluctuations in the crossovers, but when they increase, they are due for a subsequent equal decrease, and when they decrease, they are due for a subsequent equal increase. Such changes in the crossovers are met by inflows and outflows along $(S' - s'O')$ and $(S'' - s''O'')$ to and from the redistributional area and from and to basic and surplus outlay. Observe that such transfers give the redistributional area a quantity of money (so much [every so often]) but take from the circuits a volume of money (so much every so often), and vice versa.

Next, in the minor basic expansion there is no addition to existing plant and equipment but there is an addition to circulating capital: it pays for the larger turnover and the larger payroll and, as the need arises, for greater maintenance expenses. Further, inasmuch as this expansion spreads over the whole area of basic activity, the maintenance bill will include payments to surplus firms for replacements of worn parts and particular machines, so that the crossovers will begin to increase and the minor surplus expansion receive an initial impulse.

However, the minor surplus expansion properly begins when it starts attending to the widening and deepening of capital plant and equipment in the basic sphere. There is a flow of investment from the redistributional area to surplus outlay, to purchase for basic firms, old or new, new plant and more or better equipment. There is a notable increase in the crossover from wages earned in surplus activity to the basic market, to purchase a standard of living. This new demand precedes the lagging new sources of supply. Basic prices rise but basic costs for a while remain as they were, with a consequent gain in the receipts of basic firms. Such gains, when added together, would equal the sums transferred from surplus wages to basic demand. The gains incite the basic investors to support the minor surplus expansion, either directly through the compensating crossover or indirectly through the redistributional area.

A sufficiently great minor surplus expansion will encourage surplus firms to move into the major surplus expansion. In its initial phase this is an internal development of the surplus sector. It produces the means of producing the means of producing basic means of producing. The increment in surplus outlay and income is enormous. But only with a notable lag (think of a succession of five-year plans) does there begin the large-scale transformation of basic means of production. It follows that wages paid in the surplus sector will notably increase basic demand, that that demand as yet cannot be met with goods and services, that accordingly prices will rise, the difference between receipts and costs will mount, and owners in the basic sector either will invest in the surplus expansion directly along the compensating crossover or indirectly by adding their funds to the redistributional area.

Eventually, however, the major surplus expansion begins to deliver its proper fruits in an enhanced rate of widening and deepening basic enterprises. Surplus sales now have two classes of buyers: the surplus firms it has been serving in the surplus sector, and now as well the basic firms it now begins to serve. This is the transitional phase. For a while surplus outlay and income will increase. But sooner or later the self-development of the surplus sector will begin to taper off; the principal source of the basic price spread ceases to be a gusher; and at the same time the demand for labor in the basic sector will begin to exact an increase in wage rates. In this fashion begins the closing phase of the major surplus expansion and the opening of the major basic expansion.

At this point an economic system is confronted with an intrinsic test. Its success will be established if it can complete the major basic expansion and – without mishap, without inflation, without unemployment, without a break in confidence – make its way serenely into the haven of the stationary state. I mean, of course, not the stationary state of mere backwardness, not the stationary state of stagnation when a disastrous crash follows on an earlier apparent triumph, but the stationary state that preserves all the gains of the preceding major expansions. It is content to reproduce their gains at a constant rate. Its duration may be short or long, for in each case it must wait until such time as further new developments are grasped by human intelligence and eventually become practically conceived possibilities.

19   Mistaken Expectations

|1980| The transition from the major surplus expansion to the major basic expansion involves two elements: on the productive side, the major surplus expansion is tapering off; on the monetary side, the crossover from the surplus circuit to the basic is contracting.

The former element implies the latter. The contraction of surplus activity implies a contraction of surplus employment; the contraction of employment implies a contraction of surplus wages; the contraction of surplus wages implies that there is less income earned in the surplus circuit and spent at the basic final market. Just as the initial phase of the major surplus expansion paid out wages that were spent on the workers' standard of living and caused a broad spread between basic costs and basic receipts, so the closing phase of the major surplus expansion transfers workers to the major basic expansion and no longer pays them their wages. The basic price spread has to contract.

The recession has begun.

But it commonly happens in the whole of industry and commerce that some firms are more sheltered than others. They enjoy a variety of advantages that yield rents, and the rents enable them to maintain the price spread they received during the major surplus expansion. However, these rents do not bolster total basic income. They simply transfer the squeeze from the more sheltered to the less sheltered firms. The least sheltered will accumulate losses and be driven to bankruptcy. But this merely transfers the squeeze to the least sheltered of the surviving firms, and when they are driven to bankruptcy, the squeeze turns to another batch of victims.

The depression has taken over.

The ongoing process of sound firms becoming marginal and marginal firms going bankrupt provides a stimulus for rentiers to flock to a bear market. They anticipate still further losses. They sell at once their holdings in stocks and purchase the most gilt-edged of bonds.

Similarly, the bankers stiffen the conditions of granting credit and widen the range of instances in which credit is simply refused. But it easily happens that a few or even many banks find that at the clearinghouse, checks in their favor are declining and checks drawn on them are mounting. When they attempt to meet the gap, they find that collateral previously accepted has declined greatly in value or even become worthless. They may have to close their doors, and this will cause a run on other banks: depositors demand cash, and where deposits stand to cash as fifteen to one, the demand cannot be met. This only makes the tide rise higher, and sooner or later the government will be called upon to declare a moratorium.

The depression has become a crash. The accustomed lines of production and finance are snapped. Until they are reestablished or others built up in their place, an inflow of money into the economy may be described as priming the pumps but can have no effect beyond aimlessly scattering money around.

The crash yields stagnation, and a decade can go by before favorable incidents stimulate a rebirth.

Is there a moral? There is more than one.

The basic mistaken expectation rests on a failure to distinguish between normal profit, which can be constant, and a social dividend which varies. It mounts in the major surplus expansion; it declines as that expansion tapers off; it vanishes when the expansion has finished.

By constant normal profit I mean the excess of bills receivable over bills payable in the stationary state. It is an excess that must be had if the firm is not to go bankrupt and if the persons responsible for the firm's emergence and continued existence are to have a proportionate standard of living. A profit that is normal in the stationary state is no less normal in the surplus expansion.

It remains that the excess of bills receivable over bills payable during the surplus expansion is not in its entirety a contribution to personal income. The part that would be profit in the stationary state still is profit. But the excess over that part is a social dividend. It is not money to be spent. It is not money to be saved. It is money to be invested either directly or, through the redistributional area, indirectly. For it is the equivalent of the money that, if not invested, contracts surplus production, [and] that, if invested, keeps surplus production at its attained volume; [moreover,] if a further appropriate sum is added interval by interval, surplus production will not merely level off but keep accelerating.

The fact, of course, is that no difficulty is experienced in financing the surplus expansion. It is the first step towards increasing the standard of living of the whole society, and there seems to be little evidence that entrepreneurs, financiers, engineers, workers commonly are hesitant about taking that step.

The difficulty emerges in the second step, the basic expansion. In equity it should be directed to raising the standard of living of the whole society. It does not. And the reason why it does not is not the reason on which simple-minded moralists insist. They blame greed. But the prime cause is ignorance. The dynamics of surplus and basic production, surplus and basic expansions, surplus and basic incomes are not understood, not formulated, not taught. When people do not understand what is happening and why, they cannot be expected to act intelligently. When intelligence is a blank, the first law of nature takes over: self-preservation. It is not primarily greed but frantic efforts at self-preservation that turn the recession into a depression, and the depression into a crash.

It remains that mistaken expectations foster and generate a series of palliatives. The damage they do is large and multiform. It is removed only by retracing the mistaken steps of the past, and that promises to be a long, wearisome, and disheartening task. Let us say something in turn on the favorable balance of foreign trade, the colonial economy, the fate of the fatherland or the mother country, on armaments and wars, on unemployment, deficit spending, transfer payments, blocked investments, union exigences, and inflation.

20   Misadventures

This section deals with a series of palliatives that, in one way or another, divert attention away from the ineffective demand for basic goods and services and, at times, mitigate it. Of these the oldest is the favorable balance of foreign trade with epiphenomena in the colonial economy and [in] the ultimate fate of the mother country.

Originally the favorable balance of foreign trade was a doctrine that considered it advantageous for a country to export more than it imported. It was a paradoxical view, for the real advantage was with the country that imported more than it exported. Nonetheless it rested on solid empirical foundations, for the more prosperous nations were found to be those that had a more abundant supply of gold. The idea of the favorable balance was to increase the gold supply in one's own country, and on our present analysis the point to that was that an economic expansion could hardly flourish with falling prices, and so a country that wanted an increased GNP had to increase its gold supply.

With modern techniques of credit creation, this original significance is largely in abeyance. But advertence to the deficiency of basic effective demand brings to light another purpose. The first effect of a recession is that employment ceases to increase. A second effect is that unemployment swells. But when the national economy cannot manage to advance the standard of living of its own population, at least it can provide work for all that care to work. For what cannot be sold at home can be sold abroad; and what cannot be sold in more developed countries can be sold in less developed countries. It has been thought very odd that, while England began its economic takeoff (Rostow) around 1790, wages in England did not begin to rise until 1870. But it may be that a rise in the domestic standard of living is not a necessary consequence of a domestic surplus expansion. The surplus expansion may be directed to raising the standard of living in foreign countries.

Now the long-term effects of such a procedure are not without interest. Let us suppose two groups of countries, C and D. The group C is developing, first commercially and then industrially. The group D is undeveloped or underdeveloped. An initial stage is trade. The Hudson Bay Indians, for instance, were eager for muskets; the Hudson Bay traders were glad to provide them; and a musket is said to have sold for a pile of pelts as high as the musket was long. Next, say, come the planters. They know what can be produced in the country, and the natives know nothing of the demand for it and little about its production. So the planters acquire land and hire labor; this entry into the local economy invites an extension of the white man's burden into such related matters as protection, justice, and a share in government. Its precise nature varies with circumstance. In one place a sphere of influence becomes recognized; in another a protectorate is established; in the least organized communities along with traders and planters come the officials and militia of a colonial power, to be followed in due course by the dissidents, the refugees, the immigrants with their customs, their skills, their knowledge, their beliefs.

This process went forward without any grand design. It was the result of medieval commerce and travel, Renaissance voyages of exploration, the enterprise of Spain in America and of the Portuguese in the Far East. But the industrial revolution added to the profits, reaped by traders and planters, the regular flow of income from investment abroad.

The C group of developed countries had the commercial and industrial and financial capacity to supply the D group of undeveloped or underdeveloped countries with an abundance of both surplus and basic goods and services. As commercial and industrial they could supply the goods and services as items to be sold; and as financial they could supply the investments and loans that would at once foot the bill. Moreover, such production and financing could be an ongoing process. Each year the total of investments and loans would increase. Each year there would be reaped the profits from the investments and the interest from the loans, so that there would be ever more money to be invested or loaned. Finally, there was the crowning grace: a new form of surplus income emerged, and it tended to counteract the less pleasant consequences of the older form.

The latter led relentlessly from the surplus to the basic expansion. There the basic price level contracted; unsheltered firms became marginal and soon to be liquidated; the banking system was threatened and at times collapsed; unemployment mounted; investment dried up; and stagnation set in. But the new form has no tendency to expand production for domestic consumption. It consists in an increasing flow of income to be invested abroad or loaned abroad, with the investments sending home profits and the loans paying interest and amortization. So far from threatening the banking system, it generates the financial capitals of the world. So far from leading to unemployment and stagnation, it sustains employment and ongoing prosperity. The novelty in 1936 of Keynes's notion of ineffective demand finds an explanation if this superadded form of surplus income did a great deal to smooth out the fluctuations with which we since have become familiar.

If now we turn to the D group of undeveloped and underdeveloped countries, we can hardly expect them to understand what is happening to them. Because they are financed from abroad, they can come to produce not only consumer goods and services but, eventually, even surplus as well. But the profits are reaped by owners who reside elsewhere. The interest and other payments on loans are a further export. Under such a drain one cannot expect the surplus income generated in the D group to mount up to the great wealth associated with the celebrated captains of industry and masters of finance. Still less are they likely to add to the financial capitals of the world.

More complex issues supervene. The *C* group are not all equally well off. Some had a head start. Others joined the club at a later date. Rivalries develop. Navies are built not only to police the sea lanes but also to protect acquired advantages. Alliances are formed. Diplomacy aims at maintaining a balance of power, but the balance is effective only if it unquestionably favors those with much to lose and little to gain. But when that can be seriously questioned, those with much to gain, not only in wealth but also in power and prestige, will be tempted to opt for war.

A third type of surplus production and surplus income arises from anticipated and especially from actual warfare. The costs are enormous; they are paid to people. Governments naturally will aim at getting this money back, if not in taxes, at least by selling war bonds. But it does happen that this aim may not be completely successful, and so there are wartime profits with a counterpart in unbalanced budgets. Interest has to be paid on the bonds until they are redeemed or, like the unbalanced budgets, until they are consolidated into a permanent national debt. But just as the costs of war are directed to the production of munitions and casualties, so interest and amortization payments on the debt yield a surplus income.

Now this type of surplus is not confined to warlike concerns. Once the possibility of an unbalanced budget is established, the precedent can be invoked to persuade politicians to carry on other wars: wars on illiteracy, on poverty, on ill health, on unemployment, on insecurity. Where the profit motive does not prove efficacious, the state must intervene. Indeed, where higher profits are needed because workers demand higher wages, because employers insist on higher prices, or because governments are called upon to increase their benevolent expenditures, then the increasing volume of transactions requires a larger money supply, and the central bank can be persuaded to meet the demand. Finally, workers, employers, politicians can come to grasp that higher wages lead to higher prices, that higher prices in turn lead to higher wages, and that both augment the revenue from taxes, so that once more higher wages and higher prices will be called for. But it appears to be less evident that a vicious circle of ever more demands for a larger money supply with no increase in real income is inflationary.

In any case there has emerged in fact if not in name the welfare state. Its mechanism is rather strikingly similar to that of the favorable balance of foreign trade. The debt once owed by colonies to richer countries now is replaced by the national debt. The interest and amortization payments from debtor to creditor nations now are replaced by interest and amortization payments to those entitled to this third type of surplus income. The inability of colonies to surmount their burden of debt and launch their own grand-style surplus expansion now is matched by a similar burden depressing the flow of investment. Where before there was the largesse of a creditor country bestowing on a debtor an excess of imports over exports, now the long overdue basic expansion is doled out to one's own fellow countrymen under the haughty name of welfare.[95]

21 · Methodological Shifts[96]

[1980] A renewal of economic method began about 1870 and gradually transformed basic concepts. An understanding of these issues is a necessary preliminary if we are to put together the views of earlier and later economists, the innovations of the multinational corporations, and our own circulation analysis.[97]

A basic clarification results from the combination of two distinctions. The first is between *static* and *dynamic analysis* which is methodological. The second is between *stationary* and *evolutionary states* which refers to objective economic processes.[98]

In static analysis all variables have the same time subscript: they refer to price at time t, supply at time t, demand at time t; when supply equals demand at time t, there results a simultaneous equation.

In dynamic analysis consideration of the market is not restricted to the instant but goes back to influences from earlier decisions dependent on

---

95 In the 1983 version, the *Essay* ends at this point.

96 In the 1980 and 1981 versions, the section on 'Misadventures' (§ 20 of the present edition) was followed by some 39 pages that the editors regard as Lonergan's working draft of a further section, never completed. The first part of this section on 'Multinational Corporations' is entitled 'A Report' (29 pp.) and consists of Lonergan's transcriptions of other authors' works. The second and third parts, entitled 'Methodological Shifts' and 'The Position of This Essay,' are included in the present edition as §§ 21 and 22.

97 See Schumpeter, *History* 753ff. All references to Schumpeter in this section are given by Lonergan, with occasional editorial additions; the content will sufficiently identify the latter.

98 Ibid., index, pp. 1252, 1237; but Schumpeter's index gives 1256 for Static Analysis.

earlier conditions, and as well takes into account expected future values of variables, lags, sequences, rates of change, cumulative magnitudes, and so on.[99] (Note that this concept of dynamic analysis is dependent more on the preceding static view than on a study of economic actuality. Our own dynamics has the latter basis.)

A stationary state is the state of an economy that year after year keeps on reproducing itself.

An evolutionary state is a nonstationary state. More narrowly, one includes among stationary states the process of growth conceived as continuous variations of rates within an unchanging framework of institutions, tastes, technological horizons.[100]

Schumpeter observes that these distinctions were gradually worked out between 1870 and 1914 but not quickly enough or rigorously enough to take effect before 1914.

The foregoing clarification is relevant to the shift in the notion of *competition*.

Of the period 1870–1914, Schumpeter notes that the common viewpoint was that of J.S. Mill and even Adam Smith.

> No conceptual creation of the period points toward a new fact or a
> new slant. This may be illustrated by their treatment of competition.
> Their economic world ... was a world of numerous independent
> firms. To a surprising extent they continued to look upon the com-
> petitive case ... as the normal case of reality. Even the owner-managed
> firm survived much better in economic theory than it did in actual
> life.[101]

Schumpeter relates Cournot's conception of competition as starting from the case of straight monopoly, gradually adding more and more sellers, eventually reaching the point where any one seller's product is too small to affect the price or to admit of price strategy.

To this may be added Jevons's Law of Indifference that defined the perfect market as admitting only one price.

The combination of these two Schumpeter takes as the equivalent of

99 Ibid. 963.
100 Ibid. 964.
101 Ibid. 892.

Walras's *libre concurrence*, and Pareto's definition is pronounced as coming to the same thing.

It remains that such definitions pertain to the static viewpoint.

> The mechanism of pure competition is supposed to function through everybody's wish to maximize his net advantage ... by means of attempts at optimal adaptation of the quantities to be bought and sold. But exclude 'strategy' as much as you please, there still remains the fact that this adaptation will produce results that differ according to the range of knowledge, promptness of decision, and 'rationality' of actors, and also according to the expectations they entertain about the future course of prices, not to mention the further fact that their action is subject to additional restrictions that proceed from the situations they have created for themselves by their past decisions.[102]

In other words, the definitions of perfect competition regard the static case, and do not preclude the actual existence of dynamic reality.

Schumpeter distinguishes two viewpoints in this connection.

> If [he argues] we are of the opinion ... that from all the infinite variety of market patterns pure or perfect monopoly and pure or perfect competition stand out by virtue of certain properties – of which the most important is that both cases lend themselves to treatment by means of relatively simple and (in general) uniquely determined rational schemata – and ... that the large majority of cases that occur in practice are nothing but mixtures and hybrids of these two, then it seems natural to accept pure monopoly and pure competition as the two genuine or fundamental patterns and to proceed by investigating how their hybrids work out. This renders the attitude of the theorists of monopolistic or imperfect competition [that is, E.H. Chamberlain and Joan Robinson; Schumpeter, *History*, p. 975; see also pp. 1150–51]. But instead of considering the hybrid cases as deviations from, or adulterations of, the fundamental ones, we may also look upon the hybrids as fundamental and on pure monopoly and

102 Ibid. 973.

pure competition as limiting cases in which the content of actual business behavior has been refined away. This is much more like the line that Marshall took. Should the reader feel that I am laboring to convey a distinction without a difference, he is requested to ask himself whether the definition of pure competition that has been given above really fits what we mean when we speak about competitive business. Is it not a fact that what we mean is the scheme of motives, decisions, and actions imposed upon a business firm by the necessity of doing things better or at any rate more successfully than the fellow next door; that it is *this* situation to which we trace the technological and commercial efficiency of 'competitive' business; and that this pattern of behavior would be entirely absent *both* in the cases of pure monopoly and pure competition, which therefore seem to have more claim to being called degenerate than to being called fundamental cases?[103]

That is, in pure competition the seller has no alternative strategy; in pure monopoly he has no competitors; and so neither gives rise to the necessity of doing things better or at least more successfully than the fellow next door.

Schumpeter's solution is to be noted. Mathematical rigor provides a useful source for preliminary determinations of meaning, and Cournot's account of competition illustrates the point. But the economic issue arises in an ecology in which abstract relationships are complemented by concrete probabilities.[104] And it is in accord with this reality for Schumpeter to appeal to what we mean by the technological and commercial efficiency of 'competitive business.' We shall adopt a similar procedure in treating the parallel topic of equilibrium.

In a famous paper that was destined to produce the English branch of the theory of imperfect competition, Piero Sraffa[105] pointed out that [to quote Schumpeter] '*under conditions of pure competition*, a firm cannot be in *perfect* equilibrium so long as increase in its output would be attended by

---

103 Ibid. 975.

104 For Lonergan's account of this complementarity, see *Insight* 46–53/70–76, 86–97/109–20, 103–29/126–51.

105 Piero Sraffa, 'The Laws of Returns under Competitive Conditions,' *The Economic Journal* 36 (1926) 535–50, in the December issue.

internal economies.'[106] Clearly there is some connection between pure competition and perfect equilibrium, and its precise nature we shall attempt to approach through Schumpeter's presentation of Léon Walras's system.

> From the workshop of Walras the static theory of the economic universe emerged in the form of a large number of quantitative relations (equations) between economic elements or variables (prices and quantities of consumable and productive goods or services) that were conceived as simultaneously determining one another ... as soon as this Magna Charta of exact economics had been written ... a type of research began to impose itself that had been unknown in pre-Walrasian economics ... The Walrasian system of simultaneous equations ... brought in a host of new problems of a specifically logical or mathematical nature that are much more delicate and go much deeper than Walras or anyone else had ever realized ... They are much too difficult and especially too technical for us.[107]

After expounding the past and future determinants that affect a decision to buy or sell, Schumpeter notes:

> Walras was very much alive to these difficulties and in places ... he clearly saw the necessity looming in the future of constructing dynamic schemata to take account of them. For himself, however, he saw not less clearly that, absorbed in the pioneer task of working out the essentials of the mathematical theory of the economic process, he had no choice but to simplify heroically.[108]
>
> In this section we shall analyze the logical structure of Walras's system of the conditions or relations (equations) that are to determine the equilibrium values of all the economic variables, to wit: the prices of all products and factors and the quantities of these products and factors that would be bought, in perfect equilibrium and pure competition, by all the households and firms. Let us notice at once that, since the determination of these quantities implies the determina-

106 Schumpeter, *History* 1047.
107 Ibid. 967–68.
108 Ibid. 973–74.

tion of individual as well as group and social incomes, this theory also includes all that is covered by the concept of Income Analysis and that the conditions or relations to be considered, though they are fundamentally microanalytic in nature (they refer fundamentally to the quantities bought and sold by individual households and firms), also include macroanalytic aspects, for example, as regards total employment in the society. It cannot be too strongly impressed upon the reader that it is not correct to contrast income or macroanalysis of, say, the Keynesian type with the Walrasian microanalysis as if the latter were a theory that neglects, and stands in need of being supplemented by, income and macroanalysis.[109]

Finally, the task of developing a dynamic theory is very difficult and cannot be accomplished simply by adding dynamic qualifications to static theory. It requires new techniques and raises fundamental problems of its own. An example of the new techniques required is the theory of difference equations. An example of the new fundamental problems is economic equilibrium, which, if considered from a dynamic standpoint, appears in a new light.[110]

In brief, Walras's system is conceived on a static basis. Its author was aware that dynamic considerations will have to be dealt with. But he persevered in the line he had begun: at least, it would mark a turning point in the development of economic thought.

Schumpeter, though he seems everywhere to regard Walras with the highest esteem, wrote in a summary of the lectures he was to deliver at the University of Mexico of the need for new techniques and of the new viewpoint on equilibrium needed if a dynamic general theory were to be attained.

22   The Position of This Essay

[1980] While we agree with Schumpeter that Walras's system implicitly includes the aggregates commonly considered in macroanalysis, it can hardly be credited with distinctions between basic and surplus expenditure, receipts, outlay, income, and much less with an account of their various dynamic relations. But until such distinctions are drawn and their

109 Ibid. 998–99.
110 Ibid. 1143.

dynamic significance understood, the aggregates and relations cannot be contained implicitly in any system.[111]

Further, without further clarification Schumpeter acknowledged that dynamic analysis called for new light on equilibrium. Such new light arises when, over and above the equilibria of supply and demand with respect to goods and services, there are recognized further equilibria that have to be maintained if an economy chooses to remain in a stationary state, to embark on a long-term expansion, to distribute its benefits to the vast majority of its members, and so to return to a more affluent stationary state until such time as further expansion beckons.

Moreover, such macroequilibria are more fundamental than the microequilibria assembled by Walras. The former are the conditions of a properly functioning economy. In the measure such conditions are met, there result aggregates acceptable to the economic society in its entirety, while the Walrasian equilibria are confined to the distribution of receipts among producers and income among householders.

The existence of such prior and more fundamental equilibria does to some extent explain the extreme difficulty noted by Schumpeter in accounting for the determinateness, the equilibrium, and the stability of the Walrasian system since that system had overlooked such factors.[112] But there is a more radical difficulty. The period from 1870 to 1914 and later was still under the spell of classical mechanics with its ideal of exact prediction and with the complementary notion that probability was no more than a cloak for ignorance.[113] But for us quantum theory has made it possible to grasp that classical laws are abstract inasmuch as they hold only *caeteris paribus*, and that statistical laws provide a natural complement since they can reveal how often other things are likely to be equal. In a universe such as ours, with its vast numbers and its enormous time intervals, one is led to think of schemes of recurrence, whose several carriers severally follow their

111 'Contained implicitly' frequently evokes the connotation suggested by Kant's idea of an analytic a priori judgment; for example, that the predicate 'unmarried male' is 'contained implicitly' in the subject term 'bachelor.' For Lonergan, however, the phrase seems to refer to a development of understanding (and of ensuing formulations) where further insights are added to explanatory principles. See for example the case of 'concrete inferences,' *Insight* 46–47/70–71, 491–93/515–17.

112 See Schumpeter, *History* 967–68.

113 See *Insight* 53/76.

own classical laws, whose assembly follows the probability of their emergence, and whose continued functioning follows the probability of their survival. Such in a nutshell is the evolutionary view that in *Insight* I sketched out under the name of emergent probability and, earlier in this essay, I have applied to economics.[114]

For a human society, like an ecology, is an assembly of assemblies of schemes of recurrence. As interdependent they support one another. As subordinate they underpin higher orders of schemes. As higher they bring to fuller fruition their subordinates. Every scheme has had its probability of emergence, and it will last in accord with its probability of survival. How it all came about is more than we can fathom, and so with Adam Smith we may speak briefly of an invisible hand.

One set of such social schemes is the economy, the myriad interlocking recurrences of activities within and between firms, between firms and households, and within households. Each of the schemes is a possibility that occurred to someone at some point of ancient or recent human history, that has been combined with other schemes in proposed possibilities, that has been chosen with greater or less probability and maintained with greater or less deliberate choice, and any set of combinations that has existed has functioned with greater or less success for a longer or shorter period of time. In brief, an economy is just part of ongoing human history. Within that process we are born and raised. By our common sense[115] we find our place in it and work out for ourselves our sad or happy lives and thereby make sadder or happier the lives of others.

Any deeper understanding of this process is not to be ushered in solely by the techniques of mathematicians defining new variables, determining their interrelations, and establishing their 'existence.' For while it is necessary to grasp the mathematical foundations of mathematical analogies employed, it is equally necessary and more important to attend to the reality from which the analogy prescinds. That reality is human history, and it is a cord woven with three strands. The first is progress, which is the fruit of

---

114 See *Insight*, index: Recurrence, schemes of; Classical and statistical laws; Classical laws; Statistical laws; Emergent probability. There is an explicit mention of the application of emergent probability to economics in Lonergan's Preface above, which Lonergan wrote for the same 1980 version in which the present text appears for the first time.

115 *Insight* 173–81/196–204.

attention, intelligence, reasonableness, and responsibility. The second is decline, the offspring of inattention, obtuseness, unreasonableness, and irresponsibility. The third is the usually slow and long process of recovery: of removing the absurdities inflicted on the human situation by past inattention, obtuseness, unreasonableness, and irresponsibility.

Elsewhere I have distinguished between the shorter and the longer cycles of decline. The shorter cycle results from group bias, the egoism of a group that approves its own attitudes and consequent deeds. Naturally it awakens the resentment, the opposition, the hostility of other groups, and thereby creates a force for its own demise. The longer cycle results from general bias, that is, the general tendency to be content with the particular specialty, common sense, and to consider other specialties irrelevant or useless. As group bias, so too general bias awakens opposition. But the opposition is that of learned minorities, and they, when no longer simply ignored, can be put out of court by massive appeals to the masses.[116]

Now just as sustained attentiveness, insight, reasonableness, and responsibility create a situation ever more in consonance with intelligent advance and ever more responsive to it, so too every bias away from human authenticity brings about a situation ever more inhuman and intractable. It is up to man to be intelligent, act intelligently, and make his situation intelligible. On the other hand, insensitivity, oversights, the blindness of passion, the flimsy excuse, the plausible fallacy, the distortion of compromise, the waywardness of indulgence, all create a human world made in their own image and likeness.

Such is the dialectic of decline. Spontaneously it keeps making things ever worse. But reflection gives it the seven devils worse than itself. For it gives evil the status of fact. That is the way that things are, the way that things are done, the only way that one can live, indeed the way that all successful and respectable people live. One can swim against the current for a while but sooner or later one gives up. One may start to roll a rock up a mountain side, but who gets to the top and keeps the rock from rolling back again?

Now it is important to grasp that we are touching upon a very large issue. In its *fundamental* form it is the tension of liberty between grace and sin (Romans 7 and 8). In its *theological* form it is the thought of Augustine and of his commentators and continuators: I refer you to my study of Aquinas,

116 Ibid. 222–38/247–63.

Grace and Freedom.[117] In its *secularist* form it is the affirmation of the perfectibility of man by man: Leo Strauss conceives three of its waves as stemming from Machiavelli, Rousseau, and Nietzsche.[118] Economists move under this secularist mantle when they conceive economics on the analogy of natural science or, when that fails, hand the management of the economy over to the welfare state. Popular thought easily accepts secularism by its insistence that solutions to problems are sound if they obviously will work. But this, of course, is merely an unconscious shift back to Machiavelli: like him they are concerned with the factual, practical truth and not with fancies; like him they have no taste for imagined commonwealths and principalities which never were, because they look at how men in fact do live and not at such stuff as how men ought to live.[119]

Now I have been looking at the dynamic structure of the industrial exchange economy. In it I have distinguished stationary states, the increasing returns that arise when an economy is tooling up for increased production but as yet is not thereby increasing living standards, and the decreasing returns that arise for investors when tooling up is tapering off and the flow of consumer goods and services in increasing.

I beg to note that such an analysis has not been tried and found wanting. Rather, to speak with Chesterton, it has been thought hard and not tried.[120] What has been tried is roughly as follows: (1) the emergence of industrial nations as creditors and others as debtors, (2) the establishment of colonies and empires, their rivalries and wars, (3) the rise of the archsecularist Marx, the industrial development of the U.S.S.R., its diplomatic and warlike achievements, and the moral support it enjoys from secularists elsewhere, (4) the welfare state with its substitutes for a properly function-

---

117 Bernard Lonergan, *Grace and Freedom: Operative Grace in the Thought of St Thomas Aquinas*, ed. J. Patout Burns (London: Darton, Longman & Todd; New York: Herder and Herder, 1971 [CWL 1]).

118 Leo Strauss, 'The Three Waves of Modernity,' in *Political Philosophy: Six Essays by Leo Strauss*, ed. Hilail Gildin (Indianapolis and New York: Bobbs-Merrill, Inc./Pegasus, 1975) 81–98, with bibliography of Strauss's writings on pp. 239–47.

119 See ibid. 84.

120 'The Christian ideal has not been tried and found wanting. It has been found difficult; and left untried.' G.K. Chesterton, *What's Wrong with the World* (New York: Sheed & Ward, 1956) 29 (in 'The Unfinished Temple' 27–32).

ing basic phase and with its crumbling foundations in economic science, [and] (5) the multinational corporations, their flourishing but offshore economy, and the dual economies[121] they effect not only in the underdeveloped countries but also in the United States.

121 'Dual economy' is a phenomenon discussed by Richard J. Barnet and Ronald G. Müller in *Global Reach: The Power of the Multinational Corporations* (New York: Simon & Schuster, 1974) 256, where the authors credit Robert T. Averitt (*The Dynamics of the American Industrial Structure* [New York: Norton, 1968]) for coining the term. It distinguishes a 'center' economy or the few hundred firms controlling 'over 60 percent of the productive and financial resources of the country' and employing 'the bulk of organized labor'; and a 'periphery' economy 'made up of thousands of smaller firms dependent on the giants for their survival, and whose workers do not normally belong to unions.'

    'Offshore markets,' also discussed passim by Barnet and Müller, has to do with global corporations' dependence upon the raw materials and cheap labor of underdeveloped countries exploited as 'export platforms' in a strategy for worldwide profit. See especially ibid., 'Engines of Development,' pp. 148–84.

PART TWO

Healing and Creating in History

The topic assigned me reads: Healing and Creating in History.

What precisely it means, or even what it might mean, does not seem to be obvious at first glance. An initial clarification appears to be in order.

We have to do with healing and creating *in history*. But no particular kind of history is specified, and so we are not confined to religious or cultural or social or political or economic or technological history. Again, no people or country is mentioned, neither Babylonians nor Egyptians, Greeks nor Romans, Asians nor Africans, Europeans nor Americans. It would seem, then, that we have to do with healing and creating in human affairs. For human affairs are the stuff of history, and they merit the attention of the historian when they are taken in a relatively large context and prove their significance by their relatively durable effects.

Now if 'history' may be taken broadly to mean human affairs, it is not too difficult to obtain at least a preliminary notion of what is meant by the other two terms in our title, 'healing' and 'creating.' For there comes to hand a paper by Sir Karl Popper entitled 'The History of Our Time: An Optimist's View.'[122] In it he opposes two different accounts of what is wrong with the world. On the one hand, there is the view he attributes to many quite sincere churchmen and, along with them, to the rationalist philosopher Bertrand Russell. It is to the effect that our intellectual development has outrun our moral development. He writes:

122 Karl Popper, *Conjectures and Refutations: The Growth of Scientific Knowledge* (New York: Harper Torchbooks, 1968; first published, 1962) 364–76.

We have become very clever, according to Russell, indeed too clever.
We can make lots of wonderful gadgets, including television, high-
speed rockets, and an atom bomb, or a thermonuclear bomb, if you
prefer. But we have not been able to achieve that moral and political
growth and maturity which alone could safely direct and control
the uses to which we put our tremendous intellectual powers. This
is why we now find ourselves in mortal danger. Our evil national
pride has prevented us from achieving the world-state in time.

To put this view in a nutshell: we are clever, perhaps too clever, but
we also are wicked; and this mixture of cleverness and wickedness
lies at the root of our troubles.[123]

In contrast, Sir Karl Popper would argue that we are good, perhaps a little
too good, but we are also a little stupid; and it is this mixture of goodness
and stupidity that lies at the root of our troubles. After avowing that he
included himself among those he considered a little stupid, Sir Karl put his
point in the following terms:

The main troubles of our time – and I do not deny that we live in
troubled times – are not due to our moral wickedness, but, on the
contrary, to our often misguided moral enthusiasm: to our anxiety
to better the world we live in. Our wars are fundamentally religious wars; they are wars between competing theories of how to
establish a better world. And our moral enthusiasm is often misguided, because we fail to realize that our moral principles, which
are sure to be over-simple, are often difficult to apply to the complex human and political situations to which we feel bound to
apply them.[124]

In upholding this contention Sir Karl was quite ready to descend to particular instances. He granted the wickedness of Hitler and Stalin. He
acknowledged that they appealed to all sorts of hopes and fears, to preju-
dices and envy, and even to hatred. But he insisted that their main appeal
was an appeal to a kind of morality. They had a message; and they
demanded sacrifices. He regretted that an appeal to morality could be mis-

123 Ibid. 365.
124 Ibid. 366.

used. But he saw it as a fact that the great dictators were always trying to convince their people that they knew a way to a higher morality.

Now one may agree with Lord Russell. One may agree with Sir Karl. Indeed, there is no difficulty in agreeing with both, for the Christian tradition lists among the effects of original sin both a darkening of intellect and a weakening of will. But whatever one's opinion, it remains that there is a profound difference between diagnosing a malady and proposing a cure. Whether one stresses with Lord Russell the conjunction of clever but wicked or with Sir Karl the conjunction of good but stupid, one gets no further than diagnosis. On the other hand, when one speaks of healing and creating, one refers to positive courses of action. To this positive aspect of the issue, we now must turn.

The creating in question is not creating out of nothing. Such creating is the divine prerogative. Man's creating is of a different order. Actually, it does not bring something out of nothing, but it may seem to do so. William James, the American psychologist and philosopher, has described three stages in the career of a theory. First, '... it is attacked as absurd; then it is admitted to be true, but obvious and insignificant; finally it is seen to be so important that its adversaries claim that they themselves discovered it.'[125] Such a theory is creative.

Let me illustrate this need for human creating from the contemporary economic situation. Last year there was published a thick volume by Richard Barnet and Ronald Müller with the title *Global Reach* and the subtitle *The Power of the Multinational Corporations*. Its thirteen chapters fell into three parts. The first set forth the aims of the multinational corporations: they propose to run the world, for they can do the job and our little national governments are not equipped to do so. The second set of chapters delineated what the multinational corporations were doing to the underdeveloped countries: they have been making them more hopelessly worse off than otherwise they would be. The third set, finally, asked what these corporations, which in the main are American, have been doing to the United States; the answer is that they are treating the States in the same way they are treating the underdeveloped countries, and in the long run the effects will be the same as in the rest of the world.

Now, if the multinational corporations are generating worldwide disas-

125 William James, *Pragmatism* (London: Longmans, 1912) 198. Quoted by Louis Mink, *Mind, History, and Dialectic: The Philosophy of R.G. Collingwood* (Bloomington/London: Indiana University Press, 1969) 255.

ter, why are they permitted to do so? The trouble is that there is nothing really new about multinational corporations. They aim at maximizing profit, and that has been the aim of economic enterprise since the mercantile, the industrial, the financial revolutions ever more fully and thoroughly took charge of our affairs. The alternative to making a profit is bankruptcy. The alternative to maximizing profit is inefficiency.[126] All that the multinational corporation does is maximize profit not in some town or city, not in some region or country, but on the global scale. It buys labor and materials in the countries where they are cheapest. Its credit is unimpeachable, and so it can secure all the money it wants from whatever banks or money markets are in a position to create it. Its marketing facilities are a global network, and to compete one would have first to build up a global network of one's own. The multinational corporation is a going concern. It is ever growing and expanding. It is built on the very principles that slowly but surely have been molding our technology and our economics, our society and our culture, our ideals and our practice for centuries. It remains that the long-accepted principles are inadequate. They suffer from radical oversights. Their rigorous application on a global scale, according to Barnet and Müller, heads us for disaster. But as the authors also confess: 'The new system needed for our collective survival does not exist.'[127] When survival requires a system that does not exist, then the need for creating is manifest.

While it can take a series of disasters to convince people of the need for creating, still the long, hard, uphill climb is the creative process itself. In retrospect this process may appear as a grand strategy that unfolds in an orderly and cumulative series of steps. But any retrospect has the advantage of knowing the answers. The creative task is to find the answers. It is a matter of insight, not of one insight but of many, not of isolated insights but of insights that coalesce, that complement and correct one another, that influence policies and programs, that reveal their shortcomings in their concrete results, that give rise to further correcting insights, corrected policies, corrected programs, that gradually accumulate into the all-round, balanced, smoothly functioning system that from the start was needed but at the start was not yet known.

126 Where, of course, inefficiency means by definition the failure to maximize profit.

127 Barnet and Müller, *Global Reach: The Power of the Multinational Corporations* (see above, note 121) 385.

This creative process is nothing mysterious. It has been described by Jane Jacobs in her *The Economy of Cities*,[128] as repeatedly finding new uses for existing resources. It has been set forth in the grand style by Arnold Toynbee under the rubric of 'Challenge and Response' in his *A Study of History*, where the flow of fresh insights takes its rise from a creative minority, and the success of their implementation wins the devoted allegiance of the rank and file.[129]

I have spoken of insights, and I had best add what I do not mean. An insight is not just a slogan, and an ongoing accumulation of insights is not just an advertising campaign. A creative process is a learning process. It is learning what hitherto was not known. It is just the opposite of the mental coma induced by the fables and jingles that unceasingly interrupt television programs in our native land and even in the great republic to the south of us.

Again, insights are one thing, and concepts are quite another. Concepts are ambiguous. They may be heuristic, but then they merely point to unspecified possibilities, as highly desirable as justice, liberty, equality, peace – but still just empty gestures that fail to reveal how the possibilities might be realized and what the realization concretely would entail. Again, concepts may be specific, but then they are definite, rounded off, finished, abstract. Like textbooks on moral theology they can name all the evils to be avoided but get no further than unhelpful platitudes on the good to be achieved. For the good is never an abstraction. Always it is concrete.[130] The whole point to the process of cumulative insight is that each insight regards the concrete while the cumulative process heads towards an ever fuller and more adequate view. Add abstraction to abstraction and one never reaches more than a heap of abstractions. But add insight to insight and one moves to mastery of all the eventualities and complications of a concrete situation.

The creative process culminates in system, but the system is only system on the move. It never reaches static system that comes into existence and remains forever after. So it is that, when the flow of fresh insights dries up,

128 Jane Jacobs, *The Economy of Cities* (New York: Random House, Vintage Books, 1970; first published, 1969).

129 For an incomplete list of the critiques of Toynbee's *A Study of History*, see that work, vol. 12: *Reconsiderations* (London/New York: Oxford University Press, 1961) 680–90. With *Reconsiderations* available, the critics are far less impressive.

130 As the Scholastics put it: *Bonum ex integra causa, malum ex quocumque defectu.*

when challenges continue and responses fail to emerge, then the creative minority becomes the merely dominant minority and the eagerness of the rank and file, that exulted in success, turns into the sullenness of an internal proletariat frustrated and disgusted by the discovery that a country in which, more and more, everything had worked has become a country in which, more and more, nothing works. Such is the disenchantment that, to use Toynbee's terms, brings to an end the genesis of a civilization and introduces first its breakdowns and eventually its disintegration.

But, one may ask, why does the flow of fresh insights dry up? Why, if challenges continue, do responses fail? Why does a minority that was creative cease to be creative and become merely dominant?

There are many intermediate answers that correspond to the many and varied circumstances under which civilizations break down. But there is one ultimate answer that rests on the intrinsic limitations of insight itself. For insights can be implemented only if people have open minds. Problems can be manifest. Insights that solve them may be available. But the insights will not be grasped and implemented by biased minds. There is the bias of the neurotic fertile in evasions of the insight his analyst sees he needs. There is the bias of the individual egoist, whose interest is confined to the insights that would enable him to exploit each new situation to his own personal advantage. There is the bias of group egoism blind to the fact that the group no longer fulfills its once useful function and that it is merely clinging to power by all the maneuvers that in one way or another block development and impede progress. There is finally the general bias of all 'good' men of common sense, cherishing the illusion that their single talent, common sense, is omnicompetent, insisting on procedures that no longer work, convinced that the only way to do things is to muddle through, and spurning as idle theorizing and empty verbiage any rational account of what has to be done.[131]

Not only is there this fourfold exclusion of fresh insights by the neurotic, by the bias of individual and, worse, of group egoism, and by the illusory omnicompetence of common sense. There also is the distorting effect of all such bias on the whole process of growth. Growth, progress, is a matter of situations yielding insights, insights yielding policies and projects, policies and projects transforming the initial situation, and the transformed sit-

131 I have written at greater length on bias in *Insight* 191–206/214–31, 218–42/ 244–67, 627–33/650–56, 688–93/710–15. In the Hegelian-Marxist tradition bias is treated obliquely under the name of alienation.

uation giving rise to further insights that correct and complement the deficiencies of previous insights. So the wheel of progress moves forward through the successive transformations of an initial situation in which are gathered coherently and cumulatively all the insights that occurred along the way. But this wheel of progress becomes a wheel of decline when the process is distorted by bias. Increasingly the situation becomes, not the cumulative product of coherent and complementary insights, but the dump in which are heaped up the amorphous and incompatible products of all the biases of self-centered and shortsighted individuals and groups. Finally, the more the objective situation becomes a mere dump, the less is there any possibility of human intelligence gathering from the situation anything more than a lengthy catalogue of the aberrations and the follies of the past. As a diagnosis of terminal cancer denies any prospect of health restored, so a social dump is the end of fruitful insight and of the cumulative development it can generate.

I have spoken of creating in history and of its nemesis. But my topic also calls for a few words on healing. In fact, the genesis and breakdown of civilization occupy only the first six of the ten volumes Toynbee devoted to his *A Study of History*. In the last four there emerges a new factor, for out of the frustration and disgust of the internal proletariat there come the world religions and a new style of human development.

For human development is of two quite different kinds. There is development from below upwards, from experience to growing understanding, from growing understanding to balanced judgment, from balanced judgment to fruitful courses of action, and from fruitful courses of action to the new situations that call forth further understanding, profounder judgment, richer courses of action.

But there also is development from above downwards. There is the transformation of falling in love: the domestic love of the family; the human love of one's tribe, one's city, one's country, mankind; the divine love that orientates man in his cosmos and expresses itself in his worship. Where hatred only sees evil, love reveals values. At once it commands commitment and joyfully carries it out, no matter what the sacrifice involved. Where hatred reinforces bias, love dissolves it, whether it be the bias of unconscious motivation, the bias of individual or group egoism, or the bias of omnicompetent, shortsighted common sense. Where hatred plods around in ever narrower vicious circles, love breaks the bonds of psychological and social determinisms with the conviction of faith and the power of hope.

What I have attributed to love and denied to hatred, must also be denied to any ambiguous and so deceptive mixture of love and hatred. If in no other way at least from experience we have learned that professions of zeal for the eternal salvation of souls do not make the persecution of heretics a means for the reconciliation of heretics. On the contrary, persecution leads to ongoing enmity and in the limit to wars of religion. In like manner wars of religion have not vindicated religion; they have given color to a secularism that in the English-speaking world regards revealed religion as a merely private affair and in continental Europe thinks it an evil.

Again, while secularism has succeeded in making religion a marginal factor in human affairs, it has not succeeded in inventing a vaccine or providing some other antidote for hatred. For secularism is a philosophy, and, no less than religion, it may lay claim to absolutes of its own. In their name hatred can shift from the religious group to the social class. So the professions of tolerance of the eighteenth-century Enlightenment did not save from the guillotine the feudal nobility of France, and the Marxist march of history in Russia has attended to the liquidation not merely of the bourgeoisie but also of the Romanovs, the landowners, and the kulaks.[132]

As healing can have no truck with hatred, so too it can have no truck with materialism. For the healer is essentially a reformer: first and foremost he counts on what is best in man. But the materialist is condemned by his own principles to be no more than a manipulator. He will apply to human beings the stick-and-carrot treatment that the Harvard behaviorist B.F. Skinner advocates under the name of reinforcement. He will maintain with Marx that cultural attitudes are the byproduct of material conditions, and so he will bestow upon those subjected to communist power the salutary conditions of a closed frontier, clear and firm indoctrination, controlled media of information, a vigilant secret police, and the terrifying threat of the labor camps. Again, while Christians accord to God's grace the principal role in touching men's hearts and enlightening their minds, it would seem that the true believer in the gospel according to Marx must be immersed in proletarian living conditions, on the ground that only such

132   For background see the penetrating analysis by Christopher Dawson, 'Karl Marx and the Dialectic of History,' in *The Dynamics of World History*, ed. John J. Mulloy (London and New York: Sheed & Ward, 1957) 354–65. The chapter appeared originally in Dawson's *Religion and the Modern State* (London and New York: Sheed & Ward, 1935).

material conditions can confer upon him the right thinking and righteous feeling proper to proletarian class consciousness.[133]

Healing, then, is not to be confused with the dominating and manipulating to which the reforming materialist is confined by his own principles. It has to be kept apart from religious hatred of heretical sects and from philosophic hatred of social classes.[134] But besides these requirements, intrinsic to the nature of healing, there is the extrinsic requirement of a concomitant creative process. For just as the creative process, when unaccompanied by healing, is distorted and corrupted by bias, so too the healing process, when unaccompanied by creating, is a soul without a body. Christianity developed and spread within the ancient empire of Rome. It possessed the spiritual power to heal what was unsound in that imperial domain. But it was unaccompanied by its natural complement of creating, for a single development has two vectors: one from below upwards, creating; the other from above downwards, healing. So when the Roman empire decayed and disintegrated, the church indeed lived on. But it lived on, not in a civilized world, but in a dark and barbarous age in which, as a contemporary reported, men devoured one another as fishes in the sea.

If we are to escape a similar fate, we must demand that two requirements are met. The first regards economic theorists; the second regards moral theorists. From economic theorists we have to demand, along with as many other types of analysis as they please, a new and specific type that reveals how moral precepts have both a basis in economic process and so an effective application to it. From moral theorists we have to demand, along with their other various forms of wisdom and prudence, specifically economic precepts that arise out of economic process itself and promote its proper functioning.

To put the same points in negative terms, when physicists can think on the basis of indeterminacy, economists can think on the basis of freedom

133 For Marx, morality is relative to social class. As Dawson trenchantly put it: 'Hence it would seem that the only real immorality is to betray the interests of one's own class, and that a man like Karl Marx himself, or F. Engels, who serves the interests of another class even if it be the class of the future, is no social hero, but an apostate and a traitor. He has become a bad bourgeois but he can never become a good proletarian unless he is economically and sociologically absorbed into the proleteriat.' 'Karl Marx and the Dialectic of History' 362–63.

134 Of course, though racism and nationalism are prephilosophic, they can be imagined as absolutes and generate abundant hatred.

and acknowledge the relevance of morality. Again, when the system that is needed for our collective survival does not exist, then it is futile to excoriate what does exist while blissfully ignoring the task of constructing a technically viable economic system that can be put in its place.[135]

Is my proposal utopian? It asks merely for creativity, for an interdisciplinary theory that at first will be denounced as absurd, then will be admitted to be true but obvious and insignificant, and perhaps finally be regarded as so important that its adversaries will claim that they themselves discovered it.

135 Moral precepts that are not technically specific turn out to be quite ineffectual, as Christian Duquoc has pointed out in his *Ambiguité des théologies de la sécularisation: Essai critique* (Gembloux: Duculot, 1972). See his remark on *The Secular City* by Harvey Cox on p. 67; also pp. 103–12 and 113–28 on the Pastoral Constitution of the Second Vatican Council, *Gaudium et Spes*.

PART THREE[136]

23 Measuring Change in the Productive Process (II)[137]

[1944] The problem of the present section may be put as follows. Consider two successive and equal intervals of time, long enough to be representative, yet not so long that much averaging is required. Suppose that in the first of the two intervals, objects of a class i were sold in the quantity q_i and at an average price p_i, and [that] in the second interval objects in the same class were sold in the quantity $q_i + dq_i$ and at the average price $p_i + dp_i$. Suppose, further, that there are n such classes, that the aggregate payment

136 As a result of the revisions Lonergan made between 1978 and 1980, over eighty pages of the 1944 version of the *Essay* were deleted (see Editors' Preface). Many of these pages contained details and elaborations, both mathematical and prosaic, that constitute 'models' of certain features of the analysis treated in the previous sections. That is to say, certain assumptions are introduced, and the implications worked out, for such phenomena as the interrelations of surplus and basic expansions, the pure cycle, the cycles of various rates of payments, and superposed cycles. In many cases these models, though less general than the preceding analysis, assist in communicating the broad implications Lonergan envisioned for his analysis. For that reason, most of the deleted material has been restored here in order to make public those implications. Notation has been altered to conform with Lonergan's final usage.

137 This section appears in the 1944 version as 'The Theoretical Possibility of Measurement of the Productive Process.' The first paragraph of the section has already been incorporated into the present edition, at the beginning of §17.

for them in the first interval was Z and in the second interval was $Z + DZ$,[138] so that

$$Z = \Sigma \, p_i q_i \tag{13}$$

$$Z + DZ = \Sigma \, (p_i q_i + p_i dq_i + q_i dp_i + dp_i dq_i) \tag{14}$$

where all summations are taken with respect to all instances of i from 1 to n. The question is, How much does the increment in the rate of payment DZ result from price increments dp_i, and how much does it result from quantity increments dq_i? In other words, can one define two numbers, say P and Q, such that P varies with a set of numbers p_1, p_2, p_3, ... and Q varies with another set of numbers q_1, q_2, q_3, ... ?[139]

A universally valid answer to this question may be had when P and Q are not mere numbers but vectors in an n-dimensional manifold. Let $\mathbf{P}$ and $\mathbf{Q}$ be the vectors from the origin to the points $(p_1, p_2, p_3, ...)$ and $(q_1, q_2, q_3, ...)$, respectively. Then any variation in the price pattern, that is, in any ratio of the type p_i/p_j, will appear as a variation in the angle between the projection of $\mathbf{P}$ on the plane ij and the axis j. Similarly, any variation in the quantity pattern will appear as a parallel variation in an angle made by a projection of $\mathbf{Q}$. But besides such variation in price pattern or in quantity pattern there may be general increases or decreases in prices or in quantities. The latter appear as positive or negative increments in the absolute magnitudes of the vectors, for

$$P^2 = \Sigma \, p_i^2 \tag{15}$$

$$Q^2 = \Sigma \, q_i^2 \tag{16}$$

that is, the length of the vector $\mathbf{P}$ is the square root of the sum of all prices squared, and the length of the vector $\mathbf{Q}$ is the square root of the sum of all quantities squared. Thus one may suppose two n-dimensional spheres of

138 This expression and those that follow have been altered in accordance with the convention stated in note 29. In the 1944 version, Lonergan wrote $DZ + D^2 Z$.

139 This sentence and the paragraph that follows have also been inserted into §17 for the sake of clarity. They are repeated here as they appear in their original 1944 context.

radii P and Q, respectively. The vector from the origin to any point in the first 'quadrant' of the surface of such spheres represents a determinate price pattern or quantity pattern. On the other hand, variation in P and Q is variation in the size of the spheres.

Now there is a well-known theorem, called the dot product, which enables us to equate Z with P and Q, whence

$$Z = \Sigma \, p_i q_i = PQ \cos A \tag{17}$$

where A is the angle between the vectors P and Q. Thus variation in Z depends not only on the magnitude of P and Q but also on the price and quantity patterns as represented by the angle A between the vectors. This is evident enough, since it makes a notable difference in Z whether large or small instances of p_i combine with large or small instances of q_i, and such combination is ruled by the relative price and quantity patterns, to appear ultimately in the angle A.

Next, consider the second interval in which the vector P increases to $(P + dP)$, the vector Q to $(Q + dQ)$, and the angle A to $(A + dA)$. Then

$$(P + dP)^2 = \Sigma \, (p_i + dp_i)^2 \tag{18}$$

$$(Q + dQ)^2 = \Sigma \, (q_i + dq_i)^2 \tag{19}$$

$$Z + DZ = (P + dP)(Q + dQ) \cos(A + dA) \tag{20}$$

From equations (17) and (20) one obtains for DZ the expression

$$DZ = PQ[(dP/P + dQ/Q + dPdQ/PQ) \cos(A + dA) \\ - 2 \sin(dA/2) \sin(A + dA/2)].^{140} \tag{21}$$

Thus DZ depends not only on the initial quantities P, Q, A, and the increments in absolute magnitude dP and dQ, but also upon changes in the relative price and quantity patterns as represented by the angle dA.

From equations (15) to (17) it can be shown that if all prices and all quantities change in the same proportion, then there is no change in cos A, so that the angle dA is zero. Further, dA is again zero whenever there is

140 This equation has been altered; in the 1944 version Lonergan wrote
$D^2 Z = PQ[dP/P + dQ/Q + dQ/PQ) \cos(A + dA) - (\sin A \sin dA/2)/(dA/2)]$.

compensation for deviation of change from the same proportion, inasmuch as some prices or quantities change more and others less than a strictly proportionate change would require. But whenever dA is zero or very small one may write

$$DZ = PQ[(dP/P + dQ/Q + dPdQ/PQ) \cos A]\text{[141]} \tag{22}$$

so that the increment DZ then depends solely on the increments dP and dQ and the initial quantities P, Q, A.

Now the significance of the foregoing is purely theoretical. The question has been about the possibility of price and quantity indices. The only relevant common measure of tons of iron ore, ton-miles of transportation, kilowatt-hours, and so on, lies in their prices; but prices themselves are subject to change; hence if it is possible to measure the acceleration of the productive process, it has to be possible to differentiate between price variation, price pattern and quantity pattern variation, and the pure quantity variation of the productive process. The foregoing discussion has aimed at showing that, without ever lapsing into meaninglessness, it is always possible to make such distinctions.

However, the definitions that have been given are rather elaborate. When change is gradual, it will be sufficient to use the following approximate definitions of P, Q, dP, and dQ, namely,

$$PQ = \Sigma\, p_i q_i \tag{23}$$

$$PdQ = \Sigma\, p_i dq_i \tag{24}$$

$$QdP = \Sigma\, q_i dp_i \tag{25}$$

$$dPdQ = \Sigma\, dp_i dq_i \tag{26}$$

so that

$$DZ = PQ(dP/P + dQ/Q + dPdQ/PQ) \tag{27}$$

as results by referring back to equations (13) and (14) which pertain to the

141 This equation has been altered; in the 1944 version Lonergan wrote
$D^2Z = PQ[(dP/P + dQ/Q + dPdQ/PQ) \cos A - \sin A]$.

statement of the problem. On this definition one obtains different values for P and Q, and they may be termed 'weighted averages' as opposed to the previous 'vectorial averages.' The difference is most apparent in the respective equations for DZ: equations (21) and (22) contain all the relations of equation (27) but add to the latter a qualification by introducing a trigonometric function of the angle A.

The greater simplicity of the weighted averages is not without its drawbacks. Equations (23) to (26) have to be taken simultaneously; to be taken simultaneously they must be consistent; it follows that as the four left-hand-side expressions are in a fourfold proportion $(PQ/PdQ = QdP/dQdP)$, so also, for consistency, the four right-hand summations must be in a fourfold proportion. This condition obviously restricts the validity of the definition by weighted averages: in the rare cases when the summations are proportionate, the definition is exact; when the summations are approximately proportionate, the definition is no more than an approximation; when the summations are not even approximately proportionate, the definition involves a contradiction and so is meaningless.

Naturally, a theorist is ill at ease when dealing with objects whose definition can lapse into meaninglessness and usually is at best approximate, especially when there is no saying what it approximates to. On that account one may well prefer to regard equation (27) as an alternative expression for equation (22): both of these equations have parallel variables (DZ, dP, dQ), though the latter adds a further initial quantity, A, to P and Q; apart from the additional initial quantity of (22), both relate variables and initial quantities in the same way; both are in the general case approximations; and both have parallel conditions of approximation, namely, a fourfold proportion involving sets of prices, quantities, price increments, and quantity increments. This parallelism should seem sufficient to provide an answer to the embarrassing question, To what do the weighted averages approximate? One may say that they are a simplified approach to the conceptually exact vectorial averages. So much, then, for the theoretical problem of the measurement of the acceleration of the productive process: from rates of payment Z and their increments DZ, it is possible to proceed to rates of production Q and their increments dQ.

There remains the question of the application of this method of measurement to the basic and surplus stages of the productive process. In general the discussion will center on hypothetical smooth trends of expansion, so that instances of dp_i and dq_i will all be relatively small and the definition in terms of weighted averages will be available. The main indices to be employed will be P', the basic selling price index, and dP' its increment; Q', the index of basic quantities sold in the given interval, and dQ' its increment; P'', the surplus selling price index, and dP'' its increment; and Q'', the index of surplus quantities sold, and dQ'' its increment. These indices are calculated from rates of payment at the basic and surplus final markets, as follows.

$$E' = P'Q' \tag{28}$$

$$DE' = P'Q'(dP'/P' + dQ'/Q' + dP'dQ'/P'Q') \tag{29}$$

$$E'' = P''Q'' \tag{30}$$

$$DE'' = P''Q''(dP''/P'' + dQ''/Q'' + dP''dQ''/P''Q'') \tag{31}$$

At times of great and abrupt change, when weighted averages cease to have a meaning, the meaning of the indices may be salvaged by shifting to the definition in terms of vectorial averages and adding to equations (28) to (31) the appropriate trigonometric functions of A and dA. On the other hand, in discussing equations of the type of (29) and (31), one may ignore the third quotient on the right-hand side, often because it is relatively small, always because it is merely the product of the first two quotients and so does not add a further factor of variation that is different in kind.[142]

Since Q' and Q'' refer to quantities sold at the final markets, they have to be corrected by acceleration coefficients,[143] a' and a'', to give quantities under production during the contemporaneous interval. Thus, when basic quantities sold are Q', basic quantities under production will be $a'Q'$; similarly, when surplus quantities sold are Q'', surplus quantities under production will be $a''Q''$. Estimates of the acceleration coefficients proceed in two steps. First, one considers the series of indices for final sales over a number

142 It is true that the third quotient, $dPdQ/PQ$, in equations (29) and (31) does not add 'a further factor of variation that is different in kind' in the sense that its components, dP/P and dQ/Q, already occur in the first and second terms. It is not, however, clear to the editors what Lonergan had in mind by introducing this fact as a reason why the third quotient could be dropped. That the product $dPdQ/PQ$ of two small fractions will tend to be negligible seems a sufficient reason in itself.

143 Note that a' and a'' are fractions.

of intervals, say, Q'_1, Q'_2, Q'_3, ... If these are about equal, the acceleration coefficient will be unity; if they are an increasing series, then a'_1 will be greater than unity; if they are a decreasing series, then a'_1 will be less than unity. Second, one adverts to the influence of speculative anticipations: the current rate of production is based not on actual but on anticipated future rates of final sales; further, when prices are rising, there is an advantage in buying long in advance, and when prices are falling, the advantage lies with minimum inventories; finally, there is a cumulative effect whenever there is a series of transitional markets, for each successive market tends to count the speculative increments of demand of later markets as part of the objective evidence, to add on a further speculative increment, and to pass on a cumulatively inflated or deflated demand to earlier markets. Hence one may characterize the acceleration coefficients as greater or less than unity according as the stages of the process are accelerating or decelerating, as notably greater than unity when current production is expanding speculatively, and perhaps as tending to be notably less than unity in the liquidation of a crisis.

24   The Cycle of the Productive Process[144]

[1944] By a cycle is meant a more or less necessary succession of phases. By a phase is meant a series of intervals in which certain defined characteristics are verified. By a cycle of the productive process is meant a concatenation of phases defined by relations between quantity indices and their increments. The following table explores the possibility of different types of phases.[145]

144   This section is the eleventh in the 1944 version. Lonergan revised the end of it for the 1978 version and omitted it altogether beginning with the 1980 version. The 1978 revision has been included here (see note 155 below); the original 1944 ending appears below as 'Additional Note to Section 24: The Pure Cycle.'

145   Vertical strokes denoting absolute value have been added to the table that follows. 'Absolute value' means the magnitude of a quantity without the positive or negative sign; for example $|{+}5| = |{-}5| = 5$. According to Lonergan's original table, $dQ''/Q'' < dQ'/Q'$, 'neither positive,' would be a 'basic contraction'; similarly, $dQ''/Q'' > dQ'/Q'$, 'neither positive,' would be a 'surplus contraction.' The context of this section makes clear, however, that a surplus contraction is taking place when the rate of decline of dQ''/Q'' is greater than the rate

dQ'', dQ'	$\lvert dQ''/Q'' \rvert > \lvert dQ'/Q' \rvert$	$\lvert dQ''/Q'' \rvert = \lvert dQ'/Q' \rvert$	$\lvert dQ''/Q'' \rvert < \lvert dQ'/Q' \rvert$
I. Unspecified	Surplus Advantage	Proportionate Phase	Basic Advantage
II. Neither negative[146]	Surplus Expansion	Proportionate Expansion	Basic Expansion
III. Neither positive[147]	Surplus Contraction	Proportionate Contraction	Basic Contraction
IV. Both zero	—	Static Phase	—
V. One positive and one negative	Mixed Phase	—	Mixed Phase

The foregoing is simply a complete list of possibilities of a given type. The main criterion of division is derived from the relation between basic and surplus acceleration. In any given interval, dQ''/Q'' must be greater than, or equal to, or less than dQ'/Q'. If one does not specify whether dQ' and dQ'' are positive, zero, or negative, one has three generic types of phases named respectively the surplus advantage, the proportionate phase, and the basic advantage. If however one specifies that neither dQ' nor dQ'' is negative, *in the sense that at least one is positive*, the phase is respectively a surplus expansion, a proportionate expansion, or a basic expansion. On the

---

of decline of dQ'/Q', and vice versa for a basic contraction. However, when dQ'/Q' and dQ''/Q'' are negative and $dQ''/Q'' < dQ'/Q'$, then the negative quantity dQ''/Q'' is of greater magnitude than the negative quantity dQ'/Q', which is of lesser magnitude, precisely because they are both negative. This is the condition for a 'surplus contraction,' not a 'basic contraction' as Lonergan's unmodified table would imply.

    The insertion of the absolute value strokes corrects the problems in rows (I) through (IV) while preserving Lonergan's original intent. Row (V), on the other hand, presents a special problem. It seems likely that by 'mixed phase' Lonergan did mean cases where one quotient was positive and the other negative. Hence, he probably intended the 'Surplus Advantage' column to include the case where $dQ''/Q'' > 0 > dQ'/Q'$, while the case of $dQ''/Q'' < 0 < dQ'/Q'$ was to be listed under the 'Basic Advantage' column. Obviously for this row, and for this row only, the absolute-value strokes convey a different meaning from Lonergan's original, and therefore should be ignored.

146 As Lonergan notes below, the phrase 'neither negative' is to be taken in the sense that at least one is positive.

147 Again, as Lonergan notes below, the phrase 'neither positive' is to be taken in the sense that at least one is negative.

other hand, if one specifies that neither dQ' nor dQ'' is positive, *in the sense that at least one is negative*, the phase is respectively a surplus contraction, a proportionate contraction, or a basic contraction. Finally, if both dQ' and dQ'' are zero, there is a static phase, and if one is positive and the other negative, there is a mixed phase; the static phase and the mixed phase are likely to be mere theoretical possibilities.

The significance of the table is that it makes possible a distinction between different types of cycle. The trade cycle is a succession of expansions and contractions: it certainly is a movement up and down the table, and it may or may not also involve movements across the table. The contention of the present analysis is that there is a pure cycle at the root of the trade cycle. By a pure cycle is meant a movement across the table with no implication of a movement up or down the table. Thus the succession of surplus expansion, basic expansion, proportionate expansion, repeated as often as you please, would give a pure cycle. Of itself, it would not involve any contraction. It would be simply a matter of the intermittent emergence of acceleration lags in a general movement of expansion. Such a pure cycle can be shown to have an exigence for rather vigorous adaptation on the part of human agents as one phase succeeds another. It can further be shown that the lack of such adaptation transforms the pure cycle into a trade cycle: the free economies of the present day are overadapted to the surplus expansion, which they exaggerate into booms, but underadapted to the basic expansion, which they convert into slumps. Lack of adaptation thus transforms a movement across the table into a movement that also is down the table. So much, then, for the general drift of the argument in subsequent sections; present concern is the probability or necessity of pure cycles.[148]

---

148 In 1979 Lonergan distributed a supplement that gives the following schematic list characterizing the trade cycle. The other main type of cycle mentioned in the first sentence is what Lonergan terms the pure cycle; see the preceding paragraph.

'[The table] makes possible a distinction between different types of cycle: the trade cycle that actually has existed and still exists:
- it exaggerates the surplus phase into booms
- it reduces the basic expansion to a slump leaving a notable proportion of the population in the reserve army of the unemployed
- the exaggeration into booms follows from the one precept of classical economics: thrift and enterprise; then almost any enterprise will make a profit for a while, and everyone does his best to get into the act

A first preliminary point is a distinction between the several functions of surplus final products. The aggregate of surplus final products in any given interval is measured by Q''. But of this aggregate, part goes to supplying mere replacements and maintenance of existing capital equipment, while the remainder goes to supplying additional and/or more efficient equipment. Thus while part of Q'' has no tendency to accelerate the process, the remainder tends to effect a long-term acceleration in either a surplus stage or in the basic stage. Let us say that in any given interval,[149] $(1 - h) Q''$ has no accelerating effect, $h'' Q''$ accelerates the surplus stage, and $h' Q''$ accelerates the basic stage, where $h = h' + h''$.

There immediately follows a distinction between two significantly different situations. At any given time the coefficient h may be great or small. If it is small, the possibility of a long-term acceleration of the process requires that first the surplus stage accelerate itself to make Q'' and h great before turning to the long-term acceleration of the basic stage. On the other hand, if h already is great, the surplus stage may proceed at a constant rate yet have a great $h' Q''$ to effect a notable long-term acceleration of the basic stage; and in this case the basic stage will accelerate first uniformly and then with decreasing rapidity, as the lag in additional replacement requirements gradually is overcome and h decreases.

This distinction between a high and a low potential for long-term acceleration, according as h is great or small, is to be complemented with a parallel distinction between a high and a low potential for short-term acceleration. The two types of acceleration differ, it will be recalled, inasmuch as the short-term acceleration is through the more intense and more efficient use of existing capital equipment, while the long-term acceleration is through the introduction of additional and/or more efficient equipment; thus the short-term acceleration is a consequent of a previous long-term acceleration and consists in exploiting it to the full; inversely, one may say that the long-term acceleration changes the basis on which short-term accelerations operate. Now at any given time the potential of

---

- the transformation of the surplus expansion into a slump is due to the fact that the one precept works less and less well, as the above-normal profit, the social dividend, has to shift from anti-egalitarian tendency of the surplus phase to the egalitarian tendency of the basic phase'

149 Hereafter, departing from the convention explained in note 29, Lonergan's symbol H has been altered to a lower-case h, where h denotes a fraction rather than a quantity.

the economy for short-term acceleration may be high or low. One may presume it to be high when a long-term acceleration is well advanced: then there is much new equipment; many new combinations of production factors have recently emerged; and one may expect that the full potentialities of this new situation have not yet been discovered and exploited. Again, one may expect short-term potential to be high after a crisis: for then there has been a sudden contraction of rates of production, so that the material means for increasing these rates greatly are still in existence. On the other hand, short-term potential is low if a long period has elapsed since the last long-term acceleration has taken place. For if the expansion of the process has been maintained, the potentialities of short-term acceleration will in time be exhausted; and if the expansion has not been maintained but has degenerated into a slump, the potentialities of short-term acceleration will in time be destroyed by obsolescence and liquidations.

This pair of distinctions between high and low long-term and short-term acceleration potential sets the stage for a pure cycle. But the issue has yet to be clarified by [three] further considerations.

[1] It is to be expected, in the first place, that either a long-term acceleration does not occur at all or else it occurs in a massive fashion. There are three main reasons grounding such an expectation. [a] First, a long-term acceleration is a matter of long-term planning: capital formation is not worth while unless one can foresee a long period of utility for it; on the other hand, if such an anticipation is possible, then it is worth while to do the job properly while one is about it, for one is settling one's fate for years to come. [b] Second, the introduction of additional or more efficient capital equipment will not take place in isolated units here and there in the productive process; the supply of a single product depends upon the activities of many units; and if it is worth while for one of them to go in for an expansion, it is worth while for a series to do so. [c] Third, in a long-term acceleration, demand is not for some single type of surplus product but for a ramifying variety of products; thus one may expect not merely series of units but series of series of units to expand. These considerations do not make long-term accelerations inevitably massive, but they do reveal an objective logic which is verified no less in socialist planning than in capitalist free enterprise.[150]

150 Lonergan's aggregate, functional, and dynamic analysis of the pure cycle of the productive process of the economic good of order, like his idea of the good of order overall (*Insight* 213–14/238–39, 596–97/619–21, 605/628, 607/630; *Method in Theology* 47–52), may be thought of as a model, 'an intelligible,

[2] In the second place, the more massive the long-term acceleration the greater will be the expansion of surplus activity. Surplus activity supplies capital equipment to the surplus stages and to the basic stage. Hence a massive long-term acceleration is a massive development of surplus activity. Further, one is not to think of this increment in Q'' as concentrated in firms of certain types. The distinction between basic and surplus is not a material nor a proprietary but a functional distinction.[151] There are types of enterprise that in themselves are indifferently [1978] basic or surplus and turn from one stage to the other according to the use to which their products are put: such are the extraction or production of raw materials, transportation, the supply of light, heat, power, and a variety of general services. As the quantity of surplus activity expands, not merely is there a great increase in the supply of tools and machinery, in construction, and so on,

---

interlocking set of terms and relations that it may be well to have about when it comes to describing reality or to forming hypotheses,' that he thought of as more than a mere model (*Method in Theology* xii), since it also would have the hypothetical normativity of any explanatory correlations empirically verifiable in data. As explanatorily normative in this sense, it would manifest a transsocial and transcultural invariance, since it specifies the fundamental macroequilibria that 'are the conditions of a properly functioning economy' (above, p. 92). They are 'equilibria that have to be maintained if an economy chooses to remain in a stationary state, to embark on a long-term expansion, to distribute its benefits to the vast majority of its members, and so to return to a more affluent stationary state until such time as further expansion beckons.'

It follows that Lonergan, in expounding the meaning of the need for a great rate of savings required for the major surplus expansion, could write in a 1979 supplement: 'The surplus phase is anti-egalitarian, as much in Russia and socialist countries as elsewhere; there was more suffering and more deliberately inflicted suffering in Siberia at the base of the Russian surplus expansion [than] in the nineteenth-century British expansion that so raised the explosive anger of Marx.' (For the context of this quotation, see note 198 below.) This is simply an exemplification of Lonergan's understanding that his analysis would be relevant to all 'the phenomena set forth in W.W. Rostow's *Stages of Economic Growth* and *Politics and the Stages of Growth*' (above, p. 16), which is to say, relevant to *any* economy in any society or culture that has undergone a takeoff.

151 This parallels the distinction to which attention was called in note 27.

but also there is a great diversion of indifferent activities to the surplus stage.

[3] In the third place,[152] it is of the nature of a surplus expansion to prepare the way for a far greater basic expansion, for surplus activities stand to basic as a flow to a flow of flows. But a surplus expansion calls for saving, and a massive surplus expansion calls for massive saving. In contrast, the basic expansion calls for ever-increasing consumption. So the practical wisdom cherished in the surplus expansion has to give way to a quite different type of practical wisdom in the basic expansion.

The difference is not merely an internal difference, a change of mentality and attitude. For the simplest way to obtain great savings, and so promote a surplus expansion, is to increase the income of the rich, who can hardly spend more on their standard of living. Again, the simplest way to promote consumption is to increase the income of the poor, and thereby make it possible for them to improve their standard of living.

Now to change one's standard of living in any notable fashion is to live in a different fashion. It presupposes a grasp of new ideas. If the ideas are to be above the level of currently successful advertising, serious education must be undertaken. Finally, coming to grasp what serious education really is and, nonetheless, coming to accept that challenge constitutes the greatest challenge to the modern economy.

We have had the great surplus expansion of the industrial and scientific revolutions. But we have yet to master the basic expansion. First it was dodged by the worldwide pursuit of a favorable balance of foreign trade. When political economy overcame mercantilism, it clung to the practical wisdom that guided the surplus expansion and to the scientific ideal of the necessary laws of nature to be deduced from assured principles. Eventually through strikes, labor legislation, and the application of scientific ingenuity to practical inventions, the tables have been turned. In a number of countries today there is massive production of consumer goods and services. But even in them there is much poverty and backwardness. And in the rest of the world the old methods of cooperation and survival are being, or have already been, lost without the new methods effectively taking hold.

In fact, it can be argued that the new methods are flawed. For the past

152 For Lonergan's 1944 formulation of this third consideration clarifying the paired distinctions between high and low long-term and short-term acceleration potential, see the 'Additional Note to Section 24' below.

fifty years[153] the device of deficit government spending has provided an economic equivalent of the favorable balance of foreign trade; and as the latter led to an impasse so too may the former. But this topic belongs to a later stage in the argument.[154]

Additional Note to Section 24: The Pure Cycle[155]

[1944] It is to be observed that a series of intervals in which dQ''/Q'' is constant and positive is not a series of intervals with the surplus stage undergoing uniform acceleration. For dQ''/Q'' to be constant, Q'', interval by interval, has to be increasing in a geometrical progression. Thus, if in an initial interval surplus activity is Q'' and over a subsequent series of intervals dQ''/Q'' equals $k-1$, then the series of values for surplus activity will be Q'', kQ'', k^2Q'', ... k^nQ''. Inversely, if surplus activity accelerates uniformly over a series of intervals, then dQ''/Q'' is decreasing,[156] and successive values of the ratio will be

$$rdQ''/Q'', [r/(2-r)](dQ''/Q''), ... \{r/[(n-1)-(n-2)r]\}(dQ''/Q''),$$

when the initial value of dQ''/Q'' is $1/r-1$.[157]

153 The reader will recall that this was written in 1978.
154 See §31, 'Deficit Spending and Taxes.'
155 In the 1944 version, the text that follows in this additional note appears at the end of the section on 'The Cycle of the Production Process,' at the point where Lonergan discusses the third of the three considerations by which he clarified the paired distinctions between high and low long-term and short-term acceleration potential. He replaced it for the 1978 version with the ending of §24 as it appears above.
156 Here Lonergan originally wrote: 'then dQ''/Q'' is decreasing in geometrical progression; successive values of the ratio will be rdQ''/Q'', r^2dQ''/Q'', ... r^ndQ''/Q'', when the initial value of dQ''/Q'' is $1/r-1$.'
157 See Figure 24-1 and Figure 24-2.

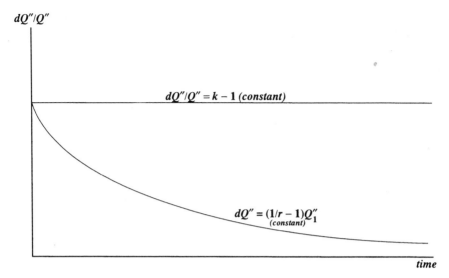

Figure 24-1 Rate of Change of dQ''/Q'' for dQ'' = constant and dQ''/Q'' = constant

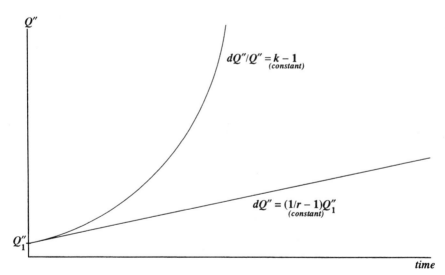

Figure 24-2 Growth of Rate of Surplus Production (Q'') for dQ'' = constant
and dQ''/Q'' = constant

Now, when the surplus stage of the process is effecting a long-term acceleration of surplus activity but as yet not affecting basic activity, one may expect successive values of Q'' to increase in a geometrical progression.

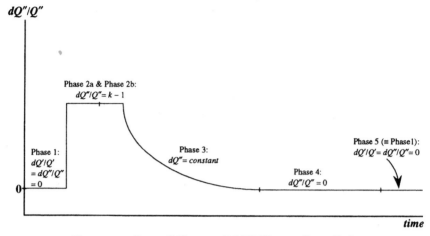

Figure 24-3 Rate of Change of dQ''/Q'' over a Pure Cycle

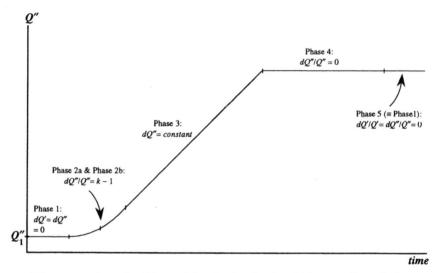

Figure 24-4 Growth of Rate of Surplus Production (Q'') over a Pure Cycle

This gives an initial period, in which the graph of dQ''/Q'' is approximately a level straight line.[158] Next, as the surplus expansion develops and devotes more and more of its activity to the long-term acceleration of the basic stage, one may expect no more than a uniform acceleration of the surplus

158 See Figures 24-3 and 24-4, Phases 2a and 2b.

stage. This gives a second period, in which dQ''/Q'' is curving downwards with successive values in a decreasing geometrical progression.[159] Thirdly, as the expansion approaches its maximum in the surplus stage, dQ'' reverts to zero and Q'' becomes constant.[160] In this third period dQ''/Q'' is again a level straight line but now coincident with the x–axis;[161] k'' is zero, but $k'Q''$ may be great for a notable period to effect a long-term acceleration of the basic stage which, however, gradually declines as replacement requirements begin to mount.[162]

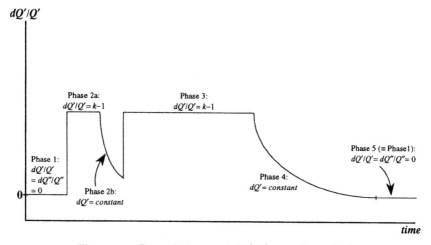

Figure 24-5 Rate of Change of dQ'/Q' over a Pure Cycle

159 See Figures 24-3 and 24-4, Phase 3.

160 See Figures 24-3 and 24-4, Phases 4 and 5.

161 By which Lonergan means the axis on which is plotted the variable 'time.' In the editors' figures 24-3, 24-5, and 24-7, the time axis has been displaced below zero, in order to allow the curve itself to be seen clearly.

162 See Figures 24-5 and 24-6, transition from Phase 4 to Phase 5.

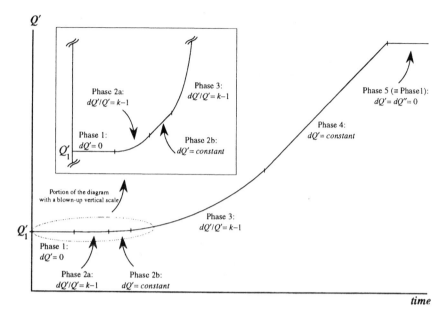

Figure 24-6 Growth of Rate of Basic Production (Q') over a Pure Cycle

The same general principles hold with regard to dQ'/Q'. When Q' accelerates in a geometrical progression, dQ'/Q' is constant. When Q' accelerates uniformly, dQ'/Q' decreases.[163] Further, one may expect the aggregate sum of values of the increments, dQ', over a long series of intervals to be approximately in the ratio Q'/Q'' to the aggregate sum of values of the increments, dQ'', over the same long series of intervals. It is indeed true that Q' is very much larger than Q'', since basic activity is to surplus as, say, volume to surface. But one may expect the increment of a volume to stand to the increment of a surface as the volume does to the surface. To suppose the contrary leads to absurd conclusions. If, for instance, dQ''/Q'' were on a long-term aggregate much greater or much less than dQ'/Q', then a series of long-term periods would make this difference multiply in geometrical progression to effect a convergence of Q'' and Q' or else a mounting divergence.[164] Such a convergence or divergence would imply that the more roundabout methods of capitalist progress were increasingly less efficient or increasingly more efficient in expanding the supply of consumer goods. Neither view is plausible. New ideas and new methods increase

163 Lonergan originally wrote 'decreases in a geometrical progression.'
164 Lonergan originally wrote 'a geometrically mounting divergence.'

existing efficiency in both the surplus and the basic stages; the ratio between the quantity of surplus and the quantity of basic products per interval is not a matter of efficiency but of the point-to-line correspondence involved in any more roundabout method, in the fact that a single surplus product gives a flow of basic products. In a word, while any concrete realization of the capitalist idea is subject first to increasing and then to decreasing returns, the series of new capitalist ideas cannot be said to be subject to either.[165]

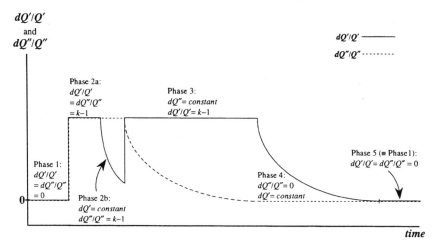

Figure 24-7 Rate of Change of dQ'/Q' and dQ'/Q' over a Pure Cycle

There is a final observation to be made. So far attention has been directed to the latter parts of the graphs of dQ''/Q'' and dQ'/Q'. It has been said that when the surplus stage devotes all its energies to self-acceleration, then Q'' will be increasing in geometrical progression and dQ''/Q'' will be a level straight line. When this period of gestation is coming to an

165 Lonergan has introduced certain assumptions about rates of growth and acceleration. These assumptions constitute something of a 'model' of a pure cycle. That model is a four-phase cycle, where the successive phases are characterized by parameters

(1) $dQ'/Q' = dQ''/Q'' = 0$; (2) $dQ'/Q' = 0$, $dQ''/Q'' = k - 1$; (3) $dQ'/Q' = k - 1$, $dQ'' = (1/r - 1)Q_1''$; (4) $dQ' = (1/r - 1)dQ_1'$, $dQ'' = 0$;

followed by a repetition of phase 1. (See Figures 24-3 through 24-7.) Such a model represents only one possible instance of a pure cycle; there are a man-end, the acceleration of Q'' tends to become uniform, and then gradually to decrease to zero; when it is uniform, dQ''/Q'' is decreasing,[166] and when it is zero, dQ''/Q'' is zero. Now, when the acceleration of Q'' is uniform, the long-term potential of the surplus stage is increasing, and so the surplus stage is devoting more and more of its efforts to the long-term acceleration of the basic stage; then Q' will be increasing at an increasing rate, and the time series of its values may stand in a geometrical progression to make dQ'/Q' a level straight line. When, however, Q'' becomes constant, the acceleration of Q' becomes uniform, and then dQ'/Q' will curve downwards;[167] and as replacement requirements begin to mount, this downward curve is accentuated until dQ' reverts to zero. Thus, both dQ''/Q'' and dQ'/Q' are described as initially level straight lines that eventually curve downwards till the acceleration ratios become zero.[168] One well may ask for an account of the movement of the acceleration ratios from their initial zeros to the level straight lines.

There are two factors in such a movement: short-term acceleration and the period of generalization of a long-term acceleration. Now any long-term acceleration has to begin as a short-term acceleration. New capital equipment does not begin to accelerate rates of production until it has been produced; its production in a series of initial cases has to be a matter of the more intense or more efficient use of existing facilities, in brief, a short-term acceleration. Further, once long-term acceleration is under way, rates of production increase increasingly; their graphs are concave upwards; but the curvature moves from being flatter to [being] rounder as the acceleration is generalized from one section to another throughout the productive process.[169] During this period of generalization, rates of production are not merely increasing in geometrical progression but moving from less to more rapid geometrical progressions.

---

ifold of other possible pure cycles, and a still larger set of possible aberrant 'trade' cycles. Lonergan's use of this model at this point in the text merely illustrates his more general principles, and is not central to his argument. In later sections of this essay, where other graphs have been supplied to illustrate Lonergan's points (for example, in § 27, 'The Cycle of Pure Surplus Income'), an effort has been made to stay as close as possible to the assumptions Lonergan introduced here.

166 Lonergan originally wrote 'is decreasing in a geometrical progression.'
167 Lonergan originally wrote 'will curve downwards in geometrical progression.'
168 See Figure 24-7.
169 Compare Phase 2b and Phase 3 in Figure 24-6.

In one very important aspect, however, the initial period of dQ'/Q' differs from the initial period of dQ''/Q''. For reasons that will appear later, the basic stage will begin a short-term acceleration as soon as there is an appreciable surplus expansion. But while the short-term acceleration of the surplus stage passes automatically into a generalizing long-term acceleration, there is bound to be a lag, equal to the surplus period of gestation, before long-term acceleration can emerge in the basic stage, and a further lag before it can be generalized there. Thus the initial period of the long-term expansion will approximate to a proportionate expansion with dQ'/Q' roughly equal to dQ''/Q''.[170] But the surplus expansion would have to be quite small, or the basic potential for short-term acceleration quite great, for this proportionate expansion to be maintained. Short-term acceleration can move dQ'/Q' up to a peak but it cannot keep it at the peak; it can move it to a peak by generalizing itself throughout the basic stage; it cannot keep it at the peak, because once it is generalized, it is apt to be exhausted, and even if it is not exhausted, it cannot make the time series of values of Q' a great geometrical progression. Thus, though dQ'/Q' initially moves to a peak, it immediately begins to descend even though Q' continues to expand at a uniform time-rate of increase. It follows that the initial proportionate expansion is succeeded by a surplus expansion: dQ''/Q'' is constant, because Q'' is increasing in some geometrical progression; dQ'/Q' is falling from a peak, even though Q' is increasing.[171] This situation, however, is bound to be temporary; its existence is the lag between the generalized long-term acceleration of the surplus stage and that of the basic stage. When that is overcome, dQ'/Q' moves again to a peak and remains there; and by the same token, dQ''/Q'' will begin to decline.[172] The surplus expansion is followed by a basic expansion. Finally, as replacement requirements begin to mount, the factor h in the product hQ'' begins to decline; the rate at which the surplus stage accelerates the basic accordingly declines;[173] and so the basic expansion approaches its end. The ultimate situation is a static phase in which dQ' and dQ'' are both zero, Q' and Q'' are on new high levels but constant, and further development is awaiting new ideas, new methods, new organization.[174]

170 See Figure 24-7, Phase 2a.
171 See Figures 24-7 and 24-6, Phase 2b.
172 See Figure 24-7, Phase 3.
173 See Figure 24-7, Phase 4.
174 See Figure 24-7, transition from Phase 4 to Phase 5.

So much for the outline of an expansive pure cycle. It assumes a long-term acceleration of the productive process and asks how such an acceleration develops. It answers by positing three periods. Generalizing short-term acceleration in both surplus and basic stages gives an initial proportionate expansion.[175] The development of long-term acceleration in the surplus stage and its lag in the basic stage gives a surplus expansion.[176] The emergence and generalization of a long-term acceleration in the basic stage, together with the impossibility of maintaining the increasing rate of acceleration in the surplus stage, gives a basic expansion.[177] At first, dQ''/Q'' is equal to dQ'/Q', then it is greater, then it is less. Without urging the necessity of such a cycle, one may say that it is solidly grounded in a dynamic structure of the productive process; and one has only to think of the practical impossibility of calculating the acceleration ratios dQ'/Q' and dQ''/Q'' to smile at the suggestion that one should try to 'smooth out the *pure* cycle.'

25   Price and Quantity Changes in Accelerating Circuits[178]

[1978] Expressions for the rate of change in prices, dP' and dP'', and in quantities, dQ' and dQ'', have now to be related to the various phases in the cycle of the productive process.[179]

Now in a surplus expansion dQ'' will be increasing, and in a basic expansion dQ' will be increasing. In either case the expansion will begin with a short-term acceleration that makes full use of already existing resources and equipment. But a movement towards long-term acceleration will be marked by an initial increase of dQ'' alone, as efforts are concentrated on widening and deepening existing capital equipment and on training employees in new skills. However, as this movement advances, the capacity for basic production will keep increasing, and as the new capacity is more

---

175 See Figures 24-3 through 24-7, Phase 2a.

176 See Figures 24-3 through 24-7, Phase 2b.

177 See Figures 24-3 through 24-7, Phases 3 and 4.

178 This section appears only in the 1978 and 1979 versions, where it follows the section on 'The Cycle of the Productive Process,' §24 above; the 1980 and later versions omit it.

179 Lonergan's sentence has been altered here to take account of the necessary renumbering of sections and pages.

fully utilized the increase of dQ' will tend to outstrip by far the increase in dQ''. For surplus stands to basic as a flow to a flow of flows, and even in part as [a flow to] a flow of flows of flows.

Increasing quantities tend to imply increasing prices. For as quantities keep increasing, competitive bidding for resources arises among those that wish to remain in the game. Such pressure will be slight or notable in accord with the scarcity of resources and the will to achieve. On the other hand, the pressure goes beyond bounds when the possibility of further expansion comes to an end, with no end imposed on the further granting of credit.

If increasing quantities tend to imply increasing prices, decreasing quantities imply decreasing prices only in truly competitive markets. Oligopolist managers can agree to prefer the prior prices, when their alternative would be to pay the higher prices for their supplies and receive lower prices when their turn to sell comes round. Similarly, labor leaders are loath to accept any appearance of declining wages and other benefits.

Now variations in dP', dQ', dP'', dQ'' involve similar variations in E', E'', R', R'', O', O'', I', I''. In brief, crossover balance has to be maintained, and any sustained imbalance will result, in the first instance, in ineffective basic or surplus demand. Further sustained imbalance in either one will lead to its breakdown and, as the two are solidary, to the breakdown of the other as well.

There follows the recession or slump. It may be mitigated by the productive process migrating from the domestic to foreign markets, by deficit government spending, and by the redistribution of income through an income tax. All three have their inconveniences, to which we revert later.[180]

To conclude, the acceleration of the productive process, if it is to succeed and not be destroyed by maladjustments to change of phase, postulates that in a proportionate expansion the rate of saving be constant, that in a surplus expansion it increase, and [that] in a basic expansion it decrease. While this decrease need not reduce the standard of living of employers or deprive them of the means to meet the costs of maintenance, it may mean that they will not have that excess of income that may be labeled 'money to invest.'

180 See especially §§ 30–31 below and also §§ 19–20 above.

Additional Note to Section 25:
The Phases in Circuit Acceleration – A Technical Statement[181]

[1944] On combining equations (28) and (29) and again equations (30) and (31) one obtains[182]

$$DE'/E' = dP'/P' + dQ'/Q' \tag{32}$$

$$DE''/E'' = dP''/P'' + dQ''/Q'' \tag{33}$$

so that, apart from price-level variations, E' varies with Q' and E'' varies with Q''. The question arises, To what extent does price-level variation offset or reinforce the concomitance of E' with Q' and E'' with Q''?

In the first place, variations in P' and P'' will not be equal and opposite to variations in Q' and Q'' to leave E' and E'' constant. This is evident from the nature of the expressions dP'/P' and dP''/P''. When Q' or Q'' is increasing in geometrical progression, P' and P'' would have to be decreasing in geometrical progression. But it is normal for rates of production to increase in geometrical progression in a long-term acceleration: the greater the rate of production, the greater the capacity to increase that rate. On the other hand, falling prices are a signal for a slump. Prices falling in a geometrical progression would soon inflict enormous losses on every entrepreneur, for entrepreneurs would be making the main part of their outlays at the higher prices but collecting their receipts at the later lower prices. Under such circumstances, the long-term acceleration, if ever it began, would rapidly come to a sudden end. The fact illustrates the value of vulgar notions of money being sound because it is rigid.

In the second place, prices tend to move in the same direction as quantities. Prices rise in a boom, when quantities increase, to fall in a slump, when quantities decrease. However, the causes of such price variations are of two kinds. There is the normal causality of increasing or decreasing scarcity. As rates of production increase, competitive demand for labor and for materials, as well as for general services such as power, transportation, credit, and so on, increase. Inversely, as rates of production decline,

---

181 The following section appears in the 1944 version with the title 'The Phases in Circuit Accelerations.' The 1978 and later versions do not include it.

182 One obtains this, however, only if the third term is dropped from equations (29) and (31), for the reasons Lonergan offers above. See note 142 above.

demand falls off. On this head, one would expect price levels to mount increasingly as the expansion developed, that is, imperceptibly in the early period, in more marked fashion once expansion becomes generalized, and in a purely inflationary manner if the maximum rates of production possible were attained yet credit continued to be expanded. Thus, so far from canceling the requirement that E' vary with Q' and E'' with Q'', one may expect price levels to reinforce and augment such variation, though in different degrees as the pressure on general markets is slight, notable, or fatuous.

These variations in E' and E'' postulate, in turn, parallel variations in I' and I''. The normal source of basic expenditure is basic income, and the normal source of surplus expenditure is surplus income. As was argued in section 15, a condition of successful circuit acceleration is that O', I', and E' keep in step, that O'', I'', E'' do likewise, that $(D' - s'I')$, $(D'' - s''I'')$, and G remain zero. Thus the long-term acceleration of the productive process with its successive proportionate, surplus, and basic expansions can be executed successfully only if the variations in the rates of payment follow the phases of the productive cycle. There would be, for instance, a radical maladjustment between circuit and productive acceleration if, when surplus rates of production were increasing more rapidly than basic, basic rates of income were increasing more rapidly than surplus. Then interval after interval, an increasingly excessive amount of monetary income would be moving to the basic final market, and there would follow a rise in prices quite different in kind from the normal rise resulting from increasing scarcity. Such a rise would not be an ordinary scarcity but at once a consequence and, as will appear, a corrective of a disproportion between monetary and real consumer income.

Not only is it true that this second type of price variation is different from the first, but also one must give it a different kind of attention. When prices rise because of real scarcity, one may speak of a requirement for variation in E' and E'' over and above the variation postulated by dQ'/Q' and dQ''/Q''. But when prices rise or fall because the distribution of income has not anticipated these requirements correctly, then price variation is not a postulate for variation in E' and E'' but rather a spontaneous effort at adjusting what should already have been adjusted. Accordingly, such adjustment variations in prices will be ignored for the moment to be considered more in detail in the next section. Present concern will be for the type of adjustment that the successive phases of the pure cycle postulate.

The central adjustment is variation in the rate of saving. This rate may be

defined, conveniently for present purposes, as the ratio of surplus income
to total income. Assuming that the rate of saving will not differ appreciably
because income is derived from basic or surplus outlay, we may denote this
rate by the symbol w,[183] so that

$$w = I'' / (I' + I'') \qquad (34)^{184}$$

The condition that w is increasing, constant, or decreasing is that surplus
income is increasing, in proportion to its size, more rapidly than basic, or
at the same rate, or less rapidly. Symbolically, if one assumes a smooth
trend and differentiates equation (34), the numerator on the right-hand
side will be $DI''/I'' - DI'/I'$ which, as it is positive, zero, or negative, makes
the differential of w positive, zero, or negative.

Now in a proportionate expansion, dQ''/Q'' equals dQ'/Q'. If price levels are rising at all, one may expect both basic and surplus levels to be rising equally. Hence DE'/E' should equal DE''/E''. Further, since rates of
income should keep pace with rates of expenditure, DI''/I'' should equal
DI'/I'. It follows that in the proportionate expansion, the rate of saving, w,
should be constant.

Again, in the surplus expansion, dQ''/Q'' is greater than dQ'/Q'; if there
is any divergence in the variation of basic and surplus price levels, scarcity
should be felt more in the surplus than in the basic stage of the process, so
that any difference between dP''/P'' and dP'/P' would have a reinforcing
and not a canceling effect. It follows, as before, that DE''/E'' should be
greater than DE'/E', that DI''/I'' should be greater than DI'/I', and so that
the rate of saving, w, should be increasing.

Inversely, in the basic expansion, the preceding argument is turned
around to give the conclusion that the rate of saving should be decreasing.
Then dQ'/Q' is greater than dQ''/Q'', prices varying from scarcity should,
if anything, reinforce this difference, and so basic income and expenditure
must be increasing more rapidly than surplus.

183 Note that in this instance the lower-case w is not a quantity but a ratio. In the
1944 version, the ratio defined by equation (34) is designated by the symbol
G. According to a page of corrigenda distributed in 1979, G should be replaced by W. The editors have used a lower-case w because a fraction, not
a rate, is being designated.

184 In the 1944 version, this equation is preceded by another, omitted here
because it involves quantities and assumptions that became obsolete once
Lonergan had introduced the quantities c', c'', i', i'', s', and s''.

To conclude, the acceleration of the productive process, if it is to succeed and not be destroyed by circulation maladjustments, postulates that in a proportionate expansion the rate of saving be constant, that in a surplus expansion it increase, that in a basic expansion it decrease. The implications of this postulate will concern us in subsequent sections on the cycle of basic income, the cycle of pure surplus income, and the cycle of price spreads.

26   The Cycle of Basic Income[185]

[1944] The purpose of this section is to inquire into the manner in which the rate of saving W[186] is adjusted to the phases of the pure cycle of the productive process. Traditional theory looked to shifting interest rates to provide suitable adjustment. In the main we shall be concerned with factors that are prior to changing interest rates and more effective.

The simplest manner of attaining a fairly adequate concept of basic

185 This section is the thirteenth of the 1944 version. In 1978 and 1979 Lonergan distributed supplemental pages prescribing a number of modifications that have been included here as indicated in notes. The 1980 and later versions, however, do not include the section.

186 In this sentence Lonergan originally wrote: 'the rate of saving, G.' A substitution of W and a change to 'social dividend' are both prescribed in the 1979 supplement mentioned in note 185 above; the original 1944 phrase 'rate of saving' has been retained throughout the present section.
  The supplement defines the social dividend as
  • 'income over and above "standard of living," "rent," interest, maintenance and replacement of capital equipment
  • [the means given] to entrepreneurs, investors, because they are the most likely to be able to interpret what it is for, namely, the successful introduction into the economic process of technological, commercial, or organizational improvements
  • who else would know which are the possible improvements that would succeed?'
  With this definition of social dividend, compare a quotation from Schumpeter, *History* 894, which Lonergan included in another supplement: '[John Bates] Clark's contribution was the most significant of all: he was the first to strike a novel note by connecting entrepreneurial profits, considered as a surplus over interest (and rent), with the successful introduction into the economic process of technological, commercial, or organizational improvements.'

income is to divide the economic community into an extremely large number of groups of practically equal income. Among these groups it will be convenient to include a zero-income group composed of dependents, the unemployed, potential immigrants, recent emigrants, the recently deceased, and so on. In any group i let there be at any given time n_i members; let each member receive an aggregate (basic and surplus) income y_i per interval, so that the whole group receives $n_i y_i$; finally, let us say that the group directs the fraction[187] w_i of its total income to the basic demand function, so that basic income per interval is given by the equation

$$I' = \sum w_i n_i y_i \qquad (35)$$

Next, let w_i increase by dw_i, n_i by dn_i, and y_i by dy_i in the immediately subsequent interval. However, since the number of income groups is extremely large, it should always be possible to represent an increase or decrease of an individual's income by his migration from one group to another. In this manner dy_i may be assumed to be always zero, and so one obtains for the increment per interval of basic income the simpler equation[188]

$$dI' = \sum (w_i dn_i + n_i dw_i) y_i \qquad (36)$$

where n_i includes the adjustment due to migration.[189] We shall consider in turn variations in basic income in virtue of dn_i and variations in virtue of dw_i.

Since there is a zero-income group one may always regard the addition of members to one group as a subtraction from other groups and vice versa. This, in fact, is always approximately true, but the presence of a zero-

---

187   In the 1944 version, Lonergan used the symbol g_i here. It has been changed so as to correspond with W, the social dividend (see notes 183 and 186 above).

188   The 1944 version of the following equation was altered by Lonergan in 1978 and again later in that year. Both of his changes have been incorporated here; in addition, the notation has been altered in conformity with the previously announced editorial practice.

189   In the 1944 version, the clause that follows equation (36) reads: 'where the component, $y_i dw_i dn_i$, is omitted as containing no new variable.' One of Lonergan's supplements appears to call for dropping this formulation, perhaps because one would ordinarily say the component is omitted because the product $dw_i dn_i$ is negligible.

income group provides a locus in which all error is concentrated without leading to any misstatement about income. Consider, then, the migration of an individual from any group i to a proximate but higher group j. Three increments are to be distinguished: the increment in the individual's total income, $y_j - y_i$; the increment in his basic income, $w_j y_j - w_i y_i$; and the increment in his surplus income, $[(1 - w_j)y_j - (1 - w_i)y_i]$. Now the higher any individual's total income, the smaller will be the fraction w of total income going to basic expenditure. Hence, in migrations from low to less low income groups, most of the increment of individual total income becomes an increment of basic income; but in migrations from high to still higher income groups, most of the increment of individual total income becomes an increment of surplus income. Evidently, then, suitable migrations are a means of providing adjustments in the community's rate of saving. To increase the rate of saving, increase the income of the rich; while they may be too distant from the current operations of the economic process to judge, at least they can put their money into the bank or bonds or stocks, and perhaps others there will see how it can best be used.[190] To decrease the rate of saving, increase the income of the poor.

The foregoing is the fundamental mode of adjusting the rate of saving to the phases of the productive cycle. It reveals that the surplus expansion is anti-egalitarian, inasmuch as that expansion postulates that increments in income go to high incomes. But it also reveals the basic expansion to be egalitarian, for that expansion postulates that increments go to low incomes which supposes that they have not already been handed over to high incomes.[191]

However, this fundamental mode of adjustment is complemented by a further mechanism of automatic correction. When savings are insufficient, too much money is moving to the basic final market, and so the basic selling-price level rises; inversely, when saving is excessive, insufficient money moves to the basic final market, and so the basic selling-price level falls. This movement of price levels has a double effect: it contracts or expands the purchasing power of monetary income; and it shifts the distribution of

---

190 The end of this sentence, beginning with 'while they may be too distant,' was added by Lonergan in a supplement distributed in 1979 (see above, note 185).

191 The end of this sentence has been altered, following a supplement that Lonergan distributed in 1979 (see above, note 185). In the 1944 version, the sentence ends: 'postulates that increments in income go to low incomes.'

monetary income to the higher or to the lower income brackets. The latter effect is less apparent but essential, for without it there results the upward or downward price spiral.[192]

When, then, prices rise, there is no tendency, at least in the first instance, for quantities to contract. It follows that rates of payment expand proportionately to the rise of prices to give a very large increase to total outlay and income. Again, in the first instance at least, this large increase of income consists in speculative profits of the entrepreneurial class, and as one may suppose this class to be already in the higher income brackets, it follows that the increment of total income resulting from rising prices is an increment in the higher income brackets and so mainly an increment in surplus income. Thus the mechanism of rising prices involves a shift in the distribution of monetary income in favor of the higher income brackets and so in favor of surplus income. This shift in distribution, of course, is achieved through increasing the money in circulation and not by decreasing the monetary income of other brackets. Nonetheless, the equivalent of that effect is had by the reduction of the purchasing power of monetary income. Now the greater the rise in prices, the greater the increase in monetary income, the greater the increase in surplus income, and the

192 In the 1979 supplement mentioned in the two previous notes, Lonergan elaborates on the 'automatic redistributional effects' as follows.

'*When* savings are insufficient, too much money is moving to the basic market; prices there are forced up; the rise in price gives a bigger price spread to entrepreneurs, and so they can invest to restore the surplus market, or increase their standard of living to increase their own windfall profits until they have a high enough standard of living and then can invest or leave the money in the bank to make 15 times as big an investment possible.

'*When* savings are too great, basic sales drop; eventually prices are forced down to reduce the price spread and correct the excessive saving.

'*Again* a rise in prices lowers the purchasing power of money to favor the rich and deprive the poor; it cuts down on basic expenditure and encourages surplus investment.

'*On the other hand*, a lowering of prices increases the purchasing power of money, to favor the poor, encourage basic expenditure, leave less for the social dividend.

'*It remains* that unless a rise in prices is accompanied by an increase in the quantity of money, the rise is blocked of its effect, and the rate of saving cannot adjust. Inversely, when prices fall, unless the quantity of money available decreases, prices will be encouraged to rise again.'

greater the reduction of the purchasing power of monetary income. Hence a sufficient rise in prices will always succeed in adjusting the rate of saving to the requirements of the productive phase. No doubt, as prices rise, the income groups increase their respective fractions w_i by some positive increment dw_i, and no doubt this involves a positive increment in basic monetary income. But also there is no doubt that as prices rise, the capacity of successive lower income groups to effect positive increments dw_i becomes more and more negligible; the fraction w_i cannot be greater than unity. Hence, as prices rise, real saving is forced upon each lower group; on the other hand, as prices rise, the consequent increment in speculative profits and so of surplus income is far greater than any greater spending effected by the small numbers in the higher brackets.

The foregoing mechanism provides an automatic adjustment to an increasing rate of saving. However, its operation is conditioned. Unless the quantity of money in circulation expands as rapidly as prices rise and, as well, as rapidly as the productive expansion of quantities requires, there will result a contraction of the process: then, instead of adjusting the rate of saving to the requirements of the productive cycle, the productive cycle is arrested to find adjustment to the rate of saving. Again, unless the increment in total monetary income goes to the higher income brackets and so to surplus income, there will be no adjustment of the rate of saving: the monetary income of the lower groups increases as rapidly as the purchasing power of monetary income contracts; no real saving is forced; and *ex hypothesi*, there is no anti-egalitarian shift in the distribution of income. It follows that basic income continues to be excessive, and so the basic price level continues to rise indefinitely.

These two types of failure of the automatic mechanism are interrelated.[193] Banks are willing to increase the quantity of money as long as

---

193 Perhaps as a replacement for the remainder of this paragraph, a supplement distributed by Lonergan in 1979 and mentioned in the previous three notes gives the following.

'Banks tend to increase the quantity of money as long as there is no appearance of uncontrolled inflation; but as soon as that menace emerges, they curtail loans.

'Further when prices rise, organized labor can point to the increased cost of living and the increased profits that prove industry's ability to pay higher wages. If industry yields, prices rise still higher, and the complaints recur with the same results. Such is cost-push inflation.

there is no appearance of uncontrolled inflation, but they curtail and even contract loans as soon as an upward spiral of prices menaces the monetary system. Thus the root of the failure of the mechanism is the failure to obtain the anti-egalitarian shift in the distribution of income. In any first instance, rising prices effect that shift. But the trouble is that, in every second instance, organized labor can point to the rising prices as palpable proof of the rising cost of living and further can point to increased profits as proof of industry's capacity to pay higher monetary wage rates. Every delay in granting wage increases is of general advantage. On the other hand, every grant of such increases may indeed shift the burden of forced saving from industrial to other lower-income groups, but certainly causes prices to spiral upwards and so hastens the curtailment of credit.

So far we have been considering the adjustment of the rate of saving in a surplus expansion when that rate is increasing. There remains the opposite situation of the basic expansion when the rate of saving is decreasing. Then the problem that arises is that insufficient income is moving to the basic final market. There is at hand the same automatic mechanism as before. Prices fall. This fall has the double effect of increasing the purchasing power of income and bringing about an egalitarian shift in the distribution of monetary income. The increase in purchasing power is obvious. On the other hand, the egalitarian shift in the distribution of income is, in the main, a merely theoretical possibility. The fall of prices, unless quantities increase proportionately and with equal rapidity, brings about a great reduction in total rates of payment. Receipts fall, outlay falls, income falls. The incidence of the fall of income is, in the first instance, upon the entrepreneurial class, and so in the main it is a reduction of surplus income. Thus we have the same scissors action as before: purchasing power of

---

'When the economy is adjusting to the shift to the basic expansion, prices should fall; the social dividend should decrease; the purchasing power of money should increase [Lonergan wrote 'decrease']; and the process will adjust to the basic phase when prices have fallen sufficiently.

'But when the only precept that is understood is 'thrift and enterprise' all these signs that the basic expansion is under way are interpreted as the signs of an impending slump; so investment drops precipitously; the available quantity of money is evaporated as banks call in loans whenever possible; prices are forced down again; consternation and panic begin, spread, justify the mistaken interpretation of the signs of the times.'

income increases, and the proportion of basic to surplus income increases; the rate of saving is adjusted to the rates of production as soon as the selling-price level falls sufficiently. But just as there is an upward price spiral to blunt the edge of the mechanism when the rate of saving is increasing, so there is a downward spiral to have the same effect when the rate of saving should be decreasing. Falling prices tend to be regarded as a signal that expansion has proceeded too far, that contraction must now be the order of the day. Output is reduced; the income of lower brackets is reduced; the adjustment of the rate of saving fails to take place; prices fall further; the same misinterpretation arises, and prices fall again. Eventually, however, the downward spiral achieves the desired effect; surplus income is reduced to the required proportion of total income; and then prices cease to fall.

An account of the crisis and slump will concern us later.[194] The present point is a very simple point. Just as the surplus expansion is anti-egalitarian in tendency, postulating an increasing rate of saving, and attaining this effectively by increasing, in the main, the income of those who already spend as much as they care to on basic products, so the basic expansion is egalitarian in tendency; it postulates a continuously decreasing rate of saving, a continuously decreasing proportion of surplus income in total income; and it achieves this result effectively by increasing, in the main, the income of those who have the maximum latent demand for consumer goods and services.

Previously I have suggested a lack of adaptation in the free economies to the requirements of the pure cycle.[195] What that lack is can now be stated.[196] It is an inability to distinguish between the significance of a rela-

---

194 See the following paragraph, together with §27. In the present edition, §19 is also relevant.

195 Lonergan is most likely referring to the preface of the 1944 version. In the present edition, §18 is also relevant.

196 In the supplement distributed in 1979, Lonergan amplified the remainder of this paragraph, from 'It is an inability' through the words 'convert the surplus expansion into a boom,' as follows.

'The misinterpretation of the signs of the times is a failure to distinguish between relative prices and absolute or general prices.

'When some prices decrease relatively to others, then production of the less wanted should be curtailed, and production of what is wanted more may well be increased.

'But when prices fall generally, it does not mean that all production should

tive and an absolute rise or fall of monetary prices. A relative rise or fall is, indeed, a signal for a relatively increased or reduced production. If the product i suffers a greater increment, positive or negative, in price than the product j, then more or less of the product i than of the product j is being demanded. As prices are in themselves relative, insofar as they express demand, so also they must be interpreted relatively with regard to expansion and contraction. When the prices both of i and of j are falling, and i more than j, it may still be true that the production of both should be increasing, though with the production of j increasing more than the production of i. For the fall of prices may be general and absolute; as such it will result not from a change in demand but from a failure in income distribution to adjust the rate of saving to the phase of the productive process; to allow such a general maladjustment to convert a basic expansion into a slump is to cut short the expansive cycle of the productive process because one has confused real and relative prices with monetary and absolute prices. Inversely, the rising prices of the surplus expansion are not real and relative but only monetary and absolute rising prices; to allow them to stimulate production is to convert the surplus expansion into a boom. This, I believe, is the fundamental lack of adaptation to the productive cycle that our economies have to overcome. The problem, however, has many ramifications of which the most important is the relativity of the significance of profits. To this we now turn.[197]

---

be curtailed. It means that the entrepreneurs are failing to understand the shift from a surplus to a basic expansion.

'Similarly, when prices rise not merely relatively but generally, it does not mean that more and more of everything is wanted; its basic meaning is the shift from a basic expansion or a slump to a surplus expansion. Such a misinterpretation encourages the boom.'

197 In a supplement distributed in 1978 (see above, note 185), Lonergan restated the problem as follows.

'The traditional doctrine of thrift and enterprise looked to the supply of and demand for money to adjust interest rates and the adjusted rates to adjust the rate of saving to the requirements of the productive process. But it can be argued that this view was not sufficiently nuanced in its estimate of the requirements of the productive process, that it missed the magnitude of the problem, and that it tended to lump together quite different requirements.

'The requirements of an expanding productive process are that pure surplus income has to keep increasing in the surplus phase of an expansion, that it has to keep decreasing in the basic phase of the expansion, and that it

Traditional theory looked to shifting interest rates to provide the automatic adjustment between the productive process and the rate of saving. In brief, the argument was that the rate of interest was the price of money: the higher the rate of interest, the greater the incentive to save and, on the other hand, the less the incentive to borrow; inversely, the lower interest rates, the less the incentive to save and the greater the encouragement to borrowers; in between these positions, it should always be possible to assign some equilibrium rate of interest equating the supply of money with the demand for it. The difficulty with this theory is that it lumps together a number of quite different things and overlooks the order of magnitude of the fundamental problem.[198] What the surplus expansion calls for is not simply more saving but a continuously increasing rate of saving: the prob-

---

vanishes when the cost of replacements and maintenance absorbs the whole of surplus. [See also the text in the next note for an especially good statement, somewhat later than the present one, of this problem.]

   'Again, it is true enough that increasing interest rates are an incentive to saving but, at the same time, they discourage borrowing; and similarly decreasing interest rates encourage borrowing and discourage saving. But the requirements of the surplus phase have to encourage not only saving but also borrowing; and it would take enormous interest rates backed by all the propaganda techniques at our disposal to bring about the ever increasing rates of surplus income proper to the surplus expansion; and some form of magic would be needed to prevent them from discouraging all borrowing. What then is needed is the at once rapid and effective decreasing purchasing power of money that brings about "forced savings." And when inevitably the surplus phase yields to its natural consequent, the basic phase, the old watchwords of thrift and enterprise become counterproductive. For then the thrift that is needed becomes less and less a matter of expected surplus income and, while enterprise loses none of its risk, it no longer lures people on with the attractions of the surplus gain to be expected during the surplus expansion.'

198 In the supplement distributed in 1979, Lonergan gave the following formulation.

   'Rates of interest, when increasing, encourage saving (but discourage borrowing). This double edge is not the per se means of effecting the enormous shift in saving to bring about the transition from a slump or a basic expansion to a surplus expansion. What is needed is a contraction of purchasing power that will direct spending from the basic market of the poor to the surplus market of the rich. The surplus phase is anti-egalitarian, as much in Russia and socialist countries as elsewhere; there was more suffering and more deliberately inflicted suffering in Siberia at the base of the Russian surplus

lem is not that the rate of saving, w, has to be bigger in a surplus expansion but that it   has to be becoming bigger and bigger all the time; w is positive as long as $dQ''/Q'' - dQ'/Q'$ is positive. Hence if there is to be any relevance to increments in interest rates, one has to envisage not intermittent increments but rather a rate of increase of interest rates. Again, to speak of interest rates providing an incentive to saving is true enough as far as it goes; but it misses the magnitude of the problem, which is to effect an anti-egalitarian shift in the distribution of income. To increase the rates of interest will effect some modification of instances of dw_i in favor of reduced basic income; but it would take enormous interest rates backed by all propaganda techniques at our disposal to effect the negative values of dw_i that are required interval after interval as the surplus expansion proceeds; what is needed is something in the order of 'incentives to save' that is as rapid and as effective as the reduction of purchasing power by rising prices.

But not only does the concept of an equilibrium rate of interest miss the magnitude of the problem. It also involves an indiscriminate lumping together of quite different things. One cannot identify a reduction of basic income with an increase in the supply of money, for a reduction of basic income is only one source of such supply; moreover, it is neither the normal nor the principal source of such supply; normally, surplus final products are purchased with surplus income, which is just as much a circular flow as the purchase of basic final products by basic income; principally the increase in the supply of money is due to the expansion of bank credit, which is necessary to provide the positive $(S' - s'O')$ and $(S'' - s''O'')$ needed interval after interval to enable the circuits to keep pace with the expanding productive process. In the concrete problem under examination there is an abundant supply of money for all purposes; the one difficulty is that the division of income into basic and surplus is not parallel to the division

---

expansion [than] in the nineteenth-century British expansion that so raised the explosive anger of Marx.

'Similarly, a lowering of interest rates may encourage the expansion of basic industry; but it also will encourage the expansion of well-intentioned but not well-thought-out innovations, the number of bankruptcies, etc. What is needed is the egalitarian shift in incomes, that will compensate for the previous and shorter anti-egalitarian shift, and will produce the things that people really need and can learn to purchase without the help of self-seeking advertisers.'

of productive activity into basic and surplus; a general operation upon the supply of money seems to be a rather roundabout and inept procedure to correct an error in distribution.

The ineptitude of the procedure arises not only from its inadequacy to effect a redistribution of income of the magnitude required but also from its effects upon the demand for money. Four types of such demand may be distinguished: demand for basic final products; demand for surplus final products; demand for maintaining or increasing the turnover magnitudes of units of enterprise; and demand for redistributional purposes. The effect of rising interest rates on consumer borrowing will be excellent as far as it goes; for it cannot but reduce consumer borrowing; on the other hand, one may doubt if such reduction is very significant, for an inability to calculate is a normal condition of consumer borrowing, and rising interest rates hardly exert a great influence on people who do not calculate.[199] The effect of rising interest rates on the demand for surplus final products is great: one may say that the initiation of further long-term expansion is blocked; to increase the interest rate from 5% to 6% increases by 10% the annual charge[200] upon a piece of capital equipment paid for over a period of twenty years. Thus rising interest rates end further initiation of long-term expansion; on the other hand, expansion already initiated, especially if notably advanced, will continue inasmuch as an increased burden of future costs is preferred to the net loss of deserting the new or the additional enterprise. The effect of rising interest rates on turnover magnitudes depends upon the turnover frequency of the enterprise. If the frequency is once every two years, 1% increase in the rate of interest is a 2% increase in costs; if the frequency is once every month, 1% increase in the rate of interest is 1/12 of 1% increase in costs. Effects of the latter order are negligible when prices are rising. Indeed, then even a 2% increase might be disregarded; but the combination of the 2% increase in costs with the uncertainty of what prices will be in two years' time is a rather powerful deterrent. The effect on turnover magnitudes, accordingly, is great when the frequency of the turnover is low, but negligible when the frequency is high. Finally, as to the effect on redistributional bor-

199   In 1944 Lonergan wrote 'cannot calculate'; the change here follows a 1978 page of corrigenda (see above, note 185).
200   That is, increases the annual charge by approximately 10%. The precise increase would be 8.557% if payments were made monthly; 8.651% if payments were made annually.

rowing, there are a variety of complications: gamblers on the stock market will continue to gamble; new flotations of stock will be discouraged for the same reason as the purchase of surplus products; the international position of the country will be affected, a point from which the argument has prescinded so far and which can be considered only later.

However, the following conclusions seem justified. When the rate of saving is insufficient, increasing interest rates effect an adjustment. This adjustment is not an adjustment of the rate of saving to the productive process but of the productive process to the rate of saving: for small increments in interest rates tend to eliminate all long-term elements in the expansion; and such small increments necessarily precede the preposterously large increments needed to effect the required negative values of dw_i. Finally, the adjustment is delayed, and it does not de-serve the name of adjustment. It is delayed because the influence of increasing interest rates on short-term enterprise is small. It does not deserve the name 'adjustment' because its effect is not to keep the rate of saving and the productive process in harmony as the expansion continues but simply to end the expansion by eliminating its long-term elements.

27   The Cycle of Pure Surplus Income

[1944] A condition of circuit acceleration was seen in section 15 to include the keeping in step of basic outlay, basic income, and basic expenditure, and on the other hand, the keeping in step of surplus outlay, surplus income, and surplus expenditure. Any of these rates may begin to vary independently of the others, and adjustment of the others may lag. But any systematic divergence brings automatic correctives to work. The concomitance of outlay and expenditure follows from the interaction of supply and demand. The concomitance of income with outlay and expenditure is identical with the adjustment of the rate of saving to the requirements of the productive process. It follows that one may legitimately project a division of expenditure into a division of income, and it is in this manner that we arrive at the concept of a pure surplus income.[201]

201 In place of the second paragraph of this section and the first sentence of the third paragraph, the supplement distributed by Lonergan in 1979 gives the following discussion of surplus income. The editors have altered the notation to conform with the final version of Lonergan's diagram of rates of flow; the whole should be read in conjunction with 'Appendix: History of the Diagram, 1944–1998,' on the successive versions of this diagram.

'Surplus Income

'Surplus income is not the same as profits. The latter are a simple matter of the excess of accounts receivable over accounts payable. They include a firm's additions to its portfolio, and living expenses (no matter how high) of the upper echelons. This accountant's concept of profit pertains not to macro- but to microeconomics.

'Surplus income as a macroeconomic concept is the social dividend [rate of saving; see note 186] that results from the functioning of an expanding econ- omy. It receives contributions from basic outlay [Lonergan wrote 'income'], $(i'O')$ as well as from surplus outlay [Lonergan wrote 'income'] $(i''O'')$. The possibility of a contribution from the basic circuit arises from the balancing contributions to basic income [Lonergan wrote 'outlay'] from surplus outlay $(c''O'')$. Without such a crossover balance one circuit is suffering an inflation while imposing a deflation on the other.

'There is a further but parallel implication. The fact that people earning their living in the surplus circuit spend a notable part of it on consumer goods gives rise to the basic price spread. This price spread is the excess of basic receipts over basic costs. In microeconomics it is interpreted as profit, and so trade-union leaders argue that commercial and industrial profits justify a rise in wages. But in macroeconomics, which is aware of the need of a crossover balance for equilibrium, the basic price spread is to a greater or less extent a part of the social dividend [rate of saving] in an expanding economy. It is only in the static economy that all of it justifies a rise in wages.

'On any turnover, then, the possible sources of surplus income are the flows of money into surplus transitional receipts, namely, (1) existing surplus firms maintaining the level of the previous turnover by spending on surplus supply the sum of $i''O''$ and $i'O'$, (2) existing surplus firms increasing the level of previous turnover by drawing on the redistributional function by $(S'' - s'O'')$, (3) emergent surplus firms drawing on the redistributional function by $(D'' - s'I'')$ to acquire plant and equipment.'

'Query: How does one distinguish surplus from basic firms?

'The distinction is not legal and to be learned by studying incorporation proceedings but functional and to be understood by distinguishing the mar- kets at which the firms' products are sold.

'While this distinction is empirical (resting on matters of fact) it is not empiricist (resting on easily ascertained matters of fact and preferably to be found in tables already drawn up and published).'

'Pure Surplus Income

'At times, when an economy is not expanding, surplus income is spent sim- ply on maintenance and replacements.

'But when an economy is expanding, a distinction has to be drawn between

Pure surplus income may be defined, for present purposes, as a fraction of total surplus income. This fraction will be denoted by the symbol v,[202] where v is the fraction of surplus expenditure that goes to new fixed investment. All surplus final expenditure may be termed a 'fixed investment' to distinguish it from the outlay of units of enterprise and their transitional payments, which may be called 'liquid investment.' Further, fixed investment may be divided into the purchase at the surplus final markets of replacements and of maintenance and, on the other hand, new fixed investment. Thus in each interval the rate of surplus expenditure E'' consists of two parts: one part, $(1 - v)E''$, goes to the replacement and maintenance of old fixed investment; the other part, vE'', goes to new fixed investment.

Now, when I'' is keeping pace with E'', so that $(D'' - s''I'')$ is zero, one may make a parallel distinction in surplus income, naming $(1 - v)I''$ as ordinary surplus income and vI'' as pure surplus income. This pure surplus income is quite an interesting object. When v is greater than zero, it is a rate of income over and above all current requirements for the standard of living, since that is provided by I', and as well over and above all real maintenance and replacement expenditure, since that is provided by $(1 - v)I''$. Thus one may identify pure surplus income as the aggregate rate of return upon capital investment: entrepreneurs consider that they are having tolerable success when they are not merely 'making a living,' no matter how high their standard of living, and not merely obtaining sufficient receipts to purchase all the equipment necessary to overcome obsolescence, but also receiving an additional sum of income which is profit in their strong sense of the term.

---

expenditure on maintenance and replacement and on the other hand the pure surplus that supports the expanding economy.

    'Let v denote the fraction of surplus income that goes to the expansion of the economy and $(1 - v)$ the remaining fraction that goes to maintenance and replacement.

    'Revert to text: "This pure surplus income is quite an interesting object ..."'

202 Lonergan originally used the symbol H. Here, as in notes 201 and 204, the symbol v has been substituted. A different letter is needed because h has already appeared in *MD:ECA*, with another meaning. Note that v denotes a fraction, not a quantity, and that this use of a lower-case letter is an exception to the convention explained in note 29.

An aggregate profit in that sense is precisely what we have found pure surplus income to be. Further,[203] unlike other income, pure surplus income need not be spent currently without effecting a reduction of total income; it is possible to divert pure surplus [income] from the circuits to the redistributional function without causing a negative $(D'' - s''I'')$ because in the redistributional function there is an organization of promoters, underwriters, brokers, and investors who there mobilize sums of money and move them along $(D'' - s''I'')$ from the redistributional function to the surplus demand function where they are spent as new fixed investment. Thus it is pure surplus income, as a concrete fact, which has given rise to and has sustained the ideal of the 'successful man' in our culture. For the 'successful man' is a man who, of course, enjoys a very high standard of living, but who measures his success in quite other terms, namely, in the industrial power of ownership which he wields, in the financial power of possession of large blocks of readily negotiable securities, and in the social prestige that may be buttressed by the purchase of the most conspicuous products of human art and ingenuity in the past history of man. For there to be successful men of this type and for them to attain their success through industry and commerce, it must be possible to derive from the circuits a rate of income that can be moved, without conflicting with circuit requirements, from the circuits to the redistributional function where alone industrial stocks, negotiable securities, and the products of the process in the remote past are now on sale.

Enough, perhaps, has been said to show that pure surplus income is at the nerve center of free economies. We have now to advert to the fact that it is subject to cyclic variation in the long-term acceleration of the productive process. The symbol v in the product vI'' has already been met. It is the measure of the long-term acceleration potential of the surplus stage of the productive process. The higher the rate of new fixed investment, the greater the rate at which long-term acceleration of the process is proceeding and, as well, the greater the rate of pure surplus income. But the long-term acceleration of the process involves a cycle,

---

203 According to the 1978 page of corrigenda (see note 185 above), the following clause, from 'unlike other income' through 'reduction of total income,' was to be deleted. The reason for deleting it may be that other income, as well as pure surplus income, can behave in this way.

and this cycle cannot but affect the rate of pure surplus income. To this we direct attention.[204]

Let the symbol f denote the ratio of pure surplus income to total income, so that

$$f = vI'' / (I' + I'') \tag{37}$$

whence, taking w as the ratio of surplus to total income,[205]

$$f = vw \tag{38}$$

204 A replacement for the next several lines of text, from 'Let the symbol f' through equation (39), was distributed by Lonergan in 1979. Note that both in the text and in the present note the symbol f is a fraction.

'Let w represent the fraction $I'' / (I' + I'')$ so that

$$f = vw \tag{38a}$$

Now a maximum is reached when the graph shifts from increasing to decreasing. Hence before the maximum, f is sloping upwards, at the maximum Δf is zero, and after the maximum f is sloping downwards. [The preceding sentence has been altered slightly.] Differentiating the product of two variables (38a), one obtains

$$\Delta f = v\Delta w + w\Delta v \tag{38b}$$

so that f will be at a maximum on the three conditions listed just above. But the key condition is that Δf equals zero so that

$$-v\Delta w = w\Delta v \tag{38c}$$

Now, if v became zero, the surplus expansion would be over, the basic expansion would be skipped, and the economy would at best be in the stationary state with surplus confined to maintenance and replacements.

'If w became zero, there would be neither maintenance nor replacements. The result would be a breakdown.

'But if Δw became zero, then pure surplus income would be at its maximum. The transition from the surplus phase to the basic phase of the expansion would begin. Maintenance in the surplus circuit would continue, and in the basic circuit it would increase. So $(1 - v)$ begins to increase, and so v has passed its maximum. At that point both terms on the right-hand side of (38b) and all terms in (38c) would be zero. Δf then is zero.'

205 The phrase 'taking w as ... income' has been added, following the 1978 page of corrigenda (see note 185 above).

On assuming a smooth trend and differentiating, one finds as a condition for a maximum of f that

$$0 = vdw + wdv \qquad (39)$$

As long as the right-hand side of this equation is positive, the ratio f is increasing; when it becomes negative, f begins to decrease.

Now the ratio w is at its maximum ($dw = 0$) when the process turns over from a surplus to a basic expansion: throughout the surplus expansion, w increases; throughout the basic expansion, w decreases. On the other hand, [since] v increases as long as Q'' increases, the maximum of v depends upon two somewhat independent factors:[206] v begins to decrease either because Q'' begins to decrease or because the rate of replacement requirements begins to rise.[207] On the assumption of the pure cycle, Q'' does not decrease but reaches a maximum and then levels off into a straight line parallel to the time axis; in that case, the maximum of v arises subsequently to the maximum of w when, during the basic expansion, the rate of replacements begins to rise or, if Q'' were still increasing, when the rate of replacements begins to increase more rapidly than Q''. If, however, the surplus expansion was over-ambitious and expanded the surplus stage of the process excessively, then Q'' is bound to fall sharply at some time or other. This will occur prior to the ordinary maximum of v to bring about a premature maximum of that ratio. It may occur after the [ordinary?] maximum of w to make the maximum of f not a smooth turning point but a sharp break and fall.[208] It may occur earlier, bringing w to a premature maximum and suddenly changing f from a rate of rapid increase to a rate of still more rapid decrease.

Thus, in general, there are three types of maxima for f. There is the ideal maximum when the turn is due to replacements absorbing the capacity of

206 According to the 1978 page of corrigenda (see note 185 above) the remainder of this sentence was to be deleted.

207 Ordinarily this will be the case, but it is also possible that v become constant while Q'' increases.

208 Lonergan's wording is somewhat ambiguous here. Since w must always begin to decrease whenever Q'' decreases (assuming $Q' > 0$), then the maximum of v cannot occur before the maximum of w. It is likely that Lonergan was referring to a maximum in v for an excessively expanded economy, which occurs prior to the 'ordinary' maximum of $w-$ that is, prior to the point in time where w_{max} would have occurred in the case of the pure cycle.

the surplus stage for effecting an acceleration of the process. There is the slightly premature maximum when the turn is due to an overexpansion of the surplus stage but occurs after the maximum of w when the rate of increase of f is already small. There is the extremely premature maximum of f when the turn is due to a great overexpansion and occurs when the rate of increase of f is still great; in this case the maxima of f, w, and v coincide. By overexpansion is meant simply the fact that the surplus rate of production Q'' falls.

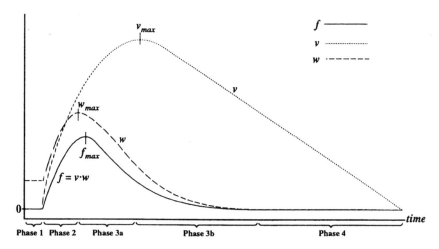

Figure 27-1 Rate of Change of v, w, and f during a Pure Cycle, Ideal Maximum f

To visualize this cycle, let us say that F_i is the pure surplus income per interval received by the unit of enterprise i, and that O_i is the outlay per interval of the same unit of enterprise. Then[209]

$$f = vw = \Sigma F_i / \Sigma O_i = F/O \qquad (40)$$

Here, ΣF_i is identical with vI'' and ΣO_i is identical with $(O' + O'')$. On the other hand, F/O may be taken as simply a representative ratio of pure surplus to total outlay among units of enterprise. In any given unit of enterprise, according to its advantages or disadvantages, the particular ratio F_j/O_j will be greater or less than the average, F/O.

209 Lonergan's notation has been altered in accordance with the editorial policy set out in note 29.

Now in the proportionate expansion at the beginning of the pure cycle, the ratio w is constant:[210] proportionately, the surplus stage is increasing as rapidly as the basic. However, the fraction v will be increasing, for the surplus stage is then increasing its potential for long-term acceleration. It follows that the ratio f and the average, F/O, are increasing as v increases. Further, since both basic and surplus stages are accelerating, ΣO_i is increasing; and so the absolute quantity of pure surplus, ΣF_i, is increasing as the product of two increasing factors, namely, v and ΣO_i. Insofar as prosperity is measured in terms of pure surplus income, prosperity has begun.

The proportionate expansion is based on the capacity of the process for short-term acceleration. If a great long-term acceleration develops, that is, a transformation of the capital equipment of the surplus stage, then dQ'/Q' will lag behind dQ''/Q'', and a surplus expansion will result. Then both w and v are increasing. The ratio f and the average, F/O, will be increasing as the product of two increasing factors, namely, both w and v. The absolute quantity of pure surplus income, ΣF_i, will be increasing as the product of three increasing factors, namely, w, v, and ΣO_i. The rewards of entrepreneurial initiative are munificent.

It is to be observed that this phase has no necessary implication of an inflationary rise in prices. That occurrence is conditioned by the failure of the rate of saving to keep increasing rapidly enough. If the pure surplus is captured by the higher income brackets alone, the anti-egalitarian shift in the distribution of income is being achieved. If not, saving is insufficient; prices rise; total income increases; and this increment, at least in the first instance when it appears as a broader price spread, will go to the higher income brackets to combine an anti-egalitarian shift with a reduced purchasing power, which pinches the lower income groups.

However, the surplus expansion is only an acceleration lag. The greater it is and the longer it lasts, the greater the potential for basic expansion that is created. Obviously, it is not created and then left unused. It is put to work as rapidly as possible, and so the basic stage accelerates at an ever greater pace while the surplus stage begins to realize that it has acquired as great a potential as possibly can be used. There results the basic expansion, with the basic stage accelerating, proportionately, more rapidly than the surplus: w has passed its maximum.

In the early part of the basic expansion, f is still increasing though at a

210 It is constant, provided certain relations among price changes obtain, as will be discussed presently.

reduced rate; for the rate of decrease of w is cutting against the rate of increase of v, which now may be less rapid. It follows that the average, F/O, is also increasing still. On the other hand, the absolute sum of pure surplus, ΣF_i, is increasing as the product of two increasing factors, namely, f and ΣO_i. On the supposition of a pure cycle, in which Q'' does not decrease, the maximum of f is intermediate between the maximum of w and the maximum of v.[211] It is a smooth turn that decreases pure surplus, not by diminishing receipts but by changing the function of surplus income from being the 'money to invest' of pure surplus to [being] the mere replacement income that has to be spent on overcoming mounting obsolescence. However, while the ratio f and the average, F/O, decrease after the smooth maximum of f, the absolute quantity of pure surplus income continues to increase up to the maximum of v, which, *ex hypothesi*, is later. Thus two periods are to be distinguished subsequent to the maximum of f: a first period, in which average pure surplus is decreasing though aggregate pure surplus continues to increase;[212] and a second period, in which both average and aggregate pure surplus income are decreasing.[213] In the second of these periods the ratio f and the average, F/O, are decreasing as the product of two decreasing factors, namely, w and v; if ΣO_i is still increasing, ΣF_i will be decreasing at a slower rate; but in any case f, v, and ΣF_i are reverting to zero, which they reach as dQ', following dQ'', reaches zero.

The foregoing is an outline of perfect adaptation to the pure cycle of the expanding productive process. However, the actual course of events is governed by the actual lack of adaptation to the pure cycle. This lack of adaptation is multiple, and so we treat successively and as distinct though conjoined phenomena the long, drawn-out depression and the short, violent crisis.

At the root of the depression lies a misinterpretation of the significance of pure surplus income. In fact, it is the monetary equivalent of the new fixed investment of an expansion: just as the production of new fixed investment is over-and-above all current consumption and replacement products, so pure surplus income is over-and-above all current consumption and replacement income; just as the products of new fixed investment emerge in cyclic fashion, so also does pure surplus income emerge in cyclic

211 See Figure 27-1.
212 See Figure 27-1, Phase 3a.
213 See Figure 27-1, Phase 3b.

fashion. It is mounting from zero at a moderate pace in the proportionate expansion; it is mounting at an enormous pace in the surplus expansion; but in the basic expansion first average, and then aggregate pure surplus income begin to decline, and eventually they have reverted to zero. Now it is true that our culture cannot be accused of mistaken ideas on pure surplus income as it has been defined in this essay; for on that precise topic it has no ideas whatever. However, the phenomena here referred to by the term 'pure surplus income' are not, as is the term, a creation of our own. The phenomena are well known. Entrepreneurs are quite aware that there are times of prosperity in which even a fool can make a profit and other mysterious times in which the brilliant and the prudent may be driven to the wall. Entrepreneurs are quite aware of the ideal of the successful man, a man whose success is measured not by a high emergent standard of living nor by the up-to-date efficiency of some industrial or commercial unit but by increasing industrial, financial, and social power and prestige. In the old days, when the entrepreneur was also owner and manager, pure surplus income roughly coincided with what was termed profit. Today, with increasing specialization of function, pure surplus income is distributed in a variety of ways: it enters into [the] very high salaries of general managers and top-flight executives, into the combined fees of directors when together these reach a high figure, into the undistributed profits of industry, into the secret reserves of banks, into the accumulated royalties, rents, interest receipts, fees, or dividends of anyone who receives a higher income than he intends to spend at the basic final market. For pure surplus income, as distributed, is the remainder of income that is not spent at the basic final market either directly by its recipient or equivalently through the action of others spending more than they earn. Thus pure surplus income may be identified best of all by calling it net aggregate savings and viewing them as functionally related to the rate of new fixed investment.

The consequence is that net aggregate savings vary with new fixed investment, and the complaint is that there exist, in the mentality of our culture, no ideas, and in the procedures of our economies, no mechanisms, directed to smoothly and equitably bringing about the reversal of net aggregate savings to zero as the basic expansion proceeds. Just as there is an anti-egalitarian shift to the surplus expansion, so also there is an egalitarian shift in the distribution of income in the basic expansion. But while we can effect the anti-egalitarian shift with some measure of success, in fact the egalitarian shift is achieved only through the contractions, the liquidations, the blind stresses and strains of a prolonged depression. Once f has passed its maximum, the average ratio of pure surplus to the outlay of an entrepreneurial unit, F_j/O_j, has to decrease. Once v has passed its maximum, the aggregate of pure surplus, ΣF_i, has to decrease. There is operative a general 'squeeze.' There is no mechanism for providing adaptation to this squeeze. There follows chaos.

In the first place, there are a number of sources of pure surplus income, as distributed, that are relatively invulnerable. Individuals may hold fixed claims of income against industrial or commercial units. In any particular case these fixed claims, whether against one or against a number of units, may amount to a claim to surplus income. The obvious instance is had in interest-bearing bonds. But there exists a series of more or less analogous instances of pure surplus income in the form of fees or of salaries, and the less these instances are directly derived from industry, commerce, or financial services, the less they can be controlled by their real though remote sources. The significance of such relative invulnerability is that such instances of pure surplus income are the last to feel the squeeze, and, what is more important, that the pressure of the squeeze is all the stronger and more relentless on other instances.

Besides this first degree of invulnerability there is a second. The same reasons that enabled some units of enterprise to recapture more than an average share of pure surplus income during the surplus expansion now will enable them to resist a proportionately more than average reduction of their share of pure surplus. Thus the squeeze is operative most of all upon the firms that have a less than average share of pure surplus. As it proceeds, it will eliminate not merely any pure surplus they receive but as well their replacement income and part of their basic income. Such relative invulnerability brings the circuits to a distorted quasi equilibrium in which an artificial rate of pure surplus income is sustained by a rate of losses. Individuals continue to receive more income than they spend at the basic or at the surplus final markets. There is no compensating rate of new fixed investment to offset this drain. There results a negative value of $(D'' - s''I'')$, but the squeeze gives positive values of $(S'' - s''O'')$ and particularly $(S' - s'O')$ as embarrassed entrepreneurs undergo a continuous and equal stream of losses. In this fashion, the required reduction of the rate of savings is effected by creating losses to supply the invulnerable rate of savings. From a different viewpoint one may say that the outlay of some firms exceeds their receipts to enable the outlay of other firms to contain an artificial pure surplus income. But however the matter is expressed, the rate of losses has to equal the emergence of more pure surplus income than the process in the given interval is generating; and if at any time the rate of losses proves insufficient, the familiar mechanism of falling prices, decreased total income, and increased purchasing power comes into play either to decrease the rate of savings or to increase the rate of losses.

Evidently, the systematic requirement of a rate of losses will result in a series of contractions and liquidations. Any particular firm may succeed in strengthening its position. But that only transfers the incidence of the squeeze elsewhere. Any number of firms may go bankrupt and be liquidated. But until the position of the strong is undermined by the general and prolonged contracting, the requirement for the rate of losses continues, and with it the depression.

It is quite true that, were a long-term acceleration to get under way, the situation would be remedied, for sooner or later the weaker firms would begin to obtain sufficient receipts to make ends meet. But the difficulty is that a long-term acceleration has been under way quite recently, that it was approaching completion in the surplus stage of the process, and that it was at least partially completed in the basic stage. Further acceleration of the process, from the nature of the development attained, would be a basic expansion, and it would have to be a short-term basic expansion before it could develop into a long-term basic expansion; things have to be going fairly well before a general movement to transform capital equipment can be initiated. Now, whenever the basic stage accelerates more rapidly than the surplus stage, the rate of savings has to decrease continuously. But in the depression there is already an excessive rate of savings, and only a distorted equilibrium is had through the simultaneous existence of a rate of losses. Further decrease in the required rate of savings only intensifies the problem; spontaneously it will work out through the mechanism of falling prices and contracting total income; that under current inadaptation an expansion could be expected against such difficulties is evidently preposterous. On the other hand, increasing contraction and liquidation tends to reduce the requirement for a rate of losses: with the surplus stage already operating at a minimum, any further reduction of the basic stage means that a zero dQ''/Q'' is greater than a negative dQ'/Q'; this postulates an increasing rate of savings, and under the circumstances, this increase of required savings (since actual savings already are too great) is a reduction of losses. Thus the greater the contraction, the less the rate of losses required; again, the greater the contraction, the weaker the position of the initially invulnerable; in the limit the rate of losses will disappear, and a dis-

torted equilibrium give place to a true equilibrium. Meanwhile, obsolescence will have mounted, and so as orders for replacements begin to
increase they will be accompanied by surplus purchases that are new fixed
investment; v begins to increase, and the proportionate expansion of the
revival is under way.

Later[214] we shall consider the effect of a favorable balance of foreign
trade or of deficit government spending in mitigating the depression's
requirement for a rate of losses. The present point, however, should be
repeated. It is that in the later stages of a long-term acceleration, even if
there is no crisis or general breakdown, there is required a continuously
decreasing rate of net aggregate savings so that, at the end of the expansion and until a new expansion gets under way, net aggregate savings or
pure surplus income have to be zero. The phenomena of our depressions
can be explained by our lack of any mechanism that will reduce net aggregate savings smoothly and equitably. There results a distorted equilibrium
conditioned by a rate of losses. This rate of losses forces the series of contractions and liquidations that characterize the depression. Further, under
such circumstances, it is vain to expect a solution or remedy by the emergence of a new cycle of expansion; that might be expected if an extremely
premature crisis arose but not if the process gets into difficulties after the
surplus expansion has largely been completed; in the latter case, suppos-
ing current adaptation, it is only the prolonged contraction undermining
the position of the strong and reducing the requirement for an impossibly
low rate of net aggregate savings that ends the depression. Even after the
distorted equilibrium through a rate of losses has been eliminated, it is
impossible for the expansion to begin if the real situation is such as to favor
a basic expansion; for that would only renew the old difficulties. But with
the passage of time, obsolescence will become great enough to make the
situation favor a surplus expansion, a great long-term acceleration; then
the trade cycle recommences.

It will be convenient to reserve to the next section an account of the
more violent phenomena of the crisis.

28   The Cycle of the Aggregate Basic Price Spread

[1944] There is a sense in which one may speak of the fraction of basic outlay that moves to basic income as the 'costs' of basic production. It is true

214 See below, §§ 30 and 31 and the Additional Note to Section 31.

that that sense is not at all an accountant's sense of 'costs': for it would include among costs the standard of living of those who receive dividends but [would] not [include] the element of pure surplus in the salaries of managers; worse, it would not include replacement costs, nor the part of maintenance that is purchased at the surplus final market, nor the accumulation for sinking funds which is a part of pure surplus income. But however remote from the accountant's meaning of the term 'costs,' it remains that there is an aggregate and functional sense in which the fraction of basic outlay moving to basic income is an index of costs. For the greater the fraction that basic income is of total income (or total outlay), the less the remainder which constitutes the aggregate possibility of profit. But what limits profit may be termed cost. Hence we propose in the present section to speak of $c'O'$, and as well of $c''O''$, as costs of production, having warned the reader that the costs in question are aggregate and functional costs in a sense analogous to that in which forced savings are savings.

In any given interval, the rates of outlay, O' and O'', are functions, not of the indices of quantities sold at the final markets, Q' and Q'', but of these indices corrected by the acceleration factors, a' and a''. Thus, when the productive process is expanding or contracting, O' is some price-level index multiplied by $a'Q'$, and O'' is some price-level [index] multiplied by $a''Q''$. In expansions, a' and a'' are greater than unity, since current production is for future greater sales; in contractions, a' and a'' are less than unity, since then current production is for future reduced sales. Let us now introduce two cost price indices, p' and p'', which are defined by the equations[215]

$$c'O' = p'a'Q' \tag{41}$$

$$c''O'' = p''a''Q'' \tag{42}$$

215 Equations 41 and 42 have been altered to conform with the notation in the final version of the *Essay*. Equation 43 was written in 1944, before Lonergan began his later revisions of the section on rates of payment and transfer and the diagram of rates of flow (§§13 and 14 in the present edition); consequently a third term that would correspond with $s'O'$ in equation (4) is missing from (43). As it stands here, equation (43) makes the tacit assumption that $s' = 0$, which is to say that $s'O'$ and $s''O''$ are assumed to be negligible throughout the present section, as Lonergan indicates in § 13 above, p. 50. See also note 57 above.

whence by equation (4)

$$I' = p'a'Q' + p''a''Q'' \qquad (43)$$

Now, when $(D' - s'I')$ satisfies general conditions of circuit acceleration by being zero, so that E' equals I', then since E' equals $P'Q'$ one may write

$$P'Q' = p'a'Q' + p''a''Q'' \qquad (44)$$

Dividing through by $p'Q'$ one may write[216]

$$J = P'/p' = a' + a''R \qquad (45)$$

where J is the basic price-spread ratio, being the selling-price index P' divided by the cost-price index p', and R is the ratio of surplus to basic activity indicated by the fraction $p''Q''/p'Q'$. It follows that the basic price-spread ratio J is the sum of the basic acceleration factor a' and of the product of the surplus acceleration factor a'' with the surplus-to-basic ratio R.

Variations in R involve no new elements. At a first estimate R will be increasing during the surplus expansion when Q''/Q' is increasing, but decreasing during the basic expansion when Q''/Q' is decreasing. Taking into account the further quotient p''/p', one would expect it to be constant, inasmuch as cost prices in basic and surplus units have the same general determinants; and inasmuch as there arose any divergence between p'' and p', one would expect it to reinforce our initial estimate; p''/p' would increase, if anything, in the surplus expansion, but would decrease, if anything, in the basic expansion.

The influence of R on the aggregate basic price spread is obvious. The greater the fraction of total basic income that is derived from surplus outlay, the less the fraction of total basic income that is derived from basic outlay. But total basic income becomes basic expenditure and basic receipts. And the source of basic price spread is the difference between basic receipts and the fraction of basic outlay going to basic income. A very rough illustration may be had if we identify basic income with aggregate wages and aggregate wages with costs of all production and, as well, with the receipts of basic sales. Then the greater the surplus activity, the greater the surplus

---

216 Note that in what follows J and R are fractions, contrary to the editorial convention explained above in note 29.

aggregate wages, the smaller the fraction of total wages paid by basic producers, the smaller the fraction of total costs paid by basic producers, and the smaller the fraction of basic receipts required to meet basic costs.[217]

The influence of the acceleration factors is also easily understood. The greater current production relative to current final sales, then the greater the price spread, provided that all current income is spent for the relatively smaller quantity that is finished and now on sale. The exact behavior of the acceleration factors, however, introduces a new element for our consideration. Introducing the symbol q' as identical with $a'Q'$, and differentiating the consequent identity, one obtains[218]

$$da' = a'(dq'/q' - dQ'/Q') \qquad (46)$$

and by changing (') to (") one has the parallel equation for da''. Hence, for the acceleration factor a' to be increasing, it is necessary for da' to be positive and so for $(dq'/q' - dQ'/Q')$ to be positive. (Note that Q', q', and a' are always positive.) This means that the acceleration factor can be positive only when the rate of current production of basic quantities is increasing more rapidly in proportion to its size than the rate of current sales of basic quantities is increasing in proportion to its size. Thus, if one supposes that q' moves ahead of Q', the acceleration factor moves above unity; but as soon as the quantities under production reach the final market, Q' accelerates; if, then, q' is accelerating at the higher rate proportionate to its greater size, a' will be at a maximum and remain constant as long as the acceleration of q' increases with a'; but as soon as the acceleration of q' ceases to mount ever more rapidly, a' begins to fall. The same holds for the surplus acceleration factor a''. Evidently, the acceleration factors are magnificently unstable. The initial lag of quantities sold behind quantities produced enables them to rise above unity. But merely to keep them constant once quantities sold begin to mount means that quantities under production have to increase in a geometrical progression for the rest of the expansion. Any failure to maintain this brilliant pace means that the acceleration factors, and so the basic price spread, drop.

217 According to a supplement that Lonergan distributed in 1978 (see note 185 above), the whole of the following paragraph (from 'The influence' through 'and so the basic price spread, drop') was to be omitted.

218 In other words, one differentiates both sides of the equation $q' = a'Q'$ and then solves for da'.

Now in any expansion it is inevitable that quantities under production run ahead of quantities sold. Current production is with reference to future sales, and if there is an expansion, then future sales are going to be greater than current sales. But in the free economies the acceleration factors are not held down to the minimum that results from this consideration. During the surplus expansion the basic price-spread ratio J will increase from an increase of R, of a'', and also of a'. The advance of the price-spread ratio will work out through a rise of basic price level, and selling prices generally will mount. Now, when prices are rising and due to rise further, the thing to be done is to buy now when prices are low and sell later when they are high. There results a large amount of speculative liquid investment. Each producer orders more materials, more semifinished goods, more finished goods, than he would otherwise. Moreover, he makes this speculative addition to a future demand estimated upon current orders received, so that the further back in the production series any producer is, the greater [will be] the speculative element contained in the objective evidence of current orders received, the more rosy the estimate of future demand, and the greater the speculative element he adds to this estimate when he places orders with a producer still further back in the series.

Thus an initial rise in prices sets going a speculative expansion that makes the acceleration factors quite notable, expands the price spread still more, and stimulates a pace of further acceleration that it will be quite impossible to maintain. Differentiating equation (45) one has

$$dJ = da' + R da'' + a'' dR \qquad (47)$$

Here the cyclic factors are R and dR: in the surplus expansion, R is increasing and dR is positive; in the basic expansion, R is decreasing and dR is negative. R is a fractional quantity, and dR the increment of a fraction. On the other hand, as long as expansion continues, the surplus acceleration factor a'' will be greater than unity. Upon this background enters the performance of da' and da'', with the former preponderant since the coefficient of da'' is the fraction R.

Now during proportionate expansion dR will be zero, but da' and da'' will be positive for a while as a short-term acceleration develops. At least in the basic stage it will prove impossible to maintain a generalized rate of expansion in a geometrical progression, so that da' will become negative.

The event will probably take place when the surplus acceleration factor a'' has reached a high-level rate so that da'' is zero. It follows that dJ becomes negative with da', and in this dJ will be all the more negative if there is any faltering in the surplus stage to give a negative da'' as well. Thus the price-spread ratio J contracts; the basic price level falls; speculators are disillusioned. There is a minor crisis: first, speculative assets are frozen as everyone wishes to sell before prices fall further, and no one wishes to buy until they fall further; then there is a period of liquidation as liquid assets are sold for whatever price they will fetch. The gravity of this first crisis will depend exclusively upon the magnitude of the speculative development, the solvency of speculators, and their ability to weather the storm without liquidating their stocks. Whether it is a squall or a tempest, the underlying long-term development soon sets things right. For as the surplus stage generalizes long-term acceleration, R increases and dR becomes positive to expand again the price spread and to keep it expanding. As this proceeds, there develops another speculative boom. The surplus acceleration factor a'' mounts and remains constant at its maximum; the basic acceleration factor a' mounts and then contracts; previous phenomena are repeated with the difference that the negative da' is mitigated by a positive dR, and that throughout this crisis there is at work a positive dR to bring things back to an even keel. When the rate of expansion is restored, the basic stage will move into a general long-term acceleration; for a while yet dR will remain positive and a third speculative boom develops. This boom suffers no restrictions from a limited potential for short-term acceleration, since both stages are now expanding in long-term style. Both acceleration factors can mount to maxima and remain at the summits with da' and da'' both zero. Further variations of the price spread thus depend exclusively upon dR, and this becomes negative as the surplus expansion gives place to a basic expansion. When then prices begin to fall to effect the continual reduction of the price spread, there follows sooner or later the real and final crash. Speculative embarrassment makes both da' and da'' negative, to augment the rate of contraction of the price spread and intensify the embarrassment. Assets are frozen and then liquidated in a great drop of prices. Worse, there is no recovery; for the remainder of the cycle should be a basic expansion which our ill-adapted economies transform into a depression.

It may be noted that the triple crisis per cycle may perhaps correspond to Prof. Schumpeter's combination of three small cycles named Kitchins in one larger cycle named a Juglar, which has a ten-year period.[219] The pattern of six Juglars in one sixty-year Kondratieff would seem to result from the quasi logical connection between successive long-term accelerations. A fundamental transformation of the capital equipment of an economy needs preparatory long-term accelerations that open the way for it; and once the fundamental transformation is achieved, there are other subsidiary transformations that for the first time become concrete possibilities. Such a time series has more affinities with a philosophic theory of history than the merely mechanical structures that we have been examining. A theory of the Kondratieff is in terms of the precise nature of the fundamental transformation, for example, railroads, but the theory of the Juglar and Kitchin that has been developed here depends solely upon the structure of the productive process and the measure of human adaptation to the requirements of an acceleration in that structure.

It is to be recalled that the account given of the cycle of the basic price-spread ratio supposes $(D' - s'I')$ to be zero throughout. A speculative boom in the stock market which encourages basic spending may be represented by a positive $(D' - s'I')$: there is an excess release of money from the redistributional function to the basic demand function. Alternatively, it may be represented by an upward revision of the fractions w_i of total current income going to basic demand, while the fact that the surplus final market suffers no contraction then results from the excess of the rate of new fixed investment over the rate of pure surplus income, so that D'' is positive. In either case, a movement of this type with its basis in redistributional optimism will offset any tendency towards a contraction of the price spread and will reinforce any tendency of the price spread to expand. On the other hand, the subsequent stockmarket break intensifies the crisis of the circuits, removing the props that had hitherto swollen expansive tendencies, and leaving the system with a greater height from which to fall.

29   Superposed Circuits

[1944] There are sets of phenomena, notably the favorable and unfavorable balances of foreign trade, deficit government spending, and the payment of public debts by taxation, that are analogous to the phenomena of the cycle. It is proposed to deal with them under the general title of 'superposed circuits.' In our general account of the monetary circulation, two cir-

---

219 See Schumpeter, *Business Cycles* 170–73.

cuits, a basic and a surplus, were distinguished. They were interconnected with a crossover. But they involved no regular flow through the redistributive function; that function stood, as it were, outside the circuits, a source of more money for expansions and a refuge for money during contractions, but not a regular stop in the circulation of money as far as the productive process was concerned.

There is, however, no impossibility of the redistributive function becoming a point through which a circuit regularly passes. On the other hand, such a circuit both presupposes and is distinct from the basic and surplus circuits already considered. Hence, the name of superposed circuits, and also the mode of treatment. For any superposed circuit may be represented by rates of payment, Z' and Z'', per interval added to variables of the circulation diagram as follows.[220]

(1) $(D' - s'I') + Z'$ — $(D'' - s''I'') + Z''$

(2) $E' + Z'$ — $E'' + Z''$

(3) $i'O' + Z'$ — $i''O'' + Z''$

(4) $(D'' - s''I'') - Z' - Z''$

The foregoing additions and, in the last case, subtractions are supposed to be made to or from the other rates, $(D' - s'I')$, $(D'' - s''I'')$, E', E'', and so on, as they are determined generally. No doubt the additions or subtractions modify these rates, reinforce or counteract the tendencies of whatever phase may be in progress. Our purpose in representing them as above is not at all to deny such interaction but rather to gain a viewpoint from which such interaction may be studied. The viewpoint adopted is that of the circuit: the circular route of Z' and Z'' is a different route from that of basic or surplus expenditure, outlay, or income; there exists a partial coincidence, but its significance varies with the nature of the superposed circuit; and there is never a total coincidence since the redistributive function is a regular port of call in the superposed circuit.

In any given interval, Z' is the same value no matter whether it is added to $(D' - s'I')$ or E' or $i'O'$ or subtracted from $(D'' - s''I'')$. Further, the addition or subtraction always occurs in each of the four cases. These two conditions are necessary to have a circular movement of a sum of money, Z', per interval. The same holds for Z''. On the other hand, from one interval

220 Throughout this and the remaining sections, notation has been altered to conform with the 1983 version.

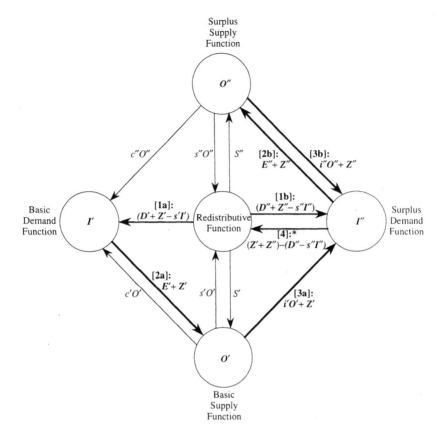

Surplus
Supply
Function

O''

$c''O''$ $s''O''$ S'' **[2b]:**   **[3b]:**
                          $E''+Z''$ $i''O''+Z''$

                           [1b]:
                         $(D''+Z''-s''I'')$

Basic   **[1a]:**   Surplus
Demand I' $(D'+Z'-s'I')$ Redistributive I'' Demand
Function   Function   Function
                                   [4]:*
                            $(Z'+Z'')-(D''-s''I'')$

          [2a]:
          $E'+Z'$
$c'O'$ $s'O'$ S'

                                [3a]:
                                $i'O'+Z'$

                  O'

Basic
Supply
Function

*The arrow for phase [4] is pointing inward in order to graphically represent the closure of
the circuits. Lonergan's plus and minus signs have been correspondingly reversed.

Figure 29-1 Diagram of Superposed Circuits

to another, the quantity represented by Z', or by Z'', may vary. However,
since our interest is to examine the superposed circuit in itself rather than
the effect of its variations, in general it will be convenient to suppose that
Z' and Z'' are constant over a series of intervals. Finally, there never is any
need of Z' and Z'' being equal.

As represented by the list of additions to the circuit diagram, a superposed circuit consists of the following eight movements per interval: from
the redistributive function Z' to basic demand and Z'' to surplus demand;
from basic demand Z' to basic supply, and from surplus demand Z'' to surplus supply; from basic supply Z' to surplus demand, and from surplus sup-

ply Z'' to surplus demand; from surplus demand Z' and Z'' to the redistributive function. In any given interval either Z' or Z'' may be zero; but if both are zero, there is no superposed circuit.

In studying the superposed circuits one may begin at any function to move in either direction. One may begin anywhere because the total movement is circular. One may move in either direction, for one may ask where the money goes or where it is coming from. Finally, one may regard the eight movements as simultaneous: they all occur within the same interval; the condition of a circulation is satisfied if they occur within the interval; and the condition of a circulation is the one condition required. In fact, a certain amount of short-term financing will be required to enable some function to pay before it receives its Z' or its Z'' either in whole or in part; or else the superposed circuit will be a circuit in virtue of a lag; but such minor phenomena need not be discussed in the general inquiry.

30 The Balance of Foreign Trade

There is an evident analogy between the rate of new fixed investment and a favorable balance of foreign trade. In both cases the rates of current production exceed, within the given area, the sum of the rate of current consumption and of the rate of capital replacements and maintenance. In both cases there results accordingly a rate of pure surplus income which really is the new fixed investment or the excess export but has as well a monetary equivalent in the difference between total outlay, which is proportionate to total production, and total consumption and replacement income, which are proportionate to a fraction only of total production.

The interest of the free economies in a favorable balance of foreign trade has a very solid foundation. Prior to the full development of monetary techniques, an excess export of goods and services was balanced by an excess import of gold; this increased the quantity of money available in the economy; and this increase in the economy made possible an equal increase in the circuits. But the expansion of the circuits is, in large part, conditioned by the possibility of increasing the quantity of money available for the transactions of the circuits. Thus a favorable balance of trade, balanced by a favorable balance of gold imports, was a means of satisfying a principal condition for economic expansion.

However, this monetary interest in a favorable balance of trade is far from the sole interest in it. The favorable balance adds an equal amount to the rate of pure surplus income; with pure surplus income at the nerve center of economies based more and more on the ideal of the 'successful man,' this addition to the rate of pure surplus was, while it lasted, an unmitigated blessing. It augmented the rate of pure surplus in surplus expansions. It offset the rate of losses in depressions, and it did this in two distinct ways: first, it tended to cancel out any rate of losses that otherwise would appear; second, it tended to prevent such a hypothetical appearance. The first point is obvious. The second follows from the fact that the rate of losses results from the economy's inability to reduce sufficiently the rate of net aggregate savings;[221] but the need of bringing about such a reduction rests on the fact that basic quantities are increasing more rapidly than surplus; evidently, in the measure in which the production of increasing basic quantities may be replaced by the production of increasing quantities of goods and services for an increasing favorable foreign balance, in that measure the turn of the process towards basic expansion is eliminated; and there follows the elimination of a tendency towards decreasing savings with the consequent rate of losses.

The theoretical significance of the foregoing is considerable. It provides an explanation both of nineteenth-century practice and of nineteenth-century theory. The nineteenth-century economy did not need, as we need, a rigorous adaptation to the pure cycle of the productive process, because then the phenomena of the pure cycle could be covered over by the favorable balance of foreign trade. Further, under such circumstances a theorist would not have his attention directed to cycles as matters of scientific

---

221 From the foregoing analysis, we know that by 'rate of net aggregate savings' Lonergan means a rate of income over and above 'constant normal profit' that has to keep pace with the flow of initial payments needed for the acceleration of the major surplus expansion. When the costs of surplus expansion and the rate of net aggregate savings shift from new fixed investment to maintenance and replacement, and the rate of savings once made possible by the basic price spread begins to vanish along with the contraction of the price spread, there is required an understanding, judging, and deciding to reduce the rate of net aggregate savings for which people have been ill-prepared by the classical slogans of thrift and enterprise; hence the ability 'to reduce sufficiently the rate of net aggregate savings' that is obviated artificially and counterproductively by the favorable balance of foreign trade.

moment, for the very good reason that, since their phenomena were covered over in part, they would be regarded naturally and spontaneously as incidental complexes of relatively arbitrary events. Accordingly, we turn to a more detailed consideration of the circuits involved in a favorable balance of foreign trade.

The assumption of the closed economy is now dropped. One supposes the existence of a number of economies, each with its redistributive function and its basic and surplus circuits. It will be convenient to assume that transactions between economies take place between their redistributive functions: thus goods and services leaving one economy for the benefit of another leave the one as redistributive goods or services and enter the other as redistributive goods or services; similarly, payments enter and leave by the redistributive function.

Consider, then, an economy that, over a series of intervals, has a favorable balance of foreign trade of $Z' + Z''$ per interval. Then in each interval, it produces, over and above all domestic requirements, Z' worth of basic goods and services and Z'' worth of surplus goods and services. Exporters purchase these products by moving from the redistributive function to basic demand Z', and to surplus demand Z''; both sums are there spent to give $E' + Z'$ and $E'' + Z''$. The resultant receipts contain $Z' + Z''$ of surplus income, that is, of income that need be spent at neither final market; hence we have the movements $i'O' + Z'$ and $i''O'' + Z''$ and then $(D'' - s''I'' - Z' - Z'')$ as the surplus income is counted pure surplus and moved from surplus demand to the redistributive function. To close the circuit it is necessary to connect this movement of pure surplus income to the redistributive function with the movement by exporters of an equal sum from the redistributive function to the final markets.[222]

222 The phrase 'close the circuit' is somewhat confusing here, since it can seem that the circuit has been closed when Z' and Z'' return to the redistributive function. Since, however, the superposed circuit in question is a circuit of foreign trade, it is not really closed until the conditions for the next round of foreign trade are reestablished. And this does not happen merely with the movement of a sum of money to the redistributive function, but when that money enables the means for another cycle of foreign trade. Loans must be repaid and working capital replenished. Since foreign currency cannot be spent at domestic final markets, foreign receipts must be in forms which will be capable of attracting investments (totaling $Z' + Z''$) from those for whom it is pure surplus income. In what follows, Lonergan considers several such investment possibilities.

Such a connection can be operated in a variety of ways. The exporters receive from abroad either a gold import or a foreign debt or the cancellation of a domestic debt abroad. For such payment to be acceptable to the exporters, it must be negotiable on the domestic redistributive market. The general condition of negotiability is that the exporters by their subsequent use of the money they receive do not drain the redistributive function of its funds. This general condition is satisfied by the movement of the pure surplus income into the redistributive function at the same rate as exporters move money out of the redistributive function. Provided then there exist markets in short-term bills and long-term securities or for gold, and provided the pure surplus is spent on these markets, the general condition will be satisfied.

The international monetary phenomena are quite simple. In a first period, payments are made in gold. The countries with the favorable balance are thus enabled to undertake expansions in virtue of their increased stocks of money. The countries with the unfavorable balance suffer equal contractions, until they discover the cause of the trouble. Then they practice the doctrine of mercantilism: foreign trade is controlled so that there is no unfavorable balance of trade. In the long run, the only countries that will balance an excess import by the export of gold are either gold-producing countries or else backward economies in which there exist stocks of gold which can be de-hoarded. In a second period, there develops the practice of foreign lending. Countries with unfavorable balances of trade have bills of exchange pile up against them in the exporting countries; these are liquidated by floating long-term foreign loans or, when an economy which previously enjoyed a favorable balance turns to an unfavorable balance, by selling domestically owned foreign securities.

Some of the domestic features of an economy enjoying a favorable balance have already been noted. The rate of excess export involves an equal rate of pure surplus income that augments the benefits of an expansion, provides a substitute for them when there is no expansion, counteracts the tendency for a rate of losses in a basic expansion, and tends to eliminate basic expansions by directing into an increasing excess export what otherwise would have been an increasing rate of domestic consumption with consequently contracting savings. Thus an economy operating with a favorable balance enjoys a cushioned domestic cycle. As far as the domestic cycle is concerned, it can proceed on the principles of increasing thrift and enterprise which are normative generally only in the surplus expansion. On the other hand, the favorable balance itself will be conditioned by the cycles in foreign economies. If the importing countries are sufficiently developed exchange economies to experience the cycle, and if the volume of international trade is sufficiently large to effect a general synchronism of cycles, then so far from mitigating domestic cycles the effect of foreign trade will be to reinforce them tremendously. On the other hand, when the synchronism is lacking, and still more when the importing countries are colonial economies with little domestic commerce or industry, such reinforcement does not occur. The existence of the cushioning effect would seem established by the fact that in England basic wage rates did not begin to rise until 1870; that would suggest that previous basic expansions had been avoided successfully by diverting increased potential into an increased excess export. And to some extent, at least, the same fact confirms the advantage of conducting foreign trade with colonies and primitive countries.

The inverse phenomena to the favorable balance result from the unfavorable balance of foreign trade. Then either or both the emergent standard of living and the increment of capital equipment of the economy are in excess of its basic and surplus rates of production. Insofar as the excess import does not enter domestic channels of industry and commerce, there is no superposed circuit: importers purchase and use or consume the excess import within the redistributive function. However, in that case they are not importers in the sense of a class of dealers; no large rate of import can be managed in that fashion, for large imports have to be sold on the regular final markets of the domestic economy. Let, then, the rate of the excess import sold on the domestic final markets be once more Z' and Z''. Then domestic entrepreneurs direct part of their gross receipts, as though they were pure surplus income, to surplus demand and thence to the redistributive function. This gives elements (3) and (4), namely, $i'O' + Z'$, $i''O'' + Z''$, and $(D'' - s''I'') - Z' - Z''$.[223] Thus domestic entrepreneurs purchase the excess import from the importers in the redistributive function and transfer it to the stocks of the domestic basic and surplus markets. There it is sold to the domestic public, to give $E' + Z'$ and $E'' + Z''$. It is true that the domestic public will pay more than Z' and Z''; however, the difference will be the wages, rents, and interest due to domestic production factors; it will circulate in the ordinary fashion; and so we need not be concerned with it. On the other hand, the Z' [plus] Z'' ends up in the redistributive function where it pays the importers who pay the foreign sellers with

223 See above, p. 163.

gold, with the contraction of foreign debts, or with the sale of domestically owned foreign securities. The problem of the unfavorable balance is to close the circuit by moving to the domestic public the money the importers receive from domestic entrepreneurs and pay to domestic sellers of gold or securities. This involves the $(D' - s'I') + Z'$ and the $(D'' - s''I'') + Z''$.

The $(D'' - s''I'') + Z''$ is analogous to the rate of new fixed investment in the domestic expansion. Domestic surplus demand is borrowing from the redistributive function at the rate Z'' per interval to purchase goods or services for the maintenance, replacement, or net increment of domestic capital equipment. But there is a grave difference. In the domestic expansion or in the purchase through borrowing (which may include borrowing from one's own holdings in the redistributive function) of domestically produced replacements, the rate of movement from the redistributive function to surplus demand is balanced by a rate of income moving from surplus demand to the redistributive function. But in the present case, the balancing movement is not a rate of income, for the goods sold were not produced domestically and so generate no income; the balancing rate is simply a rate of payment for the current supply of the goods and services of the excess import. The consequence is that, if the excess import is replacement goods, then domestic industry does not pay its own way but has to borrow, to the extent Z'' per interval, to keep its capital equipment up to date. And if the excess import is an increment of existing capital, yielding an acceleration of the process, then the economy conducts a long-term acceleration, at the rate Z'' of new capital equipment per interval, without enjoying any pure surplus income such as is enjoyed when the increment of equipment is domestically produced. Hence, the greater Z'' is relatively to E'', the greater the difficulty of investors contemplating the maintenance, replacement, or increment of capital equipment; for evidently if capital notably fails to support itself and yields only a mediocre flow of pure surplus income, investment is unattractive. Hence, just as the favorable balance of trade intensifies the joy of expansion, so the unfavorable balance dims that joy. With foreign debts mounting or foreign holdings decreasing, the economy with an unfavorable balance reacts very sluggishly indeed to opportunities for expansion. And while brilliant prospects of great developments in the future may overcome this sluggishness in a young country, the matter is quite different in an old country that once was a creditor but since has become a rentier to the world.

Even more intractable is the other component of the movement from the redistributive function to demand, $(D' - s'I') + Z'$. The possibility of

vorable balance of trade persists. In the situation of a bold monetary expansion stimulating the purchase of imports, the movement from the redistributive function is to the supply and not to the demand function; it is a $(S' - s'O') + Z'$ or a $(S'' - s''O'') + Z''$ and not a $(D' - s'I') + Z'$. This movement initially finances an increment in entrepreneurial scales of operation, but instead of this increment being sold at the final markets, there is sold the excess import. The resultant contraction may be delayed, however, by a fuller boldness of monetary policy. As long as the increment in production is to be sold at surplus markets, it can be bought by borrowers, so that the problem of providing a $(D' - s'I') + Z'$ is being solved by providing both a $(S'' - s''O'') + Z'$ and a $(D'' - s''I'') + Z'$; the former Z' expands turnover magnitudes, becomes basic income, is spent for the excess import, and so moves back to the redistributive function; the latter Z' purchases the increment in the rate of production and then circulates normally to maintain that increment. This is a case of surplus expansion not yielding pure surplus income: the Z' that moves to the redistributive function is not income but payment for the excess import; and it is accompanied by an increase in debts of $2Z'$ per interval, apart from the increase due to Z''. When, however, the domestic expansion puts goods on the basic final market, contraction results. The only escape is for these goods to be exported, and that will end the unfavorable balance of trade. Thus it should seem that a debtor country can meet the requirement for a $(D' - s'I') + Z'$ only during an expansion of the surplus stage of its productive process, and only by paying for the excess basic import by increasing its long-term capital debt by Z' per interval.

31   Deficit Spending and Taxes[225]

[1978] Government spending purports to promote the economic, social, and cultural overhead of the community. Exceptional expenditures may be funded by floating loans, but loans mean payments of interest and amortization. Ultimately, then, if not immediately, government revenues come from taxes.

Deficit spending arises when government expenditure exceeds its revenues. It may be represented by payments made to the circuits from the

225 This section appears only in the 1978 and 1979 versions. There it replaces a section of the 1944 version with the same title, which is included in the present edition as the 'Additional Note to Section 31.'

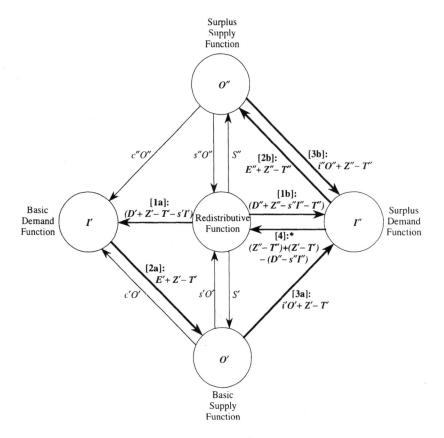

*The arrow for phase [4] is pointing inward in order to graphically represent the closure of the circuits. Lonergan's plus and minus signs have been correspondingly reversed.

Figure 31-1 Diagram of Government Spending and Taxes

redistributional area in excess of payments made from the circuits to the redistributional area.

As there are two circuits, we must distinguish in government spending in any interval Z between Z' paid into basic demand and Z'' paid into surplus demand. Similarly, in taxes T, we have to distinguish between T' withdrawn from basic demand and T'' withdrawn from surplus demand.

Now, as long as there is a deficit, Z will be greater than T. But what is true of the totals need not hold for the parts. Z' may be smaller than T' if Z'' is sufficiently greater than T''. Similarly, Z'' may be smaller than T'' when Z' is proportionately greater than T'.

But in each of these cases the balance of the circuits is upset. In the former case, the basic circuit is being drained of funds while the surplus circuit is invited to expand or inflate or deposit its excess in the redistributional area. In the latter case, the surplus circuit is being drained of funds while the basic circuit is invited to expand or inflate or enter the redistributional market.

It seems the latter alternative that is more likely to occur. Conventional wisdom favors taxing the rich and resists taxing the masses, and so T'' is encouraged to be too big and T' too small. Again it is thought that government spending should not compete against private enterprise. But then Z'' will have to be small, and from the nature of the case Z' will be the normal outlet for government spending.

There results the situation – sometimes thought mysterious – in which consumer prices continuously inflate, new enterprise is evaded, unemployment becomes chronic, and despite the inflation the value of stocks declines.

While this second alternative is most unwelcome, no doubt it is the first alternative that encouraged the advocates of the unbalanced budget and deficit spending. For the first alternative recalls the happy days of mercantilism or, rather, it appears to do so. Basic prices are held down and basic production held back by high taxation. Surplus activity is lavishly encouraged. All that is lacking is the foreign market in which the fruits of this activity can be sold.

Need the moral be repeated? There exist two distinct circuits, each with its own final market. The equilibrium of the economic process is conditioned by the balance of the two circuits: each must be allowed the possibility of continuity, of basic outlay yielding an equal basic income and surplus outlay yielding an equal surplus income, of basic and surplus income yielding equal basic and surplus expenditure, and of these grounding equivalent basic and surplus outlay. But what cannot be tolerated, much less sustained, is for one circuit to be drained by the other. That is the essence of dynamic disequilibrium.

Additional Note to Section 31[226]

[1944] Deficit spending and the taxes which sustain it reproduce simultaneously the phenomena of both the favorable and the unfavorable balance

---

226 In the 1944 version the text of this additional note appears as a section on 'Deficit Spending and Taxes.' Lonergan put '(unfinished)' after its title in his table of contents, and in the 1978 version replaced it with §31 of the present edition. Notation has been altered to conform with his latest usage.

of foreign trade. Let us suppose a public authority to borrow and spend Z' per interval at the basic final market and Z'' per interval at the surplus final market. Let us suppose that the taxation to meet interest and provide amortization against past and present borrowing is T' per interval derived from the basic circuit and T'' per interval derived from the surplus circuit. Then the superposed circuits will be

$$
\begin{aligned}
&(1)\ D' + Z' + T' &&\qquad— &&\qquad D'' + Z'' + T'' \\
&(2)\ E' + Z' + T' &&\qquad— &&\qquad E'' + Z'' + T'' \\
&(3)\ i'O' + Z' + T' &&\qquad— &&\qquad i''O'' + Z'' + T'' \\
&(4)\ D'' - Z' - Z'' - T' - T''
\end{aligned}
$$

We shall consider first the government spending, second the taxes, and third the ultimate alternative between bankruptcy and vigorous retrenchment, that is, the disappearance of Z' and Z'' and the intensification of T' and T''.

Government spending is simple. In each interval Z' is spent at the basic final market for any type of goods or services that have no tendency to accelerate the productive process, while Z'' is spent at the surplus final market for goods and services with that tendency. There results a corresponding increment in income which, as it has nothing to buy at either final market, is counted as surplus and is moved to the redistributive function where directly or indirectly it purchases government securities. Thus in each interval, labor, land, and capital are providing $Z' + Z''$ of goods and services. Those who do the required monetary saving are built into a solid and richly endowed rentier class at the rate $Z' + Z''$ per interval. The community possesses the goods and services but, unless it is going into business deliberately, their productive value will be slight. Finally, the public debt mounts by the same rate, $Z' + Z''$ per interval.

The rate of debt servicing, $T' + T''$, becomes more and more significant as the rate of deficit spending is maintained over a longer period. The movement from the circuits to the redistributive function causes no difficulty. Income is taxed, directly or indirectly, to give the third and fourth elements in this circuit. In the redistributive function, T'' per interval is paid to amortization, and T' per interval is paid as interest to the rentiers. However, if money is to be moved from the circuits to the redistributive function without causing a contracting, it is necessary that the inflow be balanced by an equal outflow.[227]

227 The 1944 version ends at this point.

Appendix: History of the Diagram, 1944–1998

Just as Lonergan greatly altered the text of his *Essay in Circulation Analysis* over the years,[1] so also the diagram of the relationships among the flows or rates of payments underwent a parallel series of revisions. Lonergan especially stressed the great significance of this diagram, and hence, the editors have felt it important to include in this appendix the six different versions of the diagram along with a brief discussion of the historical sequence of revisions. In tracing the path that leads to the final version of the diagram, we have offered a provisional interpretation of, as Lonergan would put it, 'what was going forward.'[2] While we have endeavored to be as accurate as possible, some elements of the interpretation are only the best understanding we have been able to arrive at as to why Lonergan made certain changes. Because of these hypothetical elements, the interpretation set forth in this appendix remains provisional.

To give an overview, the basic feature of the earliest diagram in this sequence, that of 1944, is the distinction of two circuits, basic and surplus, and the 'crossovers' that express their relationship of mutual dependence. Four monetary functions are implicitly defined in terms of these circuits and crossovers. A fifth monetary function, the Redistributive Function, seems to have been superimposed upon this well-thought-out scheme, along with the aggregate redistributive transactions that relate it to the other four monetary functions. This way of introducing the redistributive,

---

1 See 'Editors' Preface.'
2 Lonergan, *Method in Theology* 189.

or financial, sources of variation lacked differentiation, and gave rise to numerous questions from Lonergan's students.

There seem to have been three distinguishable sources of difficulty:

(1) While the reader was brought gradually from descriptive ideas to implicit definitions[3] in the case of the terms and relations pertaining to the circuits and crossovers, the redistributive sector was introduced solely by way of 'implicit definition.' This provided insufficient guidance to the task of bringing ranges of financial transactions ordinarily understood in a commonsense, descriptive fashion under the proper explanatory classifications.

(2) The problem of defining the explanatory relationships between surplus and basic outlays and surplus and basic incomes is fairly simple if one prescinds from the redistributive transactions; it is quite complicated when redistributive transactions are taken into account.

(3) The diagram represents the final step in preparing the heuristic structure for the circulation analysis. The first step of the analysis itself was the question of the possibility of circuit acceleration when the aggregate redistributive transactions are all zero. But when they are all zero, this is equivalent to prescinding from them. So in the sections that explain the diagram (entitled 'Rates of Payment and Transfer') there almost seems to be an uncharacteristic kind of haste to get on with the analysis. The sequence of revisions is marked by ever-increasing differentiation, and gradually chips away at these interwoven issues. Unfortunately, Lonergan did not arrive at a complete and integrated solution within his own lifetime.

A   The Significance of the Diagram

In class lectures and extracurricular conversation, Lonergan frequently adverted to the importance of the diagram for an adequate understanding of the relationships among the dynamic variables of monetary circulation. In the early texts, however, he simply wrote that the preceding explanatory material and equations 'may be resumed by explaining the diagramme on the following pages' (1944:39; 1978:41). On the other hand, in the 1982 version (40–41), the written text pointed out a broader significance. There he wrote:

3 On Lonergan's use of the terms 'descriptive,' 'explanatory,' and 'implicit,' see Lonergan, *Insight* 10–13/35–37, 37–38/61–62, 291–92/316–17.

On the basis of the foregoing definitions and relations we shall set up a diagram of the economic circulation. But it will be well at once to draw attention to J.A. Schumpeter's insistence on the merits of a diagram as a tool (HEA 241–243).

First there is the tremendous simplification it effects. From millions of exchanges one advances to precise aggregates, relatively few in number, and so easy to follow up and handle.

Next, come the possibilities of advancing to numerical theory. In this respect, despite profound differences in their respective achievements, the contemporary work of Leontieff may be viewed as a revival of François Quesnay's *tableau économique.*

Most important is the fact that this procedure was the first to make explicit the concept of economic equilibrium. All science begins from particular correlations, but the key discovery is the interdependence of the whole. While it is quite true that a *tableau* or diagram cannot establish the uniqueness of a system or rigorously ground its universal relevance, it remains that the diagram has compensating features that a system of simultaneous equations may imply but does not manifest.

I would add that the aims and limitations of macroeconomics make the use of a diagram particularly helpful, at least from the viewpoint of the present essay. For its basic terms are defined by their functional relations ...

So there is to be discerned a threefold process in which a basic stage is maintained and accelerated by a series of surplus stages, while the needed additions to or subtractions from the stock of money in these processes is derived from the redistributive area.

... it will be possible to distinguish stable and unstable combinations and sequences of rates in the three main areas and so gain some insight into the long-standing recurrence of crises in the modern expanding economy.

Thus Lonergan held the diagram to have both explanatory and heuristic significance. First, then, the later versions of the *Essay in Circulation Analysis* text draw ever greater attention to the fact that Lonergan was seeking the explanatory intelligibility underlying the ever-fluctuating rhythms of economic functioning. To that end he worked out a set of terms and relations that 'implicitly defined' that intelligible pattern. When all was said and done the relations, and the terms they implicitly defined, were markedly different from either the terms of ordinary business parlance or the terms of neoclassical and Keynesian economic theory. Moreover, not only did Lonergan's terms differ, but he also indicated that these aforementioned terms were permeated, as were the terms of Newton's theory of gravitation, with descriptive, nonexplanatory residues. Hence, just as a mathematical equation may be said to be the most adequate expression of the purely intelligible relations among explanatory terms in certain instances – for example, Einstein's gravitational field tensor equations – something closely akin to Lonergan's diagram seems necessary for the realm of dynamic economic functioning. So, for example, the existence and manner of dynamic mutual interdependence of the two circuits of payments, basic and surplus, is not adequately expressed either by descriptive terms (since this pattern does not directly relate to the senses of anyone operating in a common-sense way in a concretely functioning economy) nor by the series of equations that do not explicitly manifest the interchanging of 'flows.'

Again, the diagram can be said to have heuristic significance. In Lonergan's usage, 'heuristic' denotes the sorts of innovations that expedite the occurrence of certain acts of consciousness, particularly insights. Thus the diagram as itself a visual image can facilitate the occurrence of insights. For example, while the text of §13 works out in great detail sets of relations among *terms*, the diagram makes it easy to understand that the exchange economy consists of two *circuits* of payments, basic and surplus; that these circuits are mutually and dynamically interdependent (because of the 'crossovers'); and that these circuits are dependent upon the activities of the redistributive function. It also seems to have played an important heuristic role in helping Lonergan himself have insights into the nature of such phenomena as a 'favorable balance of trade' and 'deficit spending,' since he slightly modified the diagram in order to attain those insights. Subsequent study may reveal that there is considerable additional heuristic value to this diagram.

B   The Versions of the Diagram

The diagrams in this appendix are labeled according to the year in which they were introduced. There are the diagrams of 1944, 1978, 1979, 1981, and 1982. Finally, there is the 1998 diagram, which is §14, 'Diagram of Rates of Flow,' of this text. Unlike the other five, the 1998 diagram includes changes introduced, not by Lonergan himself, but by the editors. It differs only slightly, however, from Lonergan's own 1982 diagram.

The context and headings of the diagram also underwent revision. The 1944 and 1978 versions of the diagram appeared as the last page of the explanatory section 'Rates of Payment and Transfer,' and bore the heading 'Diagramme of Transfers between Monetary Functions.' The 1979 version, headed 'Circulation Analysis: Revised Diagram,' was distributed as an addendum to the 1978 version and was followed by a single typewritten page of explanation. The 1981 version, in turn, was distributed as a single-page addendum to the 1979 two-page addendum and bore the heading 'Diagram: Another Revision.' The 1982 version was set off in a separate section of its own, entitled 'Diagram of Rates of Flow,' which was retained by the editors as the title of the 1998 version, found in the present §14.

With these details in view, we now proceed to survey the diagram in its sequence of changes.

C   The 1944 Diagram

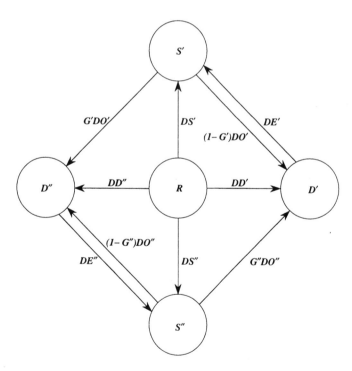

Diagramme of Transfers between Monetary Functions

The original diagram of 1944 is much simpler than the more recent versions. Let us first define the symbols employed, then summarize Lonergan's account of their relations, and finally consider some of the questions it occasioned. First, then, the symbols S', D', S'', D'', and R are to be distinguished from all the other symbols. The other symbols denote either fractions or dynamic variables of aggregate rates of payment. The symbols S', D', S'', D'', and R, on the other hand, are merely abbreviations for Basic Supply Function, Basic Demand Function, Surplus Supply Function, Surplus Demand Function, and Redistributive Function, respectively. Second, G' and G'' are fractions between 0 and 1, and are matched by their complements $(1 - G')$ and $(1 - G'')$ respectively, where $G' + (1 - G') = 1$ and $G'' + (1 - G'') = 1$. Third, DE', DO', DE'', and DO'' denote rate of basic expenditure, rate of basic outlay, rate of surplus expenditure, and rate of surplus outlay, respectively. Again DS', DD', DS'', and DD'' denote the rates of transfer from the Redistributive Function to Basic Supply, Basic Demand, Surplus Supply, and Surplus Demand, respectively. These eight symbols are all dynamic variables of aggregate rates of payments – that is, they all denote 'so and so much money every so often.' The use of the prefix D, common to all eight, is used to stress this fact. Lonergan probably used the D because, in differential calculus, it can denote a derivative, and a derivative with respect to time is a rate. Hence if E' were to be thought of as a magnitude, DE' might symbolize the rate of change of this magnitude. However, Lonergan never used terms for magnitudes, only for rates and their accelerations ('rates of rates') in the *Essay in Circulation Analysis.*

In the 1944 diagram one can discern two circuits: an upper (in *this* diagram at least), basic circuit of

$$S' \rightarrow (1 - G')DO' \rightarrow D' \rightarrow DE' \rightarrow S'$$

and a lower, surplus circuit of

$$S'' \rightarrow (1 - G'')DO'' \rightarrow D'' \rightarrow DE'' \rightarrow S''$$

These two circuits are connected by the crossover arrows, where $G''DO''$ flows from the surplus to the basic circuit and $G'DO'$ flows from basic to surplus. Thus basic outlay, DO', divides into two portions, $(1 - G')DO'$ which returns to Basic Demand, and $G'DO'$ which crosses over to Surplus Demand as surplus goods and services are purchased for maintenance, replacements, or acceleration of the basic productive process. Likewise, surplus outlay, DO'', divides into two portions: $(1 - G'')DO''$, which returns to Surplus Demand as surplus goods and services are purchased for maintenance, replacements, or acceleration of the surplus productive process, and $G''DO''$, which crosses over to the Basic Demand Function of the basic circuit as the portion of surplus outlay that is expended by surplus production's workers, managers, executives, and security holders on their standard of living.

The transfers from the Redistributive Function, DS', DS'', DD', and DD'' are net aggregates – that is, the total transfers per unit time *from* the Redistributive Function to a monetary function minus the total transfers per unit time *to* the Redistributive Function from that monetary function. Because these are net aggregates, they are undifferentiated relative to Lonergan's later revisions.

Because of that lack of differentiation, many questions arose, particularly in the first classes Lonergan taught on his manuscript. There were two basic kinds of questions: (1) how to determine which of the four rates, DS', DS'', DD', or DD'', is the appropriate classification for certain transactions, and (2) the much more knotty questions concerning how these four rates of transfer affected the division of the two rates of outlay, DO' and DO'', into basic and surplus income, DI' and DI''.[4] For example, if corporate executives of a basic enterprise decide to deposit some portion of earnings in a long-term account, or to buy stocks or bonds, or even to take over another enterprise, does this amount first 'travel' along $G'DO'$ to D'' and then 'travel' to the Redistributive Function as a negative component in the aggregate DD''? Or does it 'travel' to the Redistributive Function directly as a negative component in DS'? If the former, then $G'DO' + (1 - G')DO' \neq DO'$, and therefore $G' + (1 - G') \neq 1$, contrary to hypothesis. If the latter, then it seems there cannot be negative (deposit or repayment) components in DS', which does not seem correct. Or again, if entrepreneurs deposit receipts at the beginning of the month, and withdraw some portion of them two weeks later to purchase a small piece of capital equipment, does

4 Although the terms DI' and DI'' did not appear on the 1944 diagram, they did appear in the section of the 1944 manuscript that preceded and introduced that diagram. In that section they also appeared in equations (in many respects similar to equations (2) through (11) of §13 of this text) that relate DI' and DI'' to other terms that do indeed appear in the diagram. Hence, the confusion about their proper interpretation ensued.

the portion travel first negatively up *DS′*, then later positively back down *DS′*, then along *G″DO″* over to *D″*? Or does it travel negatively up *DS′* at the beginning of the month, and positively to the right along *DD″* two weeks later?

Thus it can be said that while Lonergan had a diagram in 1944 that expressed his basic explanatory insights into the 'system,' that is, the 'interdependence of the whole,' there were further questions that it did not answer in a definitive fashion.

D   The 1978 Diagram

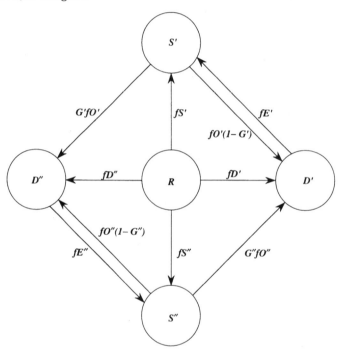

Diagramme of Transfers between Monetary Functions

The 1978 diagram is virtually identical with the 1944 diagram. The sole difference is that the prefix *D* of the dynamic variables has been replaced by an *f*. Lonergan probably did this because it was suggested that a *D* prefix commonly indicates the derivative of a variable (as in the calculus), and could lead to confusion. The prefix *f* was used to denote 'flow.' For example, *fE′* is a 'flow of basic expenditure,' that is, so much money spent on the standard of living every so often. (Lonergan replaced many of the occurrences of the term 'rate' with 'rate or flow' or simply 'flow,' in most of the explanatory sections that preceded the 1978 diagram.)[5]

The 1978 diagram did not add any further relations or differentiations, and questions about classification of certain transactions continued.

E   The 1979 Diagram

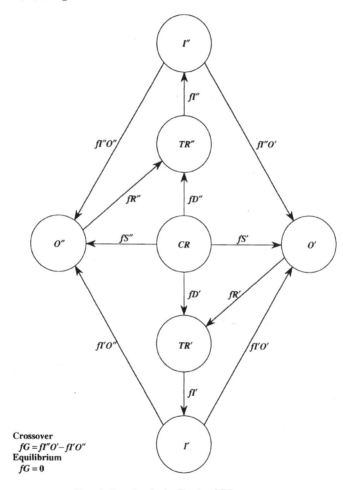

Circulation Analysis: Revised Diagram

5 It is possible that Lonergan may have been influenced to introduce the term 'flow' because of its repeated use by Robert Gordon (see Gordon, *Macroeconomics*, Boston: Little, Brown and Co., pp. 22ff of the 1978 edition that Lonergan used during the 1978 class) or Adolph Lowe (see Lowe's *The Path of Economic Growth*, Cambridge University Press, 1976).

The 1979 diagram (entitled 'The Revised Diagram') was followed by a single typewritten page of explanatory text that read:

The Revised Diagram
The basic circuit starts from outlay (O') on the far right, moves along basic receipts (fR') to the basic transitional division of receipts (TR'), where it is cushioned by additions or subtractions from the central redistributional area (CR) whence it moves along (fI') to basic income (I'), and thence along $fI'O'$ to basic outlay, where it may be increased by a positive contribution from CR along fS' or, on the other hand, decreased by the payment of a loan.

The surplus circuit starts from outlay (O'') on the far right [*sic*], moves along surplus receipts (fR'') to the surplus redistributional area (TR'') where it may be augmented by contributions from the central redistributional area (CR) or diminished by payments to it; thence it moves along fI'' to I'' and thence, in part, along $fI''O''$ to surplus outlay (O'') where it may be increased, or on the other hand diminished along fS''.

Over and above these circular movements there are the crossovers: $fI'O''$ from basic to surplus for the maintenance, widening, and deepening of basic producers' goods and services; and $fI''O'$ for the standard of living of entrepreneurs and workers in the surplus circuit.

When there occurs a crossover difference, then one circuit is accelerating by decelerating the other. The result is a very serious disequilibrium, and the longer it lasts the more deleterious are its consequences. Let us represent the crossover difference by $fG (= fI'O'' - fI''O')$. Then, once crossover equilibrium is attained, the condition of continued equilibrium will be $fG = 0$.

Again, let the basic propensity to consume, to invest, and to save be respectively: c', i', s'. Now $s'R'$ [*sic*] will be a component moving to CR along fD', so on the supposition that fD' still remains a positive total, then

$$fI' = (c' + i')(fR' + fD')$$
$$fI'O' = c'(fR' + fD'')$$
$$fI'O'' = i'(fR' + fD')$$

Similarly, in the surplus circuit

$$fI'' = (c'' + i'')(fR'' + fD'')$$
$$fI''O' = c''(fR'' + fD'')$$
$$fI''O'' = i''(fR'' + fD'')$$

Should it happen the fD'' or fD' happen to be a negative quantity, the sign in these equations changes. (1979:42b)

The 1979 diagram is clearly a substantial revision of its predecessors. First, the basic circuit

$$O' \rightarrow fR' \rightarrow TR' \rightarrow fI' \rightarrow I' \rightarrow fI'O' \rightarrow O'$$

is now shifted to the lower half of the page, while the surplus circuit

$$O'' \rightarrow fR'' \rightarrow TR'' \rightarrow fI'' \rightarrow I'' \rightarrow fI''O'' \rightarrow O''$$

is shifted to the upper half. While this might seem a fairly superficial change, it at least has the heuristic benefit of locating the symbols representing 'lower' and 'higher' levels of the circulation of money with 'lower' and 'upper' spatial areas, respectively, in the diagram. The other changes are more significant and manifest a movement in the direction of greater differentiation.

Second, then, the description of the transfers from what in this version is called the 'central redistributional area' (CR) are more nuanced. Thus, fS' and fS'' are now clearly described as contributing directly to the eventual magnitude of outlays O' and O'', respectively, through both 'positive contributions' from CR and negative 'repayments of loans.' Again, what are called 'receipts,' fR' and fR'', in this 1979 addendum are said to become the income aggregates fI' and fI'' respectively, only after being 'cushioned' by 'additions [contributions] from or subtractions [payments to]' CR in the form of fD' and fD'' respectively.

Third, several of the changes clearly have been made in order to define more precisely how the two rates of income, fI' and fI'', are constituted out of other rates. Among these, notice that the labels on the four outermost monetary functions are no longer mere abbreviations for the names of those functions – S' for Basic Supply Function, and so on. Rather, they are now labeled, as the explanatory page makes clear, in ways that connect them directly with the dynamic variables. In particular fI' and fI'' are unambiguously constituted as the sums $fI' = fR' + fD'$ and $fI'' = fR'' + fD''$ (provided one looks only at the diagram and not at the concluding paragraph and equations of the accompanying explanatory material). Then fI' and fI'' flow into the 'dynamically quiescent' monetary functions I' and I'', whence they directly become expenditures. The composition of fO' and fO'' and their relationship to other dynamic variables is not made clear from the diagram itself; in fact the 1979 Diagram sidestepped this problem.

Fourth, the vexing problem of how it could be that $G' + (1 - G') \neq 1$ and $G'' + (1 - G'') \neq 1$ has been avoided by the artifices of $fI'O'$, $fI''O''$, $fI'O''$, and $fI''O'$, which merely name those rates by their endpoints, rather than as fractions of previous rates they are derived from. (While the end of the explanatory material does begin to address this problem, the 1979 diagram itself does not.) Notice that just as fI', a symbol composed of three distinct characters, denotes a single dynamic variable, so also $fI'O'$, $fI''O''$, $fI'O''$, and $fI''O'$ are four composite symbols each denoting but one dynamic variable. As mentioned before, however, this artifice does not completely clarify the precise constitution of fO' or fO''.

Despite these developments, the diagram is far from polished. Witness the asymmetric terminology for TR' as 'the basic transitional division of receipts' *versus* TR'' as 'the surplus redistributional area.' Notice, moreover, that the basic propensity to consume, to invest, to save (that is, c', i', s') mentioned in the explanatory material have not been integrated into the diagram. Again, the meaning of 'receipts' (fR' and fR'') implicit in the 1979 diagram is not compatible with the definitions offered in the preceding section, 'Rates of Payment and Transfer.' In that section fR' is said to be identical with fE' and fR'' with fE'', while in the diagram $fR' = fI'O' + fI''O' + fS'$, and $fR'' = fI''O'' + fI'O'' + fS''$. (Recall that the 1979 diagram and its page of explanation were merely added to, but did not replace, the definitions of the 'flows' of payments set down in the 1978 version of the section on 'Rates of Payment and Transfer.') Finally, the reason for even retaining the term 'receipts' for fR' and fR'' becomes obscure, given these 1979 redefinitions.

These differentiations and confusions call for some sort of interpretation. The 1979 diagram is clearly the product of a transitional stage in Lonergan's thinking. Motivating this transition seems to have been the very complex problem of defining fI', fI'', fO', and fO'' in terms of their mutual interrelationships. The problem is triply compounded: first by the existence of time lags, second by the existence of the crossovers, and third by the transactions with the Redistributive Function.

Time lags enter into the problem of this implicit definition because in a given time period entrepreneurs make payments (transitional payments for supplies – which for the most part cancel out in the aggregate – and, as well, outlays for labor) that pertain to products not yet completed during that period. Next the recipients of these outlays take time to decide how they will make use of their incomes, thereby dividing them up into basic income, surplus income, savings, investment, and so on. Still more time may pass before they act upon these decisions and thereby turn their incomes into expenditures. But it is these expenditures (and the purposes to which the purchased items are put) that actually constitute products as basic or surplus – and that therefore actually constitute the previously-made outlays as either basic or surplus. In other words, the actual distinction between basic outlay and surplus outlay is made only once a considerable time has elapsed after the outlay itself.

Yet this particular complexity is overcome because the circulation analysis deals not with each and every series of payments, but with aggregate rates of payments. Thus in theory one can wait as long as necessary to have all the data required to determine the values and correlations of the aggregate variables for, say, the current month. In practice one may settle for approximations that choose a unit of time long enough for most outlays to be determined by incomes received in the same period, or long enough for the as yet undetermined residues of outlays to form as small a fraction of total outlays as one chooses, or long enough for determinations of outlays carried over from previous periods into the present period to be used to compensate for outlays not yet determined in the present period. Thus a little reflection reveals that this first source of complexity does not pose a serious difficulty.

Second, however, there is the problem of definition posed by the crossovers: without it one would simply have $I' = O'$ and $I'' = O''$. But when the crossovers exist, there are two possible ways of sorting out the interrelationships: either (i) the outlays are defined in terms of the level (basic or surplus) of productive activities they reward, while the incomes are defined in terms of the level of finished products (basic or surplus) they are used to purchase; or (ii) the incomes are defined in terms of the level of productive activity their recipients have contributed to, while the outlays are defined in terms of the level of receipts from which they are drawn. It is clear that Lonergan originally intended the former definition in the 1944 manuscript. There he wrote: 'DI' are the initial payments entering basic demand and DI'' are the initial payments entering surplus demand during the given interval of time' (p. 43). In such a case, outlays are then basic when they are made as initial payments to compensate the contributors to basic production, and outlays are surplus when they are initial payments for contributions to surplus production. Each of these aggregate outlays then subdivides into components in either basic income or surplus income, depending upon the decisions of their recipients.

The 1979 diagram, by contrast, appears to have shifted toward the second approach to defining the relationships between outlays and incomes, because there it is incomes, not outlays, that are subdivided. Hence in 1979 it would seem that fI' must denote the rate of income derived from work in basic production plus or minus redistributive transfers. This fI' then subdivides to flow into either O' or O'' as basic workers and entrepreneurs purchase products for their standard of living or for use in production. The same holds true for fI''. It would seem, then, that fO' should flow from O' to TR' – in other words, should be identical with fR' – and likewise for fO''. Lonergan did not do this. Why not? The reason may have to do with the fact that explanation, in his sense, presupposes but goes beyond description. This second line of defining outlays and incomes is proprietary and therefore descriptive, rather than explanatory. Incomes and outlays so defined do not correlate *strictly* with transitions in the productive process, while the former definitions do. That is, income-as-received for work on basic production does not initiate or constitute anything; it is simply the money received by a certain category of workers and entrepreneurs, it is money in relationship to them (descriptive) rather than in relationship to what it does in the dynamic whole (explanatory). By contrast, the first line of defining is dedicated to the relationships to the dynamic whole. That is, outlays as initial payments rewarding efforts in basic production initiate basic production; basic incomes as what people spend on their standard of living constitute a standard of living and determine the portion of the economic process that is functioning to support that standard. Hence, the earlier definitions of 1944, set forth in the section on 'Rates of Payment and Transfer,' stand in explanatory relationships with the key elements of the productive process itself, whereas the 1979 diagram reverted to including descriptive elements. This is probably the root of the asymmetric and incompatible uses of terms, and, as a result, of much confusion in understanding.

Why did Lonergan revert to descriptive elements? This brings us to the third complexity: the transactions with the Redistributive Function. It seems likely that in 1944 and 1978 Lonergan added the four aggregate rates of redistributive transactions *after* having sorted out the surplus and basic circuits and their interdependences. In other words, he approached the redistributive issues in terms of the way they 'fit into' the prior schema of explanatory terms and relations. He did not appear to arrive at the explanatory term, say DS', by progressing from descriptions of financial transactions toward explanatory formulation. Rather, DS' was defined as one of four natural implications of the scheme of the basic and surplus circuits. As a result, questions about how to categorize concretely described transactions were not explicitly addressed.

However, the questions that arose in Lonergan's courses all had to do with how certain savings or investment or borrowing transactions were to be classified. The basic question is, Are outlay and income aggregates determined prior to or subsequent to redistributive transactions? In order to sort this out concretely, it is probably inevitable that one think about someone making decisions about such transactions. But to think of someone saving is to think of someone doing something with what we ordinarily call their 'income,' which is a descriptive rather than an explanatory usage. Hence we have seen that Lonergan achieved some definitive clarifications by means of the descriptive reflections represented in the 1979 diagram – for example, income includes loans minus savings. Yet it seems that Lonergan had not yet shifted these clarifications back to the fully explanatory context of 1944 and 1978. Hence, the residual descriptive elements led to some odd and confusing terminology.

Some further comments need to be made about the cursory treatment in the appended explanatory material of the marginal propensities to consume, invest, and save: c', i', s' and c'', i'', s''. First, it is likely that Robert Gordon's use of similar but undifferentiated symbols (*Macroeconomics* 56–85) influenced Lonergan to introduce these symbols in place of his original G' and G''. Second, fR' is said to enter TR' where it is 'cushioned' by contributions from CR, fD'. Next, there is $s'R'$, which is said to be a component in fD'. (From the ordinary meaning of 'marginal propensity to save,' it would seem that Lonergan should have written $s'fR'$ instead of $s'R'$.) One could introduce another variable, $fX' = fD' - s'fR'$; hence $fI' = fR' + fD' = fR' - s'fR' + fX'$. This adds a further clarification: basic income is defined as the resultant *after* savings and loan transactions for the time period have been completed. The same holds for fI''. Next the symbolic artifices of $fI'O'$ and $fI'O''$ are related to fI' itself: since s' already was used in making up the aggregate rate fI', $fI' = (c' + i')(fR' + fD')$ or $fI' = c'(fR' + fD') + i'(fR' + fD')$. The two terms of this sum then become $fI'O'$ and $fI'O''$

respectively. The case for fI'' and the rest is similar. Hence, consumption and investment decisions are made out of the income of individuals, but after their wages, salaries, dividends, and so on have been augmented by savings and borrowing decisions. Still, the marginal propensities were not integrated into the diagram itself – possibly because they were fractions of a sum of two variables rather than of a single variable.

F   The 1981 Diagram

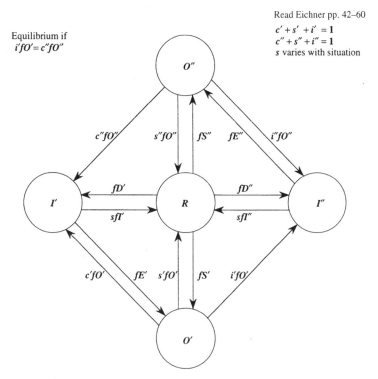

Read Eichner pp. 42–60

$c' + s' + i' = 1$
$c'' + s'' + i'' = 1$
s varies with situation

Equilibrium if
$i'fO' = c''fO''$

Surplus outlay, O'', divides into consumption, savings and investment;
          it is fed by surplus expenditure and withdrawals from R.
Basic outlay, O', divides into $c'fO'$, $s'fO'$, and $i'fO'$;
          it is fed by fE' and fS.
Basic and suplus income contribute savings to the redistributional
function and draw upon its facilities.

Diagram: Another Revision

The 1981 diagram was simply appended to the 1978 and 1979 diagrams in the 1981 version of the manuscript. While it clearly introduced significant modifications, very little additional explanatory material was distributed – only the three sentences at the bottom of the diagram. Those sentences indicate that the outward-pointing arrows represent the aggregate of positive redistributive transactions from the Redistributional Function to the other monetary functions, while the inward-pointing arrows represent the aggregates of negative transactions flowing from the monetary functions into the Redistributional Function.

The remark in the upper right-hand corner, 'Read Eichner pp. 42–60,' refers to Alfred S. Eichner, ed., *A Guide to Post-Keynesian Economics* (White Plains, NY: M.E. Sharpe, Inc., 1978, 1979). Lonergan's page references do not correspond to the 1979 edition available to these editors; pp. 42–45 come at the end of an article by Peter Kenyon, 'Pricing,' and bear virtually no relationship to Lonergan's 1981 diagram. Pages 46–60, on the other hand, refer to the entirety of an article by J.A. Kregel, 'Income Distribution.' Kregel's article includes some striking parallels to Lonergan's analysis. The article begins with a brief statement of the elements in Keynes's work that post-Keynesians (several are mentioned by name in the article) took as their point of departure for investigating the problem of income distribution. By the 'problem of income distribution' is meant the question of how income is divided between wages and profits. The 'orthodox theory' that prices determine income distribution is summarized and briefly criticized. Kregel then surveys elements from Keynes and Kalecki to provide an alternative to this 'orthodox theory.' In his survey, something very close to Lonergan's two circuits and their crossovers is described. However, the objective is quite different: Kregel describes the post-Keynesian concern to use such analysis to overturn, as far as possible, commonly advanced justifications for income differences. Finally, policy implications are drawn.

The 1981 diagram is virtually identical with the 1982 diagram (see section G below), with one notable exception. Like the 1982 diagram, the 1981 diagram contains the symbols s' and s'' for the propensity to save, but it also contains a third symbol s (without primes) absent from the 1982 diagram. According to the 1981 diagram, s' denotes the fraction of fO' diverted from the Basic Supply Function to the Redistributive Function, while s'' denotes the fraction of fO'' diverted from the Surplus Supply Function to the Redistributive Function. The symbol s (without primes) denotes both the fraction of Basic Income fI' and as well the fraction of

Surplus Income fI'' diverted to the Redistributive Function. This seems to suggest that what might be called the basic propensity to save and the surplus propensity to save are identical, namely s, while on the other hand the fractions of outlay s' deposited by basic enterprises will differ from the fractions of outlays s'' deposited by surplus enterprises. To allow for a difference in a propensity to save in one case but not in the other seems counterintuitive. However, in the upper right hand corner of the 1981 diagram, Lonergan remarked that 's varies with situation.' This could be taken to mean that the s in sfI' varies from the s in sfI''. Such a meaning would, however, be at variance not only with common convention, but with Lonergan's own general practice. The difficulty in interpreting the meaning of s disappears in the 1982 diagram when sfI' is replaced by $s'fI'$ and sfI'' is replaced by $s''fI''$. This replacement has difficulties of its own, however (see note 57). In short, the problems of fully transposing descriptive designations of financial transactions into fully explanatory categories still seem in evidence in this 1981 diagram.

Since the 1982 diagram was accompanied by new and more extended commentary, and since the 1981 diagram is equivalent to the 1982 diagram in all other respects, the remaining aspects of the 1981 diagram are covered in the next section.

G   The 1982 Diagram

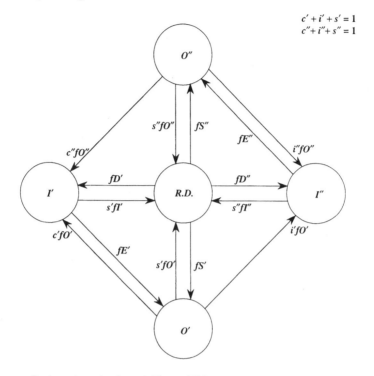

$$c' + i' + s' = 1$$
$$c'' + i'' + s'' = 1$$

Per interval, surplus demand, I'', pays fE'' for current surplus products, and receives dividends $i''fO''$ from surplus production and $i'fO'$ from basic production.

Per interval, basic demand pays fE' for current basic products and for its services receives $c''fO''$ from surplus supply and $c'fO'$ from basic supply.

Vertical arrows represent transactions between the redistributional area and surplus and basic supply; horizontal arrows the dealings of demand with the redistributional area.

12. Diagram of Rates of Flow

Besides the changes in the s symbols on the diagram itself, there are a few small differences between the 1981 and 1982 versions: the 1982 version has been retitled 'Diagram of Rates of Flow' and set off in its own separate section. The 1981 reference to Eichner's article has been dropped. The statement of the equilibrium condition has also been omitted. Finally, the three brief explanatory sentences have been altered. Whereas the explanatory sentences accompanying the 1981 diagram concerned the rates of payments centering on outlays (that is, Basic and Surplus Supply Functions), the 1982 diagram shifts its focus to the rates of payments centered on Basic and Surplus Demand Functions. While this shift in focus did little to resolve recurring questions and ambiguities regarding certain types of transactions and their relations to outlays, it did redirect attention to the two circuits and their crossovers – which was Lonergan's central concern from the beginning. The sentence explaining the arrows surrounding the 'redistributional area' [*sic*] drops the term 'savings' altogether, perhaps in an effort to remove residual descriptive connotations.

Some clarifications are to be found in the new 1982 explanatory section 'Rates of Payment and Transfer,' which precedes the diagram. The relevant passage from that section reads:

Now initial payments are income, so that in every case

$$fO' + fO'' = fI' + fI'' \tag{2}$$

Basic and surplus outlay together equal basic and surplus income together. However not a little of the income derived from surplus production is destined to be spent on [the] standard of living, and so there is some fraction, say c'' of fO'' that moves to the basic demand function. Similarly, there are large salaries and large profits to be had, at least at times, by contributors to the standard of living, and so there can be some fraction, say i', that heads to the surplus demand function. Again, there is a fraction of fO'', say i'', that goes to surplus demand, and a fraction of fO', say c', that goes to basic demand. Finally, there may be fractions of fO' and fO'', say s' and s'', intended to improve one's balance in the redistributive function, *RD*. Hence,

$$fI'' = i'fO' + i''fO'' + s''fO'' \tag{3}$$

$$fI' = c'fO' + c''fO'' + s'fO' \tag{4}$$

In these equations the crossover is represented by the inclusion in fI'' of $i'fO'$ and in fI' of $c''fO''$. Let fG represent the crossover difference in favor of basic demand, so that

$$fG = c''fO'' - i'fO' \tag{5}$$

and the condition of equilibrium will be

$$fG = 0 \tag{6}$$

On the common assumption that all savings are invested, $s'fO'$ and $s''fO''$ may be neglected unless a contrary opinion is entertained. Finally on adding both sides of (5) to both sides of (3) and then subtracting both from both of (4), we get

$$fI'' + fG = c''fO'' + i''fO'' = fO'' \tag{7}$$

$$fI' - fG = c'fO' + i'fO' = fO' \tag{8}$$

and thereby revert to the basic outlays from which we began (1982:39–40; see pp. 43–45).

While a case can be made that the diagram itself has succeeded in reaching a mature stage, the accompanying explanatory material is still in a transitional state. It sets forth another new clarification, but it is still beset with omissions and trouble spots. There is greater clarity regarding redistributive transactions, in the sense that s' and s'' are fractions of fO' and fO'', respectively, which are 'intended to improve one's balance in the redistributive function.' Thus, $fO' = c'fO' + i'fO' + s'fO'$ and $fO'' = c''fO'' + i''fO'' + s''fO''$. Therefore, as in 1981, $c' + i' + s' = 1$, and $c'' + i'' + s'' = 1$.

Unfortunately, the remainder of the passage contains further trouble spots. Second, then, the nature of fS', fS'', fD', and fD'' is not clarified at all. Are they withdrawals from savings accounts? Loans? And where do repayments of principal or interest fit in? Third, as a consequence of this omission, the claim of equation (2), 'initial payments are income, so that in every case $fO' + fO'' = fI' + fI''$ is not true in *every* case; not, that is, when fS', fS'', fD', or fD'' is non-zero. Fourth, along the same line, does the aggregate $fO' = fR' + fS' = fE' + fS'$ while $fO'' = fR'' + fS'' = fE'' + fS''$? And if so are the marginal propensities to save, s' and s'', calculated on the basis of the sums $fR' + fS'$ and $fR'' + fS''$? Fifth and more serious yet, equations (3) and (4) do not correspond with the diagram at all. According to the diagram, even neglecting fS', fS'', fD', and fD'',

$$fI'' = i'fO' + i''fO''$$

and not $fI'' = i'fO' + i''fO'' + s''fO''$ as equation (3) claims,

while $fI' = c'fO' + c''fO''$,   not $fI'' = c'fO' + c''fO'' + s'fO'$

as in equation (4). This would be a rather unusual way to calculate s' and s''. Sixth, there is introduced the assumption that the s' of $s'fO'$ is identical with the s' of $s'fI'$, and similarly with the two occurrences of s''.

Part of the problem, arguably, is that Lonergan was writing with an eye on his next section – the possibility of circuit acceleration when the net redistributive transactions are zero: when '$s'fO'$ and $s''fO''$ may be neglected unless a contrary opinion is entertained.' Tacitly, the same holds true for $s'fI'$, $s''fI''$, fS', fS'', fD', and fD'' as well: they are neglected until a 'contrary opinion is entertained.' There is a similar problem with the three sentences at the bottom of the 1981 diagram. Lonergan seems to have been doing two things at once, but not clearly differentiating them. The first is to give a system of explanatory definitions expressing the system of dynamic relationships among the variables. The second is completing the heuristic preparation for the first step in the analysis proper: the question of acceleration when net redistributive transactions are all zero. In fact, this preoccupation had probably been responsible for the lack of differentiation all the way back to 1944.

H   The Editors' Diagram of 1998

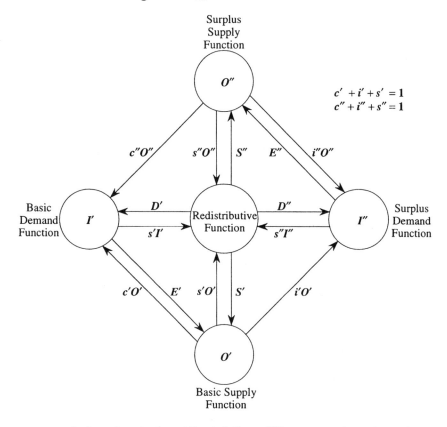

Per interval, surplus demand [function], I'', pays E'' for current surplus products, and receives dividends $i''O''$ from surplus production [i.e., surplus supply function] and $i'O'$ from basic production [i.e., basic supply function].

Per interval, basic demand [function, I',] pays E' for current basic products and for its services receives $c''O''$ from surplus supply [function] and $c'O'$ from basic supply [function].

Vertical arrows represent transactions between the redistributional area and surplus and basic supply [functions]; horizontal arrows the dealings of demand [functions] with the redistributional area.

Figure 14-1 Diagram of Rates of Flow

The editors have made only minor changes to the 1982 diagram: the five monetary functions have been explicitly labeled; and the prefix f has been deleted from the symbols for the dynamic variables of aggregate rates.[6] This implicitly turns the 1998 diagram's symbols O', O'', I', and I'' into both dynamic variables and dynamically quiescent quantities. In fact, however,

6 See note 29.

this is the way things tend to be: money for outlays and money for expenditures does tend to be held onto for some subdivision of the measuring time period, but then spent or saved. (In fact one could even define money not actually deposited, but held for, say, the whole quarter or year, as 'saved.')

Although the editors' version of the explanatory material set forth in §13 of this text has been as faithful as possible to Lonergan's own writing, some of the questions remain. What follows is one possible way of resolving these questions.

First, then, S' has both a negative and a positive component: the positive component is the aggregate of loans made for the purpose of basic outlays, and the negative component is the aggregate of repayments of principals of such loans. Second, interest on such loans can be considered payment for surplus services (that is, services for facilitating the financing of basic production), and it therefore enters into E''. Third, something similar holds for S''. Fourth, D' also has a positive and negative component: the positive component is the aggregate of loans made for the purpose of expenditures on the standard of living, while the negative component is repayment of principal. Fifth, interest paid on consumer loans should be regarded as payment for basic services – that is, for services provided as part of the completion of the basic purchase – and, therefore, regarded by definition as completion of the basic product. Hence such interest payments are part of E'. Sixth, D'' is parallel to D', except that it is loans and repayments for expenditure on surplus services and equipment, and its interest payments, like those associated with S' and S'', enter as part of E''. Seventh, the aggregate $s'O'$ also has positive and negative components: positive are deposits, and negative are withdrawals. Eighth, $s''O''$ is similar. Ninth, since the tacit assumption of the identity of the s' in $s'O'$ and the s' in $s'I'$ is not completely general – and may well be counterfactual – the symbols need to be altered, so that $s'O' \rightarrow s_o'O'$, and $s'I' \rightarrow s_I'I'$. Similarly, $s''O'' \rightarrow s_o''O''$, and $s''I'' \rightarrow s_I''I''$.

The net result of all this is that the variables O', O'', I', and I'' are to be regarded as aggregates that are 'completed' only after all redistributive transactions have been taken into account. Thus

$$O' = R' + S' - s_o'O'$$

so that

$$s_o' = [(R' + S')/O'] - 1$$

and

$$O'' = R'' + S'' - s_o''O''$$

so that

$$s_o'' = [(R'' + S'')/O''] - 1$$

Moreover,

$$E' = c'O' + c''O'' + D' - s_I'I'$$

which seems to imply that

$$I' = c'O' + c''O''$$

and if so, then

$$s_I' = 1 - [(E' - D')/(c'O' + c''O'')]$$

and likewise

$$E'' = i'O' + i''O'' + D'' - s_I''I''$$

while

$$I'' = i'O' + i''O''$$

so that

$$s_I'' = 1 - [(E'' - D'')/(i'O' + i''O'')]$$

Now, while admittedly this is a somewhat unorthodox way of conceiving of s_o', s_o'', s_I', and s_I'', it is not an inconsistent or contradictory way. If the strangeness of these definitions should prove troublesome, they can be redefined along more conventional lines, such as

$$O' = R' + S' - s_R'R'$$

so that

$$s_R' = [\text{aggregate deposits from } R' \text{ minus withdrawals for } O']/R'$$

and

$$O'' = R'' + S'' - s_R''R''$$

so that

$s_R'' = $ [aggregate deposits from R'' minus withdrawals for O''] / R''

Something analogous could be done for the two remaining s symbols.

Of course this would mean changing the corresponding symbols associated with the arrows pointing inward toward the Redistributive Function circle of the diagram, but that would be a relatively minor change.

Finally, it should be noted that, when Lonergan did eventually 'entertain a contrary opinion' to the assumption that all net redistributive transactions are zero,[7] it was always the differences $(S' - s'O')$, $(S'' - s''O'')$, $(D' - s'I')$, and $(D'' - s''I'')$ that entered into the analysis. (However, Lonergan did not modify the later sections of his 1982 manuscript to take into account the changes in the 1982 diagram. The editors have made the corresponding changes.) While there will no doubt be questions for future research in which fluctuations in the components of the parenthetical quantities will need to be studied separately, the purposes Lonergan himself focused on in this *Essay* did not necessitate so fine-tuned a degree of differentiation.

PATRICK H. BYRNE

7 See note 58.

Glossary of Symbols

In preparing the present edition, the editors have endeavored to make the symbolic notation (which varies between, and within, the successive versions of Lonergan's *Essay in Circulation Analysis*) consistent throughout. (See Editors' Preface, p. xxii, and 'Appendix: History of the Diagram, 1944–1998.') Each of the symbols used in parts one and three is listed here in alphabetical order, with the number of the page where it first appears in the present edition and a brief explanation of its meaning.

Symbol	Page where introduced	Explanation
a'	112	Basic acceleration coefficient. When Q' basic quantities are sold over an interval, $a'Q'$ basic quantities are under production during that interval.
a'_1	113	Basic acceleration coefficient for interval number 1; when Q'_1 basic quantities are sold over interval number 1, $a'_1 Q'_1$ basic quantities are under production during that interval.
a''	112	Surplus acceleration coefficient; when Q'' surplus quantities are sold over an interval, $a''Q''$ surplus quantities are under production during that interval.
A	109	Angle between vectors P and Q in n-space.

Symbol	Page where introduced	Explanation
A'	74	Angle between vectors P'_j and Q'_j in n-space.
A_n	37	Measure of short-term acceleration of the rate of production on the nth level. (A_1, A_2, A_3 are specific instances of A_n.)
a, b, c	37	Time lags between rate of production of the nth level and the acceleration of the $n-1$ level.
B_n	37	Measure of rate of production on level n that is effecting merely replacements on the $n-1$ level. (B_1, B_2, B_3 are specific instances of B_n.)
c'	49	Fraction of O' that goes to the basic demand function.
c''	49	Fraction of O'' that goes to the basic demand function.
D'	51	Aggregate of rates of transfers from redistributive function to basic demand function, over and above $s'I'$.
D''	51	Aggregate of rates of transfers from redistributive function to surplus demand function, over and above $s''I''$.
da'	159	Differential of a'; defined by equation, $da' = a'(dq'/q' - dQ'/Q')$
da''	159	Differential of a''; defined as analogous to da'.
dA	109	Change in angle, A, between vectors P and Q over two successive intervals.
DE'	112	A 'weighted average' (p. 111) increment in E' over two successive intervals; defined by equation $DE' = P'Q'(dP'/P' + dQ'/Q' + dP'dQ'/P'Q')$.
DE''	112	A 'weighted average' (p. 111) increment in E'' over two successive intervals; defined by equation $DE'' = P''Q''(dP''/P'' + dQ''/Q'' + dP''\,dQ''/P''Q'')$.
dI'	134	Change in I' over a given interval; defined by equation $dI' = \Sigma\,(w_i dn_i + n_i dw_i)\,y_i$.
DI'	132	Change in I' over a given interval.
DI''	132	Change in I'' over a given interval.
dJ	160	Differential of J; defined by equation $dJ = da' + Rda' + a''dR$.

Symbol	Page where introduced	Explanation
dn_i	134	Change in n_i over a given interval.
dp_i	107	Variation in average price of products (in class i) sold in two successive intervals.
dP	109	An approximate variation in prices; by implication, defined by equation $dP = \Sigma\, q_i dp_i / Q.$
$d\boldsymbol{P}$	109	Variation in vector $\boldsymbol{P}$ over two successive intervals. $d\boldsymbol{P}$ is itself a vector, an ordered n-tuple: $d\boldsymbol{P} = (dp_1,\, dp_2,\, dp_3,\, ...).$
dP'	112	A 'weighted average' (p. 111) increment in basic selling price index, P'.
dP''	112	A 'weighted average' (p. 111) increment in surplus selling price index, P''.
dq_i	107	Variation in quantity of products (in class i) sold in two successive intervals.
dq'	159	Differential of q'.
dQ	109	An approximate variation in quantities; by implication, defined by equation $dQ = \Sigma\, p_i\, dq_i / P.$
$d\boldsymbol{Q}$	109	Variation in vector $\boldsymbol{Q}$ over two successive intervals. $d\boldsymbol{Q}$ is itself a vector, an ordered n-tuple: $d\boldsymbol{Q} = (dq_1,\, dq_2,\, dq_3,\, ...).$
dQ'	112	A 'weighted average' (p. 111) increment in index of basic quantities, Q'.
dQ''	112	A 'weighted average' (p. 111) increment in index of surplus quantities, Q''.
dv	149	Differential of v.
dw	149	Differential of w.
dw_i	134	Change in w_i over a given interval.
dy_i	134	Change in y_i over a given interval.
DZ	108	Variation in aggregate payments for goods and services between two successive intervals; defined by equation $DZ = \Sigma\, (p_i dq_i + dp_i q_i + dp_i dq_i)$. (Roughly equivalent to variation in Gross Domestic Product, without identifying whether basic or surplus.)
E'	46	Aggregate of rates of basic expenditures (aggregate of rates of consumers purchasing goods and services for their standard of living).

206 Glossary of Symbols

Symbol	Page where introduced	Explanation
E'	112	Alternate definition of E' above; here defined by equation $E' = P'Q'$.
E''	46	Aggregate of rates of surplus expenditures (aggregate of rates of producers purchasing surplus goods and services for use in their enterprises).
E''	112	Alternate definition of E'' above; here defined by equation $E'' = P''Q''$.
f	148	Ratio of pure surplus income to total income; here defined by equation $f = vI''/(I' + I'')$.
Δf	148 n.204	Variation in f; used as practically identical with the differential of f.
f_{ij}	65	Final payments (receipts) received by enterprise i during turnover j.
$f_n'(t)$	37	Measure of the rate of production of the nth level of production; first derivative with respect to time of $f_n(t)$. ($f_1'(t), f_2'(t), f_3'(t)$ are specific instances of $f_n'(t)$.)
$f_n''(t)$	37	Measure of the acceleration of production of the nth level of production; first derivative with respect to time of $f_n'(t)$; second derivative with respect to time of $f_n(t)$. ($f_1''(t), f_2''(t), f_3''(t)$ are specific instances of $f_n''(t)$.)
F_i	150	Rate of pure surplus income (see vI'') received by unit of enterprise i.
F/O	150	Ratio of pure surplus income to total outlay; defined by equations, $F/O = \Sigma F_i / \Sigma O_i = vI''/(O' + O') = vw = f$. (Although by implication, $F = \Sigma F_i$ and $O = \Sigma O_i$, Lonergan used neither F nor O apart from their combination in this ratio.)
F_j/O_j	150	Ratio of pure surplus income to total outlay for enterprise j.
G	49	Crossover difference of aggregate of rates of payments; defined by equation $G = c''O'' - i'O'$. ($G > 0$ implies a crossover difference in favor of basic demand; $G < 0$ implies a crossover difference in favor of surplus demand.)
h	116	Overall long-term acceleration coefficient; h is the

Symbol	Page where introduced	Explanation
		fraction of Q'' that accelerates either basic or surplus production; $h = h' + h''$.
h'	116	Basic long-term acceleration coefficient; h' is the fraction of Q'' that accelerates basic production.
h''	116	Surplus long-term acceleration coefficient; h'' is the fraction of Q'' that accelerates surplus production.
i	29	When used as a subscript, denotes a particular instance, product, enterprise, turnover, or axis.
i'	49	Fraction of O' that goes to the surplus demand function.
i'	65	When used in appendix to § 15 as a limit of summation, denotes total number of enterprises engaged in basic production.
i'	74	When used in § 17, denotes a class of basic products for sale.
i''	49	Fraction of O'' that goes to the surplus demand function.
i''	74	When used in § 17, denotes a class of surplus products for sale.
I'	46	Aggregate of rates of basic income (aggregate of rates of monies available to consumers of basic goods and services).
I''	46	Aggregate of rates of surplus income (aggregate rates of monies available to consumers of surplus goods and services).
j	29	When used as a subscript, denotes a particular instance, product, enterprise; turnover, or axis.
j'	66	When used in appendix to § 15, denotes turnover immediately preceding turnover j (i.e., $j' = j - 1$).
J	158	Basic price spread ratio; defined by equations $J = P'/p' = a' + a''R = a' + a''(p''Q''/p'Q')$.
k	30	When used as a subscript, denotes a particular instance, product, enterprise, interval, turnover, or axis.
k	120	When used as a coefficient, k is the multiplier in a geometrically increasing series of Q'' (e.g., where $dQ''/Q'' = (k - 1)$ and Q'', kQ'', k^2Q'', k^3Q'', etc.). Used only in additional note to § 24.

Symbol	Page where introduced	Explanation
k_n	37	Multipliers that connect the rate of production (on level n) effecting long-term acceleration (on the level $n-1$) to the rate of acceleration so effected. (k_2, k_3, k_4 are specific instances of k_n.)
M'	51	Aggregate of rates of monies added to the basic circuit; defined by equation $M' = (S' - s'O') + (D' - s'I') + G.$
M''	51	Aggregate of rates of monies added to the surplus circuit; defined by equation $M'' = (S'' - s''O'') + (D'' - s''I'') - G.$
n	37	When used as a subscript in § 11, denotes a particular level of production.
n	65, 108, 120	When used as either a limit of summation or as a subscript in appendix to § 15 or in § 23, or as a coefficient or exponent in additional note to § 24, denotes total number or last item in a finite series of turnovers, intervals, etc.
n_i	134	Number of members of group i, all of whose income is 'practically equal' to y_i.
o_{ij}	65	Initial payments (outlays) made by enterprise i during turnover j.
O_i	150	Rate of outlay of unit of enterprise i.
O'	46	Aggregate of rates of basic outlay (aggregate of rates of initial basic payments).
O'	65	Alternate definition of O' above; here defined by equation $O' = \Sigma\Sigma\, o_{ij}.$
O''	46	Aggregate of rates of surplus outlay (aggregate of rates of initial surplus payments).
p_i	72	Initially, just a number; subsequently, a component of vector $\boldsymbol{P}$. (p_1, p_2, p_3, are specific instances of p_i; p_j is an equivalent alternate expression.)
p_i	107	Average price of a class of products, i, sold during an interval. (Differs from the definition of p_i above only by the added interpretation of the components of vector $\boldsymbol{P}$ as average prices of class of products i.)

Symbol	Page where introduced	Explanation
p'	157	Basic cost price index; defined by equation $c'O' = p'a'Q'$.
p'_{ij}	74	Price of basic products in class i' sold during interval j (p'_{ik} is an equivalent alternate expression).
p''	157	Surplus cost price index; defined by equation $c''O'' = p''a''Q''$.
p''_{ij}	74	Price of surplus products in class i'' sold during interval j (p''_{ik} is an equivalent alternate expression).
P	71	Price level of standard macroeconomic theory. (See Robert J. Gordon, *Macroeconomics* [Boston: Little, Brown & Co., 2nd ed., 1981], chapter 2.)
P	72	Initially, just a number that varies with a set of numbers, $p_1, p_2, p_3, \ldots$ (i.e., $P = \Phi(p_1, p_2, p_3, \ldots)$ where Φ is some function of several variables); subsequently (p. 73) elaborated as $P = |\boldsymbol{P}| = \sqrt{P^2} = \sqrt{\Sigma p_i^2}$.
$\boldsymbol{P}$	73	A vector, an ordered n-tuple: $\boldsymbol{P} = (p_1, p_2, p_3, \ldots)$.
$\boldsymbol{P}$	108	A vector elaborated as a price index with price components p_i.
P'	71	Basic price level; defined by equation $Y' = P'Q'$ (note 87).
P'	112	Basic selling price index – a 'weighted average' (p. 111) compared to the definition of P above; defined by the equation $E' = P'Q'$.
P'_j	74	Basic price index during interval j; defined by equations $P'_j = \sqrt{P'^2_j} = |\boldsymbol{P}'_j| = \sqrt{\Sigma p'^2_{ij}}$.
$\boldsymbol{P}'_j$	74	Basic price index vector during interval j; $\boldsymbol{P}'_j = (p'_{j1}, p'_{j2}, p'_{j3}, \ldots)$.
$\boldsymbol{P}'_{kj}$	75	Basic price index vector difference over successive intervals j and k; defined by the equation $\boldsymbol{P}'_{kj} = \boldsymbol{P}'_k - \boldsymbol{P}'_j$.
P''	71	Surplus price level; defined by equation $Y'' = P''Q''$ (note 87).
P''	112	Surplus selling price index – a 'weighted average' (p. 111) compared to the definition of P above; defined by the equation $E'' = P''Q''$.

Symbol	Page where introduced	Explanation
P''_j	74	Surplus price index during interval j; defined as analogous to P'_j.
$P'_{kj}Q'_{kj}$	75	Difference between basic final sales in interval k and basic final sales in interval j; defined by the equation $P'_{kj}Q'_{kj} = (P'_k \cdot Q'_k) - (P'_j \cdot Q'_j)$.
q_i	30	Quantity of some ultimate product, whether service or material object, in class i, sold during an interval.
q_i	72	Initially, just a number; subsequently, a component of vector Q. (q_1, q_2, q_3, are specific instances of q_i; q_j is an equivalent alternate expression.)
q_i	107	Quantity of a class of products, i, sold during an interval. (Differs from the definition of q_i on p. 72 only by the added interpretation of the components of vector Q as quantities of class of products i.)
q_{ij}	30	Contribution by enterprise j to q_i.
q_{ijk}	30	Contribution of factor of production k (labor, management, capital, etc.) within enterprise j to ultimate product q_i.
q'	159	Rate of quantities of basic products under current production; defined by equation $q' = a'Q'$.
q'_{ij}	74	Quantity of basic products in class i' sold during interval j (q'_{ik} is an equivalent alternate expression.).
q''_{ij}	74	Quantity of surplus products in class i'' sold during interval j. (q''_{ik} is an equivalent alternate expression.)
Q	71	Real income of standard macroeconomic theory. (See Robert J. Gordon, *Macroeconomics* [Boston: Little, Brown & Co., 2nd ed., 1981], chapter 2.)
Q	72	Initially, just a number that varies with a set of numbers, q_1, q_2, q_3, ... (i.e., $Q = \Psi(q_1, q_2, q_3, ...)$ where Ψ is some function of several variables); subsequently (p. 73) elaborated as $Q = |Q| = \sqrt{Q^2} = \sqrt{\Sigma q_i^2}$.
Q	73	A vector, an ordered n-tuple: $Q = (q_1, q_2, q_3, ...)$.
Q	108	A vector elaborated as a quantity index with quantity components q_i.
Q_i	30	Rate or flow ('so many every so often') of ultimate product q_i.

Symbol	Page where introduced	Explanation
Q_{ijk}	30	Rate or flow of the contributions of factor of production k (labor, management, capital, etc.) within enterprise j to ultimate product q_i.
Q'	71	Basic real income; defined by equation $Y' = P'Q'$ (note 87).
Q'	112	Index of basic quantities – a 'weighted average' (p. 111) compared to the definition of Q above; defined by the equation, $E' = P'Q'$.
Q'_j	74	Basic quantity index during interval j; defined by equations $Q'_j = \sqrt{Q'^2_j} = \lvert \mathbf{Q}'_j \rvert = \sqrt{\Sigma q'^2_{ij}}$.
$\mathbf{Q}'_j$	74	Basic quantity index vector during interval j; $\mathbf{Q}'_j = (q_{j1}, q_{j2}, q_{j3}, \ldots)$.
$\mathbf{Q}'_{kj}$	75	Basic quantity index vector difference over successive intervals j and k; defined by equation $\mathbf{Q}'_{kj} = \mathbf{Q}'_k - \mathbf{Q}'_j$.
Q''	71	Surplus real income; defined by equation $Y'' = P''Q''$ (note 87).
Q''	112	Index of surplus quantities – a 'weighted average' (p. 111) compared to the definition of Q above; defined by the equation $E'' = P''Q''$.
Q''_j	74	Surplus quantity index during interval j; defined as analogous to Q'_j.
r	120	A factor in a coefficient of constant surplus acceleration; that is, acceleration, $dQ'' = \text{constant} = (1/r - 1)Q_1''$, where Q_1'' is the rate of surplus production in the first interval in the period of constant acceleration. Used only in additional note to § 24.
r_{ik}	68	Payments received by (receipts of) enterprise i during turnover j from previous turnover $k(k = j - 1)$.
R	158	Ratio of surplus to basic activity; defined by equation $R = (p''Q''/p'Q')$.
R'	46	Aggregate of rates of basic receipts (aggregate of rates of receipts of E' by final agents of supply of basic goods and services).
R'	65	Alternate definition of R' above; here R' defined as $R' = \Sigma\Sigma f_{ij}$.

Symbol	Page where introduced	Explanation
R''	46	Aggregate of rates of surplus receipts (aggregate of rates of receipts of E'' by final agents' supply of surplus goods and services at all surplus levels).
$\Delta R'$	66	Difference in turnover magnitude of aggregate of basic final payments at beginning and end of an interval; defined by equation $\Delta R' = \Sigma\ (f_{in} - f_{i0})$.
s'	49	Fraction of O' that goes to the redistributive function.
s''	49	Fraction of O'' that goes to the redistributive function.
s_{ij}	65	Net increase in monetary circulating capital received by enterprise i during turnover j (e.g., net remainder of savings withdrawals, savings deposits, loans received, and loan-principal payments by enterprise i during turnover j).
S'	51	Aggregate of rates of transfers from redistributive function to basic supply function over and above $s'O'$ (e.g., loans to expand or retool basic enterprises).
S'	65	Alternate definition of S' above; here S' defined by equation $(S' - s'O') = \Sigma\Sigma s_{ij}$.
S''	51	Aggregate of rates of transfers from redistributive function to surplus supply function over and above $s''O''$ (e.g., loans to expand or retool surplus enterprises).
t	37	Time variable.
t_{ij}	66	Transitional payments made by enterprise i during turnover j.
T	174	Rate of total tax payments; $T = T' + T''$.
T'	174	Rate of tax payments withdrawn from basic demand.
T''	174	Rate of tax payments withdrawn from surplus demand.
$\Delta T'$	66	Difference in turnover magnitude of aggregate of basic transitional payments at beginning and end of an interval; defined by equation $\Delta T' = \Sigma\ (T_{in} - T_{i0})$. (Not related to T'.)

Symbol	Page where introduced	Explanation
T_{ij}	66	Transitional payments received by enterprise i during turnover j.
v	146	Fraction of surplus expenditure (E'') that goes to new fixed investment.
Δv	148 n.204	Variation in v; used as practically identical with dv, the differential of v.
vI''	148	Pure surplus income; product of v and I''.
w	132	Ratio of surplus to total income; defined by equation $w = I'' / (I' + I'')$.
w_i	134	Fraction of aggregate income y_i, of group i, directed to basic demand.
W	133	Social dividend; 'income over and above "standard of living," "rent," interest, maintenance and replacement of capital equipment.' (See note 186.)
x	69	When used as a limit of summation, denotes total number of turnovers.
x	123	Used on this page only as a symbol for the time axis.
x	75	Used on this page only as a symbol for an algebraic unknown number.
y	75	Used on this page only as a symbol for an algebraic unknown number.
y_i	134	Magnitude of the 'practically equal' income of the n_i members of group i.
Y	71	The Gross Domestic (or National) Product of standard macroeconomic theory. (See Robert J. Gordon, *Macroeconomics* [Boston: Little, Brown & Co., 2nd ed., 1981], chapter 2.)
Y'	71	Basic gross product; defined by equation $Y' = P'Q'$ (note 87).
Y''	71	Surplus gross product; defined by equation $Y'' = P''Q''$ (note 87).
Z	108	Aggregate payment for goods and services in an interval; defined by equation $Z = \sum p_i q_i$. (Roughly equivalent to a Gross Domestic Product, without identifying whether basic or surplus.)
Z	174	Rate of total government spending; $Z = Z' + Z''$.

Symbol	Page where introduced	Explanation
Z'	163	Basic superposed rates of payments; i.e., monies per interval injected into the basic circuit over and above classes and rates of payments defined in §§ 2–14. (In § 30, Z' derives from rates of foreign-trade balance payments; in § 31, Z' derives from government spending.)
Z''	163	Surplus superposed rates of payments; i.e., monies per interval injected into the surplus circuit over and above classes and rates of payments defined in §§ 12–14. (In § 30, Z'' derives from rates of foreign-trade balance payments; in § 31, Z'' derives from government spending.)

Index

146, 158, 163, 172–73, 175, 182, 184, 200

Exploitation, 33 n. 34

Factors, xlv, xlix, lxiii, 30, 32, 42, 47, 58, 60, 62, 90, 92, 117, 126, 133, 149, 151–52, 157, 159, 160–61, 169

Factory, 15, 24, 27, 44

Family wage, xxviii, xl, xliv

Fascism, xxxii

Favorable balance of foreign trade, lxiv, lxix, 5, 17, 64, 70, 82, 85, 119–20, 156, 165–67, 170, 180

Fichte, Johann Gottlieb, 9

Final basic operative payment, 46, 48

Final market, 33, 57, 64, 67, 71, 80, 112, 131, 135, 138, 146, 153–54, 157, 159, 162, 167, 169, 172–73, 175–76

Final surplus operative payment, 46

Finance, xxix, xxxi, xliv, xlix, 16, 81, 85

Financial, 13, 16, 43–44, 77, 84–85, 96, 100, 147, 153–54, 178, 191, 194

Firm(s), lviii, lxv, 4, 12, 26, 69–70, 78–81, 84, 87, 89–90, 93, 96, 104, 118, 145, 154–55

Five-year plan, xxxix, lxvii, 33, 79

Flanagan, Joseph, x, lxxiv

Flow(s), vi, xv, xxii, xlvi, lviii, lx, lxviii–lxvi, 16–17, 29–30, 45–55, 66, 77–79, 84, 86, 95, 101–102, 119, 125, 129, 142, 144–45, 157, 163, 166, 170, 177, 180–85, 188, 190, 195

Forced savings, lxix, 141 n. 197, 157

Foreign, vii, lxiv, lxvi, 12–13, 17, 39, 63–65, 70, 82–83, 85, 119–20, 129, 156, 162, 165–72, 175–76

Freedom, xxxi–xxxiii, xxxvii–li, liv, lv, lxxi, 6, 95, 105; f. of exchange, 6

Free enterprise, xxxiii, xxxiv, xxxvi, xxxvii, 117

Frequency, 54, 56–60, 63–64, 67–69, 73, 143

Function(s), xx, xxxvi, xlv–xlvi, lv, lix, lxi, lxviii, 5, 18, 23 n. 25, 24, 27–29, 37, 40, 48–56, 60–65, 70, 72, 76, 88, 102, 111–12, 116, 134, 145, 147, 152–53, 157, 162

Functional, ix, xxxiv, lvi, lx, lxi, lxii, lxv, lxviii, 17, 26–27, 54, 56, 72, 117–18, 145, 157, 179

Galileo, xlvi

Gaudium et Spes, 106 n. 135

General bias, xxxv, lxiv, lxix, 94, 102

Generalization, xxxix, lv, 18, 126

GNP, 72 n. 87

God, love of, lxxi

Going, Cathleen, xxviii, xl

Gold, 61, 78, 83, 165, 168, 170–71

Good of order, xxxii, 117

Gordon, Robert J., xlii, lii, 71 n. 87, 185 n. 5, 191

Government(s), xxxiii, xxxv, xxxvi, xliii, xlvii, xlix, l, li, 12, 23, 63–65, 70, 81, 83, 85, 99, 120, 129, 156, 162, 172–76

Government spending, l, li, 64–65, 70, 120, 129, 156, 162, 173–76

Grace, xxxi, liv, lv, lxxi, 84, 94–95, 104

Graham, Nicholas, x, xxxv, lxxiii

Group bias, xxxviii, xlvii, lxiv, 94

Group egoism, 102–103

Gutierrez, Gustavo, xl

Hansen, Alvin H., xlix

Hayek, Frederick, xxx n. 20

Hefling, Charles, iii, v, ix–x, xxiii

Hegel, G.W.F., xxvi, 9, 102 n. 131

Heythrop College, xxvii

Hilbert, David, lv, 26 n. 27

History, vii, x–xxiii, xxvi–xxvii, xxx–xxxi, xl, xliii, xlvii, lii–liii, lx–lxi, lxviii, lxx–lxxii, 4, 7–8, 10–11, 14, 27, 36, 49, 50–55, 61, 68, 86, 88, 90, 92–93,